TO THE
SWIFT

S TO THE WIFT

Classic Triple Crown Horses and Their Race for Glory

EDITED BY JOE DRAPE

St. Martin's Press ≈ New York

www.stmartins.com

Book design by Phil Mazzone

Library of Congress Cataloging-in-Publication Data

To the swift : Classic Triple Crown horses and their race for glory / edited by Joe Drape.—1st ed.
   p. cm.
  ISBN-13: 978-0-312-35795-5
  ISBN-10: 0-312-35795-8
  1. Race horses—United States—History. 2. Triple Crown (U.S. horse racing)—History. 3. Horsemen and horsewomen—United States—History. I. Drape, Joe.
  SF338.T6 2008
  798.400973—dc22

                                                            2008006244

First Edition: May 2008

10 9 8 7 6 5 4 3 2 1

To all the Horse Lovers
and Horseplayers
gripped by this majestic
sport

CONTENTS

PART II

PART III

INTRODUCTION:
MAN HERE LOVES HIS HORSE

BY JOE DRAPE

JUNE 10, 1978— *"As all readers of bad fiction know, horsemen are callous schemers steeped in guile, to whom a thoroughbred of royal lineage and generous courage is merely a tool to be used while it can produce money and then discarded or destroyed. In movies they wear a snap-brim hat over eyes that regard the world with a larcenous stare. They talk out of the corner of the mouth, almost always in conspiratorial tones because they are almost always conspiring to fix a race, break a jockey's arms, swindle a sucker or nobble another man's horse. When they aren't talking, a cigarette droops from the corner of the thin-lipped mouth. Lazaro Sosa Barrera could be a hell of a horseman, except that he is hatless, amiable, patient, humorous, warm, cooperative and accommodating, looks like Cupid with a suntan and doesn't smoke. Probably his trouble is that he is a Latin, for Latins are notoriously emotional. This Latin is openly and unashamedly emotional about a horse name Affirmed, who may or may not add victory in the Belmont Stakes this afternoon to his scores in the Kentucky Derby and Preakness and thus become history's 11th winner of the triple crown, the third in five years and the second in 12 months..."*

In 208 words, Red Smith conjured horse racing's lawlessness and romance, its majesty and passion—all the elements that force even the casual sports fan to stop everything on the first Saturday in May and pay attention to the Kentucky Derby. Beneath the iconic twin spires of Churchill Downs in Louisville, Kentucky, the best 3-year-old horses in the world break from the gate in America's most famous race. A little more than two

1

minutes and a mile and a quarter later, only the winner can chase immortality.

Over the next five weeks, it must capture the mile and three-sixteenths Preakness Stakes at Pimlico Racecourse in Baltimore and the grueling mile and a half distance of the Belmont Stakes in New York. Three consecutive victories at three different distances and at three different racetracks, add up to a Triple Crown championship.

It is only appropriate that Red Smith gets the first words in this collection from *The New York Times* on thoroughbred racing's most grueling and hallowed series. Whether or not you agree that he is America's greatest sportswriter, Smith was unparalleled when it came to matters of the turf. He often said the beat provided the best stories in all of sports, and proved it time and again.

In a way, Smith also gets the last word—Affirmed outdueled Alydar to win the Belmont in 1978 and remains the sport's eleventh and last Triple Crown champion. The ensuing 29 years have hardly been uneventful. Ten horses have captured the Derby and Preakness but failed to win the Belmont Stakes. In 2006, the Kentucky Derby winner Barbaro shattered his leg in the Preakness, and for eight months waged a gallant battle for his life before having to be put down humanely. Last year's Triple Crown provided three memorable races, each with a different winner. Rags to Riches' victory in the Belmont was only the third in that race by a filly and the first in 102 years.

Red Smith is in good company among *Times* columnists and reporters who for more than 130 years have covered America's oldest sport and written with ardor about fast horses and the colorful characters who have owned, trained, cared for and ridden them. Some of them are revered—Arthur Daley and Dave Anderson, like Smith, are Pulitzer Prize winners. Some are current—William C. Rhoden and George Vecsey. Some are known and respected within the sport—Steve Cady and Steven Crist. Some are familiar but perhaps out of context: Linda Greenhouse, who covers the United States Supreme Court, and William Grimes, a book critic, have written frequently about horses and are included here.

In fact, *The New York Times* is filled with folks who know their way around the racetrack (among them executive editor Bill Keller), and believe that racing is home to compelling and uniquely American stories. It is perhaps why the paper pulls out all the stops when it comes to covering the Triple Crown. One of those folks, Alex Ward, asked me to root around in the *Times* archives and put together this book. I've covered the horses for the paper since 1999, have written two books about the sport, and could not have dreamed up a more rewarding endeavor. When you are a horseman, mucking a stall—whether of a Derby winner or $5,000 claimer—is not a chore, it is a cherished part of life. And when you are a turf writer, mucking through great writing about horses is another reason to count your blessings that you do not have a real job, especially when you have the help I did. I thank Tomi Murata for her assistance in negotiating the archives and Maggie Berkvist for coming up with fresh photographs.

Beyond their expertise in horse racing and narrative skills, each of the writers featured here shares something far more important: they wanted their readers to love horse racing as much as they did. This, of course, is not a trait exclusive to the staff of *The Times*. Over the years, some of America's best writers, such as Laura Hillenbrand and Stephen Dobyns, have weighed in on their passion for the sport. They are here, too. In addition, Jane Smiley, Bill Barich, Jim Squires, Steven Crist and others have written new essays about a sport that there are hardly enough words for to describe.

This book is not meant to be a comprehensive history of horse racing, or the definitive word on the great horses or horsemen of our times. It offers snapshots of the sport's different eras, a showcase for terrific storytelling, and, it is hoped, an entertaining look at how what was once a pastime has evolved into a business.

PART I

---◆◆◆---

"This most remarkable of all hoss extravaganzas . . ."
—ARTHUR DALEY ON THE KENTUCKY DERBY

Churchill Downs. An exuberant Kentucky Derby bettor, May 3, 2003 (following Funny Cide's win). RICK RICKMAN/NEW SPORT/CORBIS

On June 18, 1874, Colonel M. Lewis Clark gathered Louisville's richest citizens to a meeting at the Galt House Hotel and presented his vision of an organization and racetrack that would be the envy of the world. Two days later, he filed articles of incorporation for the Louisville Jockey Club and Driving Park Association. Clark leased 80 acres three miles south of downtown that his uncles, John and Henry Churchill, owned. He raised $32,000 by convincing 320 other horsemen and businessmen that a $100 subscription to his racetrack would make Louisville synonymous with world-class horse racing. By May 17, 1875, a clubhouse, grandstand, porter's lodge, six stables and the track's signature race, the Kentucky Derby, was in place.

On May 18, 1875, *The New York Times* reported on opening day of the inaugural meeting of the Louisville Jockey Club: "The great event of the day was the Kentucky Derby, which was won by Aristides, making the fastest time ever made by a three-year-old, and is only second to the time made by Tom Bowling as a four-year-old," wrote the unnamed correspondent. "The fifteen horses started at the first tap of the drum and got away in beautiful style."

Like England's Epsom Derby, the Kentucky version was for three-year-old colts competing at a distance of one and a half miles that not only was intended to test a horse's endurance and speed but also to identify a potential

7

stallion in the future. In 1896, the race was shortened to a mile and a quarter after complaints that three-year-olds—barely teenagers in equine evolution—were not developed enough to go the greater distance.

More than 10,000 people showed up to watch Aristides pick up the $2,850 first place check. But Clark was a better visionary than businessman: he ran into financial problems and was bought out by another group of wealthy men in 1894. They, too, made an eternal contribution to Louisville and horsemen the world over when they hired Joseph Dominic Baldez to design a new grandstand.

Just 24 years old, the draftsman worried that his original plans were not grand enough for a landmark. Baldez wanted horse country to remember him so he drew a pair of hexagonal spires that towered over Churchill Downs like two sentinels guarding the gates of horse heaven.

It would be decades before this little race became one of the most famous in the world, and Baldez's towers would become known as the Twin Spires.

As the following *Times* articles illustrate, Churchill Downs, Belmont Park (and to a lesser extent Pimlico Race Course) are far more than just racetracks. They are transformed each spring into temples where horses and horsemen chase the Holy Grail that is a Triple Crown Championship.

LOUISVILLE JOCKEY CLUB—
OPENING MEETING

LOUISVILLE, MAY 17, 1875—The inaugural meeting of the Louisville Jockey Club opened to-day under more favorable auspices than was hoped by the most sanguine of its managers. Upward of 12,000 spectators were in attendance. The grand stand was thronged by a brilliant assemblage of ladies and gentlemen. The quarter stretch and other stands were crowded, and the centre field was filled with hundreds of carriages. The order was perfect, and every arrangement carried out to the letter.

The great event of the day was the Kentucky Derby, which was won by Aristides, making the fastest time ever made by a three-year-old, and is only second to the time made by Tom Bowling, as a four-year-old. The fifteen horses started at the first tap of the drum, and got away in beautiful style.

The mile-heat race won by Fairplay was also made in almost unprecedented time.

Altogether to-day's meeting was extraordinarily successful. The weather was everything that could be expected, the track was in fine order, and there was everything to indicate an eminently satisfactory meeting.

RUN FOR THE ROSES

BY ARTHUR DALEY

LOUISVILLE, MAY 4, 1946—The stands were crowded to capacity. Some of the spectators had been up at the crack of dawn in order to get places of vantage at Churchill Downs. They traveled by mule car and they came in their carriages or on horseback, with the gay young blades riding their hunters. Kentucky never had a gathering to compare with it in size. There were at least 12,000 persons present on Derby day. Can you imagine that?

But before you strain your imagination entirely out of joint, it had better be explained hastily that this is a flashback to the first Kentucky Derby of 1875 and that any resemblance to today's show is purely coincidental. On that day the landed gentry in its careless extravagance paid as high as a dollar for seats in the grandstand, while the common people got into the infield for free.

There have been some minor changes since then. The clubhouse chairs now cost $6.15 per copy ($75 each on the scalper's black market) and general admission is $2.55. The crowds have likewise expanded a trifle, going from 12,000 to 100,000. The purse has mounted from $1,000 added to its present total of a giddy $100,000 added.

Only one thing remains constant in this most remarkable of all hoss extravaganzas, the remarkable man, Col. Matt Winn. He saw it grow. He made it grow. The Derby is his baby. Without him Churchill Downs would be just another country racetrack, unwept, unhonored and unsung.

But this fabulous character has parlayed this one event into the most pretentious thing of its kind in the country.

Much of the romance that the colonel imparts to the now-classic Run for the Roses traces back to that first Derby of 1875. He saw it, just as he has watched every one of its successors—except that he now rates a much better view of the proceedings. But, when Aristides, the "little red horse," romped home on top in the inaugural, a wide-eyed boy of 13 was standing on the seat of his father's grocery wagon, taking in the scene. Today he was taking it in from the clubhouse, a wide-eyed, cherubic-faced man of almost 85—strong, vigorous and energetic, a living lie to his rightful age, since he looks and acts at least thirty years younger.

The colonel was a bit disappointed with that first Derby, but he's hardly had a disappointment since—unless it could have come in 1920 when Samuel D. Riddle refused to start his colt, a fair-to-middling nag named Man o' War. That 1875 affair, however, was a grievous disappointment. The colt the boy on the grocery wagon wanted to win was Chesapeake, who was supposed to be the greatest 3-year-old in the world.

No one paid much attention to his stablemate, an undersized little fellow named Aristides. Despite the Grecian sound to his name, Aristides was not owned by William Helis, the Golden Greek. He was owned by a chap named McGrath, whose ancestors obviously didn't come from Athens. The jockeys on both steeds wore the McGrath colors, green with an orange belt.

The starting line was drawn in the back stretch with the butt end of the starter's flag. And when that flag flashed down one set of green and orange colors foundered while the other set out in hot pursuit of the others. That couldn't be mighty Chesapeake back there, thought the anxious boy. But it was. Eagerly he awaited that famed home-stretch drive of his equine hero. The jockey's whip struck, and struck again. But, even at the age of 13, youthful Matt recognized a beaten horse when he saw one.

But wait! Up in front raced a horse carrying a jockey in green and orange. That must be vaunted Chesapeake. Yet could it be? This one was a little chestnut, the other a big bay. With sinking heart the youngster on the seat of the grocery wagon nudged his father. "That wasn't Chesapeake, was it?" he asked. "No, son," was the answer. "That was his stablemate, Aristides, and he just set a world record for the distance."

When the first Kentucky Derby was run Ulysses S. Grant was the President of the United States and the Indians were causing unrest in the sparsely settled West. The world has had considerable changes since then and made considerable progress. So has the Derby.

Some of the spectators still get up at the crack of dawn in order to get vantage points. But none of them ride out there in tallyhos, surreys, broughams or fashionable carriages. None come on horseback nor travel by mule-drawn street cars. Their methods of transportation now are powered by electricity or gasoline. A few still use the time-honored system of shanks' mare, walking out to Churchill Downs, which no longer is situated on the outskirts of the town, but is in the heart of the city.

The stands have expanded and spread. If the original ones couldn't contain those 12,000 customers, neither can the present ones hold the 100,000 in attendance today. They flow over into the infield, where that 13-year-old boy watched his first Derby seventy-one years ago, then swarm under the cavernous clubhouse with its spired towers.

They find restaurants, bars and taverns every way they turn. Confidentially, Churchill Downs seems to have more oases than Fifty-second Street. They encounter barkers, vendors and peddlers. As one astonished gentleman of the press gasped, "It's Coney Island—with horses." It's all of that, a perfectly incredible scene of bustling humanity with mild equine overtones.

Most of the spectators (?) never even saw the seventy-second Kentucky Derby run. For the benefit of those who might have missed it, it would be churlish, indeed, not to let the secret out. Hold fast, folks. The winner was Assault.

A DAY AT CHURCHILL DOWNS

BY ARTHUR DALEY

LOUISVILLE, MAY 8, 1955 — "He's an observant horse," said Mickey Tenney the other morning. "He notices everything." The slow-speaking Tenney should know because he trains Swaps, the colt from California.

On his way to the starting gate today the curious Swaps noticed the blanket of roses which was awaiting the winner of the eighty-first Kentucky Derby. He had a hankering for it. A few minutes later the rose blanket was draped tastefully around his neck.

Thus did the colt from the coast take the measure of the two titans, Nashua and Summer Tan. He didn't do it by any fluke either. With Willie Shoemaker giving him a handsome ride, he let Nashua, a fierce competitor, come up to him in the stretch and then he beat back the big son of Nasrullah for a solid, convincing victory.

Not many Derbies have been as spectacular as this one. Thunder rumbled and lightning flashed on and off all during the major part of the show. Rain sprinkled after a day of sunshine. It almost was like one of those large screen super epics from Hollywood. And Swaps, a California horse, won it. This wasn't in the original script but it sure meant a surprise finish.

There is always a Runyonesque flavor to a Derby Day crowd and many of the racegoers look as though they'd stepped off the stage from *Guys and Dolls*. There is, for instance, the totally implausible Diamond Jim Moran of New Orleans. He has diamond fillings in his teeth, diamond-encrusted eye glasses and diamonds for buttons. And some of the stories a Blue Grass tourist hears sound suspiciously as though Damon Runyon wrote them.

The tale was being told in the barn area this morning of the guy who had been coming to the Kentucky Derby for twenty years. Never once in that time does he bring his everloving wife with him. And finally his old lady insists that she accompany him. This is slightly more than somewhat embarrassing to the guy because his everloving might interfere with his drinking. But he orders a mint julep anyway. "Let me taste that," she says, reaching for the glass with the grass in it.

"Ugh," she says, making a face. "That is horrible."

"You said it," he says bitterly. "And all these years you have been thinking that I have been having fun."

A guy can buy a mint julep at Churchill Downs almost anywhere on the premises and the price of $1.35 entitles the purchaser to keep the suitably-inscribed glass as a souvenir. Not long before the Derby was run one bleary-eyed patron was discovered arguing with his rather irate spouse.

"Whash you so mad at?" he muttered. "I'm doin' thish for you. You said you wanted a set of mint julep glasses, didn't you?"

There was a party the other night at one of the baronial mansions which dot the Blue Grass country. And one guest was an ex-cowpoke from Texas, new to the Derby and a stranger to the dynamite lurking at the bottom of julep glasses. It was a garden party beneath gay parasols and awnings. The tyro from Texas didn't miss a food course or a julep. Just before the end of the meal he slid gently beneath the table and off to sleep.

The other guests eventually departed and no one realized that the Texan was missing. At 6 A.M. the servants began cleaning up the debris and one stumbled over the ex-cowpoke. He shook him.

"What are you doing here?" demanded the unbelieving servant.

The cowpoke groped his way back out of the fog.

"I reckon I'm still waiting for dessert," he said.

Note to all members of the Baseball Writers Association: Please send your check immediately for $5. It will entitle you to membership in "The Happy Club." This is an organization which is collecting campaign funds for Happy Chandler.

The unfrocked baseball commissioner is now running for Governor of Kentucky. And, so the advertisements in the paper say, needs all the financial help he can get. His old buddies from the baseball press box won't desert their once beloved leader in his time of stress—or will they?

The house rules for the Derby prohibited from admission to the clubhouse guys not wearing coats or dolls wearing slacks or shorts. The closest to circumvention of this edict came when two college boys appeared at the clubhouse entrance. The ticket-taker blinked twice but decided they qualified. They were wearing jackets, all right, but they also were clad in Bermuda shorts.

The attraction of the Kentucky Derby is one of sports' most extraordinary phenomenons. It is to be doubted that half of the usual crowd of 100,000 even sees the race run. Thousands don't even try. They sit in the garden behind the stands, watching the race by ear—using the public address system for their eyes.

All of them would be far more comfortable at home in front of television sets—for free, too. But they pay money to be uncomfortable and unseeing. However, they can feed their money into the maw of the mutual machines here and they can't do it at home. Maybe that's the explanation.

MILE AND A QUARTER OF MEMORIES

BY RED SMITH

LOUISVILLE, APRIL 30, 1979 — This is the week when dear little old ladies in Shawano, Wisconsin, get to know about sports figures named Spectacular Bid and Flying Paster. Spectacular Bid and Flying Paster are thoroughbred racehorses, and there are vast and sinless areas in this country where they and their like are regarded as instruments of Satan 51 weeks a year. Then comes the week of the Kentucky Derby, and sinless newspapers that wouldn't mention a horse any other time unless he kicked the mayor to death are suddenly full of information about steeds that will run and the people they will run for at Churchill Downs on the first Saturday of May. In cities all over the land stenographers invest their silver in office pools, in cities and towns and on farms the sinless old ladies study the entries and on Saturday almost everyone tunes in on television.

Nobody has ever explained satisfactorily why the Derby is the most famous race in the Western Hemisphere and, in the view of many, the only race of any year. The easy explanation is that Col. Matt Winn, who operated Churchill Downs for half a century, was a master showman but the truth is he wasn't. He was a tailor who promoted racing at Empire City in Yonkers and Juarez in Mexico as well as in Louisville. Empire City is now Yonkers Raceway, where jugheads pace and trot. Juarez is for gila monsters.

"In my home town," says Johnny Rotz, the former jockey who is now a steward in New York, "the only times the newspaper mentioned racing was to tell who won the Derby and how much money Eddie Arcaro had."

As everybody knows by now, or will know before the week is out, the 105th Derby is widely regarded as a match between Spectacular Bid and Flying Paster, with everything else last. It could turn out that way, as it did last year when Affirmed and Alydar were considered best of the 3-year-old crop and proved it again and again.

Affirmed and Alydar had hooked up four times as 2-year-olds. Spectacular Bid and Flying Paster have never laid eye on each other. While Flying Paster was establishing himself as the top horse in California, Spectacular Bid was rampaging through the East in a bold charge to the Eclipse Award as champion 2-year-old.

Starting last September, Spectacular Bid has won 10 stakes in a row. He started his 3-year-old campaign by sweeping four races in Florida—the Hutcheson Stakes, the Fountain of Youth, the Florida Derby and the Flamingo—and last Thursday he tuned up for the Derby by winning the Blue Grass Stakes with his ears pricked.

He could go to the post Saturday as the shortest-priced favorite in—well, in three years.

In 1976 there was a favorite who, like Spectacular Bid, had waited until September to take command of the 2-year-olds. Once he started winning the big ones he seemed invincible. He, too, took the Florida stakes route at 3, and he, too, cleaned up everything in sight, including the Florida Derby and the Flamingo.

"Who does he remind you of now?" his trainer was asked on television as he watched a tape of his horse winning the Flamingo by the widest margin ever.

"Well, right now," the trainer said, and you could hear him gulp on the air, "Secretariat."

That colt went into the Derby at 40 cents to $1, joining Bimelech, Count Fleet and Citation as one of the four shortest-priced favorites. His name was Honest Pleasure and he finished second to Bold Forbes, who had done most of his running in Puerto Rico. Which probably proves that although memory may be short, a mile and a quarter can be a long, long way.

Up to now, this Derby field has not been ornamented by horses that were nominated because the trainer's wife was told by her departed Aunt Minnie at a table-rapping séance that the beast could sweep the Triple Crown like breaking sticks. Maybe the presence of Spectacular Bid and Flying Paster will scare that sort away, but it is hard to discourage dreamers.

More often than not, a few owners show up so eager to see their colors in the Derby that they will tear their pants getting up entry and starting fees. The fact that the bettors rated A Dragon Killer no better than a 294 to 1 chance didn't discourage that noble creature's owner in 1958, and the same field included Chance It Tony at 243 to 1.

Historians steeped in Derby folklore like to repeat the story of One-Eyed Tom, who had lost an eye when he ran into a tree on a Nevada ranch and had been left out to die until a ranch hand took pity on him. The horse had never broken from a starting gate, and his owner was persuaded to withdraw him when other owners vowed that they wouldn't allow their horses on the same track with him.

Another year a creature named Gift Silver came out of Iowa with an own-er-trainer whose regular job was piloting a locomotive. Gift Silver had never raced, but his owner swore by the striped cloth cap on his head that he had clocked the horse in track-record time going a mile and a half in the snow.

Management contrived to talk the engineer out of starting Gift Silver but nobody protested three years ago when a little guy named Tony Battaglia flew in with Bidson, a colt who had never won until five weeks earlier.

Ed Ways of Park Ridge, Ill., paid $6,500 to charter a plane from Florida and $7,600 more to start Bidson who got up to sixth place in the first quarter-mile but faded to last, beaten 17 lengths at 72 to 1.

SYMPATHY FOR DERBY "MUSKRATS"

BY GEORGE VECSEY

LOUISVILLE, MAY 6, 1989 — The Kentucky Derby would be such a wonderful event if only they didn't let all these horses in it.

Sixteen of them will clutter up the start of the Derby this afternoon, many of them as intrusive as fighting in hockey, television timeouts in basketball, cheerleaders in football, the wave in baseball.

That's what the purists have been saying this week as the Derby shaped up as one of those wagon stampedes when the Western frontier was opened to homesteaders.

The loquacious D. Wayne Lukas even came up with a new word for these interlopers: "muskrats," those lumpy woodland critters not known for their speed. Of course, Lukas stopped talking so derisively when William T. Young, a member of the Churchill Downs board of directors and a Lukas customer, asked the trainer to handle Shy Tom in the Derby. As D. Wayne explained it, "It was hard to say no."

After all, if the lords of racing have eagerly sold breeding shares, allowed hordes of fans to squat in the precious infield, allowed the grubby legions of the press to stroll in the barn area, then they can make room for muskrats, too.

There is no other place like Lou-uh-vul on the first Saturday in May when they sing "My Old Kentucky Home," but this is also America, where everybody is equal.

The eighth race is not exactly first-come, first-served, either. Since 23 horses went off in the 100th running in 1974, the Derby is now limited to the 20 top 3-year-old stakes winners whose owners put up the $20,600 entry fee.

That $20,600 sounds impressive unless you have watched visiting swells in blinding green jackets and yellow pants parading through Standiford Field, ready to spend that much money for Derby Week room rates, larcenous cabbies, gaudy hats, tacky gimcracks, Derby souvenirs, hot Brown sandwiches (don't ask) and mint juleps (don't drink).

Besides, ever since Dr. Kalarikkal Kunhiraman Jayarman, a cardiologist, and his wife, Dr. Devi Jayarman, a pathologist, arrived from India in 1964, they have believed America is a democracy.

They were standing in the damp dawn yesterday, wearing identical red silk jackets that read "Tiffany Stables," named after their pet poodle, and proudly watching Irish Actor try to kick his groom.

"He's never finished worse than fourth," the husband said. "He finished third behind Easy Goer in the Champagne last fall. There were only four horses, of course, and he finished 19 lengths back. Personally, I don't like races with a few horses. Kind of boring." What better fun than watching 16 horses acting like commuters funneling into the door of a railroad train? Particularly with some of those muskrats linked into field and entry bets?

"Only three field horses have ever won the Derby," said Dr. Howard Hoffman, one of three psychiatrists who own Northern Wolf. "One was in 1971, one in 1951, one in 1925. We think it's time for it to happen again."

The three amigos like sports, as well as the intellectual challenge of racing, and they don't mind in the least that Deep Silver Stable has shown a profit for more than a decade.

Besides, Dr. Hoffman noted, people in his field are known to have a "strong sense of fantasy." And Dr. Allen Cahill smiled as he described his friend having a temper tantrum after finishing second: "But I wanted to win!"

Every owner will say the horse has a chance to win. Jack Kent Cooke, who does not dictate the lineup to Washington Redskins coach Joe Gibbs, as far as we know, apparently told Jay Robbins to enter Flying Continental.

Hank Allen, who played major league baseball for parts of seven years, will be the first black American trainer in the Derby since Ned Gaines saddled King Clover for C. C. Boshamer in 1951.

Allen is too gracious to tell newcomers that he is weary of talking about the race. By yesterday, he also was more than a tad tired of being asked if Northern Wolf had a shot.

"Have you ever seen a horse pay $100 or $200 to win?" Allen answered. "Obviously, long shots sometimes win."

Sometimes the immensity of the Derby strikes newcomers without warning. Randy Williams of Pasadena, Md., operates a ceramic-tile business when he is not escorting his wife, Patsy, and Wind Splitter to the Thursday draw for post positions.

Surrounded in the darkened Churchill Downs museum by a gaudy slide show of lush cinematic roses, galloping hooves, shiny coats, blaring trumpets and clips of past winners, Patsy Williams burst into tears.

"That's why we never watch the race together," said her husband, not without affection. "I wonder where she'll be on Saturday?"

Not in the winner's circle, the experts say with certainty. The muskrats have no chance. Easy Goer can't lose the Derby. But guess what? They're gonna hold it anyway.

SIGHTS AND SOUNDS AT
THE PREAKNESS

BY JOHN KIERAN

BALTIMORE, MAY 10, 1941 — Pulling away from the railroad station and heading for the Pimlico track the taxi driver turned around and said, confidentially:

"Trip before this I took out Whirlaway's jockey, Eddie Arcaro. Yeah. He's a little black-eyed guy. He told me the only horse that worried him in the Derby was Our Boots. He thinks he'll win today on Whirlaway. You can't blame him for that. It's his horse. I like Dispose myself."

The man from Philadelphia, who was sitting up front with the driver and had the taxi meter for a chest decoration, said stoutly (he was a stout man):

"Dispose. That's something to put away and forget. Our Boots will win all the money today."

This seemed to discourage the taxi driver, who said no more until he reached the clubhouse gate, at which strategic point he announced:

"Fifty cents each, gents. Thank you."

The man from Philadelphia said to him, with a grin: "This is like throwing money away."

There was a clear sky and a cool breeze for the big day. The regulars were predicting a fast-drying track. The breeze was supposed to help a lot. The Pimlico working force had given the racing strip a good going-over about 10 A.M.

A man in the paddock said:

"I hear Ben Jones doesn't like Whirlaway's post position. He's the inside horse. Might get shut off right at the start."

"Shucks!" said his neighbor. "What's the difference about the start. Whirlaway's a stretch runner."

Director Dave Woods of the Maryland Jockey Club, who is also chairman of the library committee, commented on the fine weather, but he didn't claim credit for it. Asked about the horses in the big race, he said:

"I like all of them, and I wish there were more."

Probably he was thinking about the starting fees.

Sunny Jim Fitzsimmons, the veteran trainer, said cheerfully that he thought King Cole had a chance. By a curious coincidence Sunny Jim is King Cole's trainer.

"Well, King Cole is a fast breaker," said Sunny Jim. "He ought to get away well and this is a hard track to catch up on a leading horse."

Maxey Hirsch, trainer of Dispose, was glad to see the sun and feel the breeze. He said that the faster the track the better he liked the chances of his horse.

After the third race a sprinkling cart went up the stretch in front of the clubhouse. Some suspicious persons said it was sent out there by Silent Tom Smith, trainer of Porter's Cap, the horse that likes heavy going.

Of the chances of Kansas, the outsider in the field, a local Democrat said scornfully: "Kansas! He'll probably run like Alf Landon."

The Marylanders liked Ocean Blue, the nearest thing to a Maryland horse in the Preakness. Ocean Blue hails from Virginia, a neighboring and passably friendly state.

Larry MacPhail, Brooklyn baseball magnate, was sitting in a box near the finish line. Asked who would win, he said loudly:

"The Dodgers!"

United States Senator Happy Chandler was sighted in the clubhouse. He wouldn't name his choice, but he looked like a man who was backing Whirlaway.

The laugh of the afternoon came with the announcement that the handlers of Dispose had forgotten to bring the King Ranch colors to Pimlico and were scouring around to borrow a set for Carroll Bierman, the rider of Dispose.

"Lucky they didn't forget to bring the horse," said President Alfred Gwynne Vanderbilt of the Maryland Jockey Club.

Everybody was talking of the Preakness from noon on, but they must have been thinking about the earlier races, too. The mutual play on the earlier races was brisk. Still, maybe they bet without thinking. It has been done.

The King Ranch colors being a brown and white combination, they did well enough in borrowing a jockey's weskit and cap for Bierman, who was up on Dispose. They were the colors of Mrs. Patrick Brady—white jacket with brown stripes, and a brown cap. Not exactly the King Ranch arrangement of the colors, but good enough to pass in a crowd.

While white roses are the official badges of office and symbols of authority worn by the stewards at Pimlico, the winner of the Preakness is always decorated with a blanket of black-eyed susans. The flowers are not home-grown. They are brought in from California. Later in the year they can be picked free of charge in Maryland meadows. But the Preakness couldn't wait for that, so California got the trade.

When Jockey Arcaro left his contract stable (Greentree) in New York to make the Baltimore trip, Trainer Johnny Gaver of Greentree said to him: "Hurry back!" Those were the same instructions that Trainer Ben Jones gave Arcaro as he put him up on Whirlaway for the start of the Preakness.

Out came the eight starters in the big event, with the rush at the mutual windows showing Whirlaway on top, followed by Our Boots, Porter's Cap and Ocean Blue in the investment rating. Well, Sir, Whirlaway was bashful about getting into the starting gate and slow getting away from it, but the Derby winner just ran over the field when he got ready and breezed to a glorious victory in the Preakness. Now for the Belmont and the triple crown of the turf.

DOWDY IMAGE OVERSHADOWS ROLE OF PIMLICO

BY JOE DRAPE

BALTIMORE, MAY 16, 2003 — Lore has it that the name, Pimlico, comes from the English settlers who inhabited the 129 acres on which the racetrack was built. They were a nostalgic bunch and yearned for the famous landmark near London that they had left behind: Olde Ben Pimlico's Tavern.

Since opening its doors in 1870, Pimlico Race Course has been visited by history in odd and significant ways.

The United States House of Representatives adjourned on Oct. 24, 1887, so the distinguished gentlemen could watch a horse named Parole beat Ten Broeck and Tom Ochiltree in what has become known as the Great Race.

Pimlico was the proving ground for an Italian automobile driver named Emmanuele Cedrino in 1908. He set a world record of 51 seconds for a mile on a circular track, but he lost control of the vehicle, was thrown from it and was fatally injured.

Then there are the 11 horses—the last being Affirmed in 1978—that arrived here as Kentucky Derby winners, captured the Preakness Stakes, which will be run Saturday for the 128th time, and prevailed in the Belmont Stakes to earn the Triple Crown.

What is missing at this granddaddy of a racetrack, as Maryland officials are reminded each May, is some charm. In an annual rite of spring, some reporters, as well as some patrons, note the track's ramshackle condition, criticizing Pimlico for being a run-down, soulless factory, an eyesore and an unfit host for the second jewel of the Triple Crown.

Some wacky recent events at the Preakness have exacerbated the perception that Pimlico, a once-proud monument to the golden age of swells, has become hopelessly down and out. On a sweltering day in 1998, a power outage left more than 91,000 people without air-conditioning, working elevators, working escalators and, worst of all, some working betting machines for several hours.

The next year, three races before Charismatic secured a Preakness victory for two-thirds of the Triple Crown, a man made his way onto the track from the infield to face down a thundering herd of nine horses in the stretch and take a punch at the 4-5 favorite, a horse named Artax.

"Clearly, everyone involved with the racetrack, the employees, the horsemen and breeders and management, do not enjoy having people say these things," said Tim Capps, executive vice president of the Maryland Jockey Club. "Yes, it would be nice if you had a nicer building. Gee, we know that."

Last year the pieces appeared to be falling in place for the track to receive a facelift when the Magna Entertainment Corporation bought a controlling interest in Pimlico and its sister track, Laurel Park. The company, led by the horse racing aficionado Frank Stronach, has been aggressively acquiring racetracks with the two-pronged intention of transforming them into entertainment destinations and offering year-round horse racing for its fledgling television and Internet networks. Hopes were further raised when the Maryland General Assembly seemed ready to embrace slot machines for the state's racetracks.

But this spring doubts arose about the renovation of Pimlico. A committee in the Maryland House of Delegates killed the bill on slot machines, and Magna announced it would first concentrate its money on rebuilding the barn area at Laurel Park. There has been speculation that Magna may consider moving the Preakness, Maryland's biggest race, to one of its other racetracks—namely to Santa Anita Park in Arcadia, Calif., one of the 15 tracks that the company owns, operates or manages.

"How can you move history?" said Stronach, Magna's chairman, who won the 2000 Preakness with a colt named Red Bullet. "We intend to restore Pimlico to a world-class facility when the time is right. Slots are not the final answer, but it will help."

Jim McAlpine, president and chief executive of Magna, said the company would soon release plans for updating Pimlico, but he also indicated an overhaul of the track's facade would take a backseat to improving its infrastructure.

"We're in the entertainment business, and the No. 1 rule is that the show must go on," said McAlpine, noting that Maryland had 220 racing dates. "We're going to do the things first that insures we have horses racing on the days we have available to us."

Besides a long, colorful history, Pimlico also offers a rich tradition of quality horses. Funny Cide, the Kentucky Derby winner and the Preakness favorite, is trained by Barclay Tagg, who honed his craft in Maryland for 30 years before moving to New York. Another New York transplant from Maryland, Edgar Prado, who won 14 riding titles here, will ride the morning line's second choice, Peace Rules.

Despite Pimlico's reputation, horsemen eagerly anticipate their stop at the racetrack along the Triple Crown trail. Bob Baffert, who has won four of the last six Preakness Stakes, especially likes the old stakes barn behind the grandstand, where the majority of the contenders are stabled. The Hall of Famers like D. Wayne Lukas and Bobby Frankel sip coffee with younger trainers.

"It's like going to camp," Baffert said. "You're close to your colleagues and regular fans, and the people could not be nicer down here. It's way more relaxed than the Derby and the surface is in incredible shape. It's an honest racetrack."

The Maryland Legislature is expected to take up the issue of slot machines in its next session, and most people here appear confident that the slots will eventually be authorized, bringing more money for purses, as well as a track makeover. But Pimlico's most immediate hope for a renaissance may come this summer with the release of a movie based on the book *Seabiscuit: An American Legend*.

It was here that Seabiscuit defeated War Admiral in a celebrated match race in 1938. Alfred G. Vanderbilt, a former prep school bookie and a sporting scion of one of America's most celebrated families, orchestrated the race for the track he owned and a sport he dearly loved.

"Pimlico is more than a dirt track bounded by four streets," he once said. "It is an accepted American institution, devoted to the best interests of a great sport, graced by time, respected for its honorable past."

When the field of 10 horses springs from the gate in the Preakness, the grandeur Vanderbilt spoke of will be visible—for at least the two minutes it takes to determine the winner.

THE BELMONT STARTS WITH GEORGE

BY RED SMITH

ELMONT, N.Y., JUNE 6, 1973 — George Bennett Cassidy, ruddy, smiling and faultlessly tailored, climbs a short flight of stairs beside the inner rail at Belmont Park and stands watching while assistants lead the horses into the starting gate. The moment the doors are closed, four or five urgent voices rise: "No, boss, not yet!" "No chance, boss!" "Not ready!" Almost immediately, Cassidy's thumb presses the button at the end of an insulated cord. A strident bell rings, doors fly open with a metallic clang, the jockeys whoop like Comanches. They're off in the 105th Belmont Stakes. "In gate at 5:35," the chart in Sunday morning's paper will report. "Off at 5:35 Eastern Daylight Time. Start good." With only minor variations, charts have been saying this about every Belmont since June 7, 1930, when Cassidy sent a field of four away and saw Gallant Fox come home in possession of the Triple Crown.

The race that sends Secretariat off on the same mission Saturday will be George Cassidy's 44th Belmont. He has let horses go from walkup starts, from a belt of webbing stretched across the track, from the Australian barriers—six strands of rope designed to trip horses and strangle jockeys—and from the infernal machines that were the immediate precursors of today's electric gate. Five times while Belmont Park was closed for reconstruction he started the stakes of Aqueduct's stretch turn, where a race of a mile and a half had to start on a track measuring a mile and an eighth.

"Start good," 42 of the charts reported. "Start good for all but Determined Man," read the single exception in 1964 when Bill Boland's mount reared just as Cassidy hit the switch.

In Cassidy's time the Belmont has had as few as three starters—in 1931 when only Sun Meadow and Jamestown chased Twenty Grand—and as many as 13—in 1954 and 1971. If Secretariat can add this race to his Kentucky Derby-Preakness double he will become the first Triple Crown winner in 25 years, so Cassidy will take special pains to get a clean start.

He does not anticipate trouble, even though Secretariat is habitually nonchalant leaving the gate. "I can't remember any Belmont that was trouble," he said yesterday, "since the early days before we had the gate. There's just a little more tension than the ordinary race. I guess the year Canonero was here [1971] was our biggest field, plus the fact that there were so many of those South Americans hopping around.

"Canonero was supposed to be a bad actor in the gate. They had to blindfold him and load him last, but in New York we load 'em by post position, from the inside out. We blindfolded Canonero but loaded him seventh, when his turn came. Once he was standing, we took the blindfold off and he never made a move."

It doesn't worry Cassidy that $6 million or more may be riding on the races he starts Saturday. He is a blithe spirit, as patient as he is good-humored, and responsibility rests lightly on those exquisitely groomed shoulders. Experience has polished a gift that Eddie Arcaro likens to the split vision of a quarterback surveying all his receivers in one glance. "He seems to sense the instant when a bad horse is going to stand," the former jockey says. "Sometimes, sitting on a skittish 2-year-old in the old Widener chute, I'd marvel at how he could get 28 of us off together."

Maybe this is because Cassidy, like Secretariat, was bred for his job. In 1890, his father, Mars, who owned and trained thoroughbreds and trotters, was pressed into service as a starter at Iron Hill, a Maryland track now lost from memory. In 1903 Mars was invited to New York, and he worked the big wheel until his death in 1929.

Mars was distinguished by a high bowler hat, handlebar mustaches, a temper that boiled at 98.6 degrees and a vocabulary that would bring blushes to the foredeck of a Portuguese freighter. All three of his sons worked as his assistants but only George stayed with it. Marshall became a steward and Jockey Club official highly influential on the national scene.

A variety of adventures at the post convinced Wendell that his future lay in the oil fields.

Once, as occasionally happens with a horse notoriously reluctant to start, Wendell was assigned to stand behind a sluggard and encourage him with a bullwhip. He slipped his wrist through the thong at the butt of the whip and, on signal, fetched the steed a manly swat. The lash took a half-hitch round the horse's tail. "Wendell went the first eighth in a little better than 12," George says, "before the whip pulled free."

When George was 22 and schooled in esoteric wiles like biting a rogue's ear to make him stand, the stewards at Saratoga sent word for him to start the first race in the absence of his father, who had been unavoidably detained. In those days, a talent for beating the start was esteemed as the loftiest refinement of the equestrian art. Riding in the first race were Pony McAtee, Leverne Fator, Earl Sande, Mack Garner and Jim Burke, all capable of removing a starter's coat and vest without getting caught.

They walked up to the tape, George shut his eyes and let them go. The stewards couldn't believe their binoculars. It was the best start of the meeting. The desperadoes had made a compact: "Good kid, young Cassidy. Give him a break." After that beginning it was inevitable that George would succeed his father.

Soon after he did, an owner named Riley demanded that his horse be removed from the schooling list of bad actors forbidden to start until their manners at the post improved. "We had prohibition then," Cassidy says, "with rum runners and hijackers, and this Riley belonged to the armpit artillery. He said he'd make it tough for me. His horse stayed on the list but I had Riley insomnia for a few weeks."

As far as the jocks were concerned, all friendship ceased when the Cassidy kid officially became The Man. The first to test him was Earl Sande. He tried to beat the barrier and Cassidy gave him a five-day suspension. He tried again and got five days more. This cost him a stakes assignment on Gallant Fox.

"I stopped in a butcher shop," Cassidy says, "and here was this guy with a white apron and red arms, horse player, whacking up a side of beef with a cleaver and saying how he'd like to get his hands on the louse that took Sande off Gallant Fox. I took my business elsewhere."

THESE DAYS IT ISN'T JUST
"THE EIGHTH AT BELMONT"

BY STEVE CADY

ELMONT, N.Y., JUNE 10, 1978—Sports fans who do not understand horse racing tend to see it as little more than a numbers game supported by unshaven derelicts with nothing better to do.

But there's another side to racing, a side filled with color and drama and tradition and that is the image the public will see today when the 110th running of the Belmont Stakes takes place at Belmont Park, on the edge of Queens.

Hard-core horseplayers, touts and even pickpockets will all be part of the scene. But so will the sightseers, socialites, celebrities and working folks who regard horse racing as a pleasant diversion. If the sun stays out, a crowd that could surpass the Belmont Park record of 82,694 will be playing horses, listening to music or relaxing on the grass in the midst of trees, flowers and shrubs.

Meanwhile, house detectives will be keeping an eye out for the 30 to 40 pickpockets they expect to pick up.

"They usually work in pairs," said Bill Billing of the Thoroughbred Racing Protective Bureau, "and they're usually most effective during the running of a race. We spot most of them after the announcer says, 'It is now post time,' because they're the only ones that aren't watching the race."

Nobody will drink a mint julep today or sing "My Old Kentucky Home" or drape a blanket of red roses over the winning horse, as at the Kentucky

Derby. Today it will be "The Sidewalks of New York" and a blanket of white carnations.

Fittingly, the dance band that will be playing the theme song, a group called Bo and Generation II, has a reputation for blending the old with the new. That's what Belmont is all about—yesterday and today. When 18-year-old Steve Cauthen rides his 3-year-old colt, Affirmed, out of the paddock in search of a Triple Crown sweep, they will be parading past a 150-year-old white pine. The prospect of another duel between Affirmed and Alydar, the colt who chased him in the Derby and the Preakness, has produced a record number of requests for dining reservations.

"I've been begging everybody to cut off the reservations," said Tony Triola, the track's maitre d'hotel, "because the demand is bigger than we had for Secretariat or Seattle Slew," the two previous equine superstars of the Belmont.

"I'm overchairing everything now," he added, "turning four-seat tables into sixes, and sixes into eights. I'm even setting up private buffets in some of the executive offices."

Socialites who paid $125 a ticket to attend last Tuesday's black-tie Belmont Ball will be at the track today, along with other celebrities who didn't make the ball. Governor Carey and other Albany dignitaries are expected.

"We have Pete Rozelle, Al Rosen, Phil Rizzuto and Wellington Mara on the Terrace," a reservations aide reported. "And George Steinbrenner's going to be with us, and let's see . . ."

Management calls its mile-and-a-half stakes race the "test of the champion," and horse breeders tend to agree. Nobody calls it just the "eighth race at Belmont" anymore, as racing's aristocracy did in stuffier days. Changing promotional attitudes have turned the Belmont into a genuine happening that comes as close as New York gets to a world-famous yearly sporting event. As one rail-bird put it, "The Belmont is annual proof that New York City still lives."

BELMONT MAKES THE HEART BEAT FASTER

BY STEPHEN DOBYNS

ELMONT, N.Y., APRIL 24, 1988—From the window of the placing judges booth, a hundred feet above the finish line at Belmont Park, the horses look like canoes as they pass beneath on the post parade to the starting gate—canoes with bright colors at their centers, the silks of the jockeys, the red jackets of the outriders, the green jackets of the pony boys and girls. Some horses seem relaxed, several prance sideways, flicking their heads; one sprints forward as its jockey stands in the stirrups. Beneath the booth, thousands of spectators watch the horses—amateur handicappers ranging from the happy beginners with $40 for the day, more interested in the outing than the betting, to the passionate horse-players who hardly notice the beauty of the track as they search for that last detail that might give them an edge.

"What I look for in a winning horse is fluidity of movement," says Sonny Taylor, one of the three placing judges in the booth perched on the roof of the clubhouse. "I mean, the horse just seems to flow. If the horse has it, you spot it right away."

"Belmont puts you in mind of a racetrack," Taylor says. "It's simply the best racetrack in the country."

Situated just across the line in Nassau County, Belmont Park is bounded on three sides by the Cross Island Parkway, the Jericho Turnpike and Hempstead Avenue. It was built by a group of financier-sportsmen headed by August Belmont 2d, a wealthy breeder and chairman of New York State's second racing commission. The track opened on May 4, 1905, when a crowd of 40,000 saw one of August's horses, Blandy, win the first race of the day. Belmont Park covers 430 acres and has an attendance capacity of about 90,000. Its biggest crowd was on June 5, 1971, when 82,694 came to see Canonero II try for the Triple Crown in the Belmont Stakes (he lost). The average daily crowd at the 1987 fall meet was 13,000. As much as $7,895,946 has been wagered in a single afternoon. The average daily handle during the 1987 fall meet was $2.9 million.

Like most New York Racing Association employees, Sonny Taylor moves between three tracks—in 1988, 114 days of racing at Belmont, divided between the spring and fall meets, 174 at Aqueduct during the winter, and 24 days in August at Saratoga. Two other placing judges also work in the booth, Lee Buonagura and John Hennegan, as well as the official timer, Steve Foster.

Races can range from five furlongs (five-eighths of a mile) to two miles. The race we are watching today is seven furlongs, and the starting gate is on the far side of the infield. From the placing booth one sees every inch of the main track, then the two turf, or grass, courses. Four white railings circle the three tracks. Just past the Inner Turf Course (the other is called the Widener Turf Course), the three green tote boards face the grandstand and clubhouse.

Two great horses are buried in the infield at Belmont. To the left, within a horseshoe-shaped hedge under the American flag, is the grave of Timely Writer, who went down with a broken left foreleg during the Jockey Club Gold Cup in October 1982, in a pile-up that killed another horse and badly injured four jockeys. To the right, within another horseshoe-shaped hedge and under the Racing Association flag, is buried Ruffian. The unbeaten three-year-old filly was destroyed after breaking two bones in her right foreleg in a match race with a Kentucky Derby winner, Foolish Pleasure, in July 1975.

Today the grass of the infield is filled with Canada geese, at least 500 of them. On either side of the infield are ponds, each roughly the shape of a bowling pin. Beyond the starting gate is a thick line of trees in varying shades of green. The air is smoky, the sky blue. A dirt road wanders along the edge of the infield past a row of shrubs. About three miles away stand the three tall apartment buildings that make up North Shore Towers. Sonny Taylor lives in the center one, and as he follows each race, his binoculars sweep across his living room window just above the trees.

Belmont has the biggest track in the country. The main course is a mile and a half, while those at Aqueduct and Saratoga are a mile and an eighth. According to some handicappers, this gives them an edge at Belmont, since it means that in most races the horses only go around one turn and stand less chance of being blocked. This is also what can make the Belmont

Stakes, the last leg of racing's Triple Crown, such a heartbreaker. As the only mile-and-a-half race for three-year-olds, it is longer than the Kentucky Derby (a mile and a quarter) and the Preakness (a mile and three-sixteenths). Such favorites as Carry Back and Northern Dancer failed to win the Triple Crown because they tired on the Belmont track. In some 70 years, only 11 horses have won the Triple Crown, perhaps the most decisive victory being won in 1973, when Secretariat beat Twice A Prince in the Belmont Stakes by 31 lengths before a crowd of 70,000, to set a track record time of 2:24. As the horses approach the starting gate, Sonny Taylor picks up his binoculars and moves to the big window. Lee Buonagura steps over to her computer. Taylor focuses his glasses and as the last horses are being urged into place, he says, "O.K., lock it."

Lee Buonagura touches her keyboard, and beneath us the betting machines are closed down at the 789 parimutuel windows. One imagines the groans of the people still waiting in line.

Now Taylor, John Hennegan and Steve Foster all have their binoculars trained on the starting gate. There is no noise in the booth, seemingly no noise anywhere. Then, as if from far away, we hear the voice of Marshall Cassidy, the track announcer, over the public-address system: "They're off!"

ESSAY: WHAT'S IN A NAME? IN THIS CASE, THREE BIG WINS

BY DOROTHY OURS

When Sir Barton swept the Kentucky Derby, Preakness and Belmont Stakes in 1919, the Roman Catholic Church had featured a literal "triple crown" for about six hundred years. It was a headdress sporting three coronets and worn by the Pope.

So the concept of three crowns being better than one took root long before British horse racing birthed the St. Leger (1776), Epsom Derby (1780), and Two Thousand Guineas (1809). When West Australian in 1853 became the first horse to sweep these classics, however, his feat wasn't officially labeled the Triple Crown. In fact, fifty years and ten sweeps later, the very proper *Times* of London still didn't use the popular term "triple crown" in its coverage or celebrate the achievement.

While London's newspaper of record spurned the term, the phrase "triple crown" had caught on with sports fans. On March 12, 1894, the *Irish Times* rejoiced that, "Ireland has achieved the triple crown honours of Rugby football." That summer, *The New York Times* reported "a Triple Crown" for jockey Fred Taral, who had just won the Brooklyn, Metropolitan, and Suburban handicaps—with two different horses at three different New York tracks—in the same year.

Those races were for older horses, however, and when the New York tracks failed to popularize a three race series for 3-year-olds racetracks in Kentucky and Maryland stepped in to fill the void with richer purses. So New York sportsmen took some of their best young stock on the road, winning the 1915 and 1916 Derbys with Eastern imports Regret and George Smith.

Local limitations had opened the way for ambitious risk—and, ultimately, a championship quest with wider appeal. Spanning a region roughly twice the size of England, the Kentucky Derby, Preakness Stakes, and Belmont Stakes had not made a natural series. By railroad train, about 650 miles separated Churchill Downs from Pimlico, and more than 200 additional miles separated Pimlico from Belmont Park. Long-distance travel dangers were so daunting that between 1875 and 1917, only three horses ran in both the Kentucky Derby and the Preakness Stakes.

But suddenly the incentive changed. In 1918, the Preakness purse surged from $5,000 added to $15,000 added. War Cloud, beaten favorite in the muddy Derby, popped up at Pimlico only four days later to win a division of the oversubscribed Preakness.

Chasing maximum money and prestige, War Cloud went on to New York's Belmont Stakes and ran second to rising champion Johren. He had won only one-half of one classic—but by running fourth, first, and second in Kentucky, Maryland, and New York's top springtime races for three-year-olds, War Cloud radically expanded the racing world.

So when Sir Barton won the 1919 Derby in a canter, trainer Guy Bedwell quickly shipped him to Baltimore for the now $25,000-added Preakness. Again, only four days separated the Kentucky and Maryland classics—but three other Derby starters joined Sir Barton at Pimlico but were unable to deprive him of a wire-to-wire victory. Like War Cloud the year before, he invaded New York.

From his Maryland home base to Louisville, back east to Baltimore, then north to Long Island, Sir Barton had traveled more than a thousand miles in less than three weeks. This rugged schedule didn't seem to faze him. Only ten days after winning the Preakness, the short but muscular grandson of English "triple crown" champion Isinglass romped home first in the Withers; then, a mere month and one day after his Kentucky Derby, Sir Barton scored his fourth straight victory, taking the Belmont Stakes. The *Daily Racing Form* noted that the champion colt, ". . . added another jewel to his crown when he captured it in the same easy fashion that signalized his triumphs in the Derby, Preakness and Withers."

Horsemen admired his talent and envied his accomplishment. So a magic spell took hold. In 1920, although grand champion Man o' War skipped the Kentucky Derby, an unprecedented five Derby starters faced "Big Red" in the Preakness. Winning both classics was no longer out of the question—Sir Barton had made it part of the question, and inspired a red-hot quest.

When Gallant Fox became the first to match Sir Barton, sweeping the 1930 Preakness, Kentucky Derby, and Belmont Stakes, *The New York Times* echoed backstretch talk and hailed his feat as "the 'triple crown.'" Twenty years later, sanctified by the Thoroughbred Racing Associations, the popular nickname finally lost its quotation marks and gained capital letters.

Almanacs now make it look as if an existing triple crown was Sir Barton's target in 1919. Actually, the Triple Crown had resisted conscious design. Later would come a three-cornered Tiffany trophy, and a multimillion-dollar bonus. Still, Sir Barton had snagged these three great races for one simple reason: to strike while the iron is hot. His striking success changed our ideas of what is possible.

Dorothy Ours wrote Man o' War: A Legend Like Lightning.

PART II

---◆◆◆---

"There is class in every line of his body."
—FROM THE *TIMES* ACCOUNT OF SIR BARTON'S
WIN IN THE BELMONT STAKES

Sir Barton, first winner of the Triple Crown in 1919. AP IMAGES

AFTER 1919, when Sir Barton demonstrated that winning the Derby, Preakness and Belmont was not only a practical feat but also a prestigious one, the great names in American racing bore down on the sweep. William Woodward, who was chairman of the Central-Hanover Bank of New York, owned Belair Stud, which produced the next two Triple Crown champions, Gallant Fox in 1930 and Omaha in 1935.

Samuel Riddle swept it in 1937 with War Admiral, a son of the great Man o' War, the winner of 20 of 21 races. But Riddle had refused to run Man o' War in the 1920 Derby because he considered Churchill Downs an unworthy "western" track, and the Derby's mile and a quarter distance too taxing for three-year-olds.

Warren Wright Jr., the breeder and operator of the legendary Calumet Farm, campaigned Whirlaway to the 1941 Triple Crown championship. In 1943 Count Fleet captured the trio of classics for owner Fannie Hertz, the wife of John D. Hertz, the founder of Yellow Cab and the Hertz rental car agency.

Much like the vast fortunes in America, the best horses and bloodlines were in the hands of the privileged few, most of whom were Easterners. *The New York Times* coverage of these five Triple Crown champions focused as much on the horses' owners as it did the animals. The owners were sportsmen who did not mind running their horses frequently: Whirlaway, for example, raced as a five-year-old and chalked up sixty career starts, thirty-two of them victories. Assault, the 1946 champion, was still racing as a seven-year-old. In fact, the eleven Triple Crown winners together made 104 starts at age four or older, and won fifty-seven of them.

In 2006, however, thoroughbreds of all abilities averaged just 6.37 lifetime starts. While the most recent Kentucky Derby winners have hinted at their forerunners' brilliance, they have not come close to their longevity. The call of lucrative breeding fees is irresistible to most owners now, and it's rare to see a top stakes winner race beyond four. Only the 2003 Derby winner Funny Cide, a gelding, continued to race at the age of seven.

These owners were the closest things the nation had to aristocracy, which struck an uncomfortable nerve in Depression-era America. In 1938, as an entire nation listened on radio, a California-based five-year-old named Seabiscuit became a hero for working America when he defeated the great War Admiral in their wildly anticipated match race at Pimlico. Unspectacular as a three-year-old, Seabiscuit was never even considered for any of the Triple Crown races. But his win two years later over War Admiral confirmed him as racing's most renowned late bloomer.

SIR BARTON EASILY WINS
THE BELMONT

ELMONT, N.Y., JUNE 12, 1919 — Sir Barton set the seal on his greatness at Belmont Park yesterday, where 25,000 persons made a midweek holiday to see Commander Ross's colt capture the historic Belmont Stakes in the easiest possible manner, at the same time setting a new track record of 2:17 ⅖ for the mile and three furlongs. This supplants the mark made by August Belmont's Hourless two years ago, but how much faster Sir Barton could have traveled if pushed is a problem that may vex racegoers for some time. He was not extended for more than a furlong, and at the finish was almost pulling Jockey Loftus out of the saddle as he breezed past the judges five lengths in front of W. R. Coe's Sweep On, with the same owner's Natural Bridge, the only other starter, eight lengths farther back.

Vociferous were the greetings which welcomed the new three-year-old champion as he returned to the stand where Commander Ross was waiting, bubbling over with joy, to shake the hand of Loftus and playfully pat his peerless thoroughbred. Encomiums on the son of Star Shoot, which varied from the "horse of the decade," to the more extravagant praise of "horse of the century," were meted out by experienced turfmen who are used to weighing brilliant performances with calm judgment. One thing is certain—of all the good horses which have won this classic for three-year-olds at Belmont Park only James R. Keene's Colin, the victor in 1908, will bear comparison with yesterday's winner. Colin was beaten and was the last American three-year-old whose winnings reached $100,000. This mark in all probability will be equaled by Sir Barton, for the Belmont was worth $11,950 net to the winner, which, added to the moneys won in the Kentucky Derby, Preakness and Withers Stakes, brings his total earnings in four races up to $64,950.

The certainty that Sir Barton would be a starter was sufficient to attract more than double the usual Wednesday crowd to see the closing card of the successful Westchester Racing Association meeting run off under ideal weather conditions, and of these many hoped that the champion would be extended by Sweep On, which ran such a great race in the Suburban. This hope led to the extremely liberal odds of 2 to 5 being offered against Sir Barton, but it was futile, for there never was a point in the race that held danger for the champion.

Thousands made the trip to the track just to get a look at the horse that leaped into fame by graduating from the maiden ranks in the Kentucky Derby. Of these a goodly proportion visited the paddock to obtain a close-up view of the new racing wonder. As soon as Sir Barton appeared he was surrounded by a dense throng. Sir Barton is superbly muscled, with quarters that indicate strength, and strong, straight legs that taper to the fine point desirable in a horse bred for speed. There is class in every line of his body, and the well-rounded barrel suggests stamina to reinforce the speed guaranteed by his shoulders and hindquarters.

Sir Barton was so eager for the fray that he leaped into the lead at the start of the race. He was immediately pulled back by Loftus, and Natural Bridge set out to make the pace to suit Sweep On, his stable companion. Before they had gone half a mile Natural Bridge had a lead of two lengths, with Sir Barton the same distance in front of Sweep On. Thus they ran until they disappeared from view behind a clump of trees at the end of the hairpin turn.

Natural Bridge held his advantage when they reappeared, with Sir Barton striding along behind under a strong pull. The racers were headed then for the main course, and it was in the middle of his turn that Sir Barton was let down for a short burst of speed. In less than a furlong he had shot by Natural Bridge and assumed a lead of two lengths before Loftus again put him under restraint. The last turn into the stretch saw Sir Barton still rating along two lengths in front, and at that moment Sweep On was let down to make his bid for victory. A slight motion of Loftus's hands provided all the urging needed for Sir Barton. His stride lengthened and he shot away from Sweep On, only to be checked again by his careful rider. During the last eighth Loftus sat still as a statue, holding his mount back as well as he could, but the beautiful chestnut could not be restrained entirely. He was endowed with the spirit of competition and ran straight and true to the end, pulling up without showing the least trace of weariness.

PREAKNESS, GROSSING $61,925, WON BY GALLANT FOX, SANDE UP

BY BRYAN FIELD

BALTIMORE, MAY 9, 1930 — William Woodward won his first Preakness and Earl Sande rode his first Preakness winner when Gallant Fox captured Maryland's greatest turf classic before 40,000 persons at Pimlico today.

The son of Sir Galahad III and Marguerite came from next to last position at the half-mile mark to the heels of Thomas Cassidy's pacemaking Crack Brigade at the mile. Three-sixteenths further, the end of the race, and Gallant Fox was the winner by three-quarters of a length and had earned $51,925. The time was 2:00 ⅗.

Cassidy's horse was six lengths in front of Walter J. Salmon's Snowflake, which led Michigan Boy by a length, while seven others trailed. The gross value of the race was $61,925, the second, third and fourth horses dividing $10,000.

Gallant Fox was an even money favorite and he and Sande paraded to the post to the cheers of the great crowd. They came back after the victory to more cheers and a great clattering of camera shutters. A moment before the two had rushed past the winning post, the roar of cheering was overwhelming, with a faintly hysterical note, for there were comparatively few in the great throng who gave Gallant Fox much chance when he had coasted past the grand stand the first time, in a pocket, and trailing by many lengths his chief competitors.

The snapping of pictures at the finish and a talk over the radio took considerable time and quite obscured the quiet stroll in from the infield of a smiling, middle-aged figure. It was Sunny Jim Fitzsimmons, trainer of the winner. Asked if he ever worried when Gallant Fox's prospects looked so poor, he said:

"No, he's a fine colt and when he got close to the leaders I knew it was all over. He's a fine colt. But that Crack Brigade is a nice horse, too."

Sande was sweat-streaked and dust-covered when he got to the jockey room after the race, the mixture making a fudge-like covering over his face. He, too, praised Gallant Fox.

"I didn't call on him until we hit the furlong pole," he said. "Then he came on with a rush and hung it on Crack Brigade."

The eleven lined up at the start with comparatively little trouble. Armageddon was somewhat fractious, but the field was at the post only about six minutes. At the break Gallant Fox from his number one post position next to the rail, broke smartly. But he lacked early foot and the ten others outside of him swung past and around so that the first rush down past the grand stand found Gallant Fox securely pocketed on the fence, behind Tetrarchal, Crack Brigade, Sweet Sentiment and Gold Break and fenced in from the outside by most of the others.

Going around the clubhouse turn, Sande lost more ground keeping his horse out of trouble and when straightened out in the backstretch there was only one horse back of him.

Then began the most electrifying dash that has been seen in Maryland in many a day. Finding a hole here and a gap there, Sande snaked his way through the field and was third at the far turn. As he was going through and past many other horses his colors were concealed and there were few who knew the great riding until the white silks and red spots appeared third at the far turn.

Third though he was, Gallant Fox still had his race to win, for the two in front were Tetrarchal and Crack Brigade—the latter considered his chief competitor. And they were several lengths ahead.

The short swing around the bend found Tetrarchal at the end of his stride. He dropped back fast, but Crack Brigade was coming on as strong and fast as ever. At the top of the stretch Gallant Fox was second, but there was still daylight between his nose and Crack Brigade's heels.

Coming to the outside, Sande let Gallant Fox run on his own courage and the Belair color bearer ranged alongside of the others. George Ellis, on Crack Brigade, went to the whip and Crack Brigade held Gallant Fox even. Again it looked like Gallant Fox was beaten despite his courageous dash. But Sande called on his mount at the exact moment and on he came, never faltering a stride.

Crack Brigade could not stand the strain and gave, just a trifle. That was right in front of the stand and hats, programs and people were in the air—the fans jumping up and down in an effort to get a fleeting glimpse of the finish over the heads of those in front. The two horses swept over the line lapped on each other, only three-quarters of a length apart, but the winner was going away and Crack Brigade was a gallant and tired second.

Gallant Fox came out of the race in fine shape as near as could be judged from a superficial examination. If it is found by tomorrow that he still is in tip top condition he will be shipped on to the Kentucky Derby. His owner never has won a Derby or a Belmont. Gallant Fox will return to New York after the Derby to be fitted for the $30,000 test at Belmont Park.

GALLANT FOX TAKES DERBY AS LORD DERBY AND 60,000 LOOK ON

BY BRYAN FIELD

LOUISVILLE, MAY 17, 1930 — Gallant Fox swung into the top of the stretch at Churchill Downs today, running free in the van of the Kentucky Derby field, while a quarter of a mile away in a glass enclosed pagoda near the finish line a big-shouldered man dropped a pair of binoculars from his eyes with a throaty exclamation:

"Fine stuff! I'm glad!"

It was Lord Derby of England turning to William Woodward, owner of the horse, which stands alone tonight as the champion 3-year-old in America.

Sixty thousand persons massed at the track were still roaring themselves

hoarse for Gallant Fox or for one or the other of the fourteen thoroughbreds back of him when Lord Derby made his remark to Mr. Woodward.
The race was far from over, but Lord Derby's ancestors have been racing
horses for centuries and he had seen the best in the Derby field challenge
Gallant Fox only to be beaten off in the backstretch and on the bend.

And a driving, pouring rain did not obscure the vision of this tilted
gentleman, who has raced his silks in many countries and all weathers.

He knew the race was over and said so. Perhaps ten seconds later the
big bay colt swept past the little glass house to the finish line—ten seconds
which had held much of drama for thousands who had hoped for Gallant
Fox to falter. But the judgment of Lord Derby was vindicated and the
fifty-sixth Kentucky Derby became history with the winner taking the major share of the $60,725 purse.

The victory was worth $50,725 and the three horses which finished
next in order back of the winner divided $10,000. They were the Audley
Farm's Gallant Knight from Virginia, G. W. Foreman's Ned O from
Maryland and William Ziegler Jr.'s Gone Away from New York. Tannery,
pride of the Blue Grass and the horse counted on to beat Gallant Fox, was
raced into submission in the backstretch and finished eighth.

Earl Sande was the rider of the winner and Lord Derby waved his hand
to him as squads of special policemen drove away thousands who had
swarmed over the racing strip.

Gallant Fox and Sande saluted the stewards, were drawn into the tiny
protected oblong of greensward next to Lord Derby's pagoda and Mr.
Woodward stepped out into the rain. Without a topcoat, he strode across
the lawn and grasped Sande's hand and congratulated him on riding his
third Derby winner, the first jockey to do this since Isaac Murphy turned
the trick in the previous century.

Then he caressed Gallant Fox, undefeated this year and previously
winner of the Wood Memorial in New York and the Preakness Stakes in
Maryland.

Photographers by tens scaled the fence and in three minutes Mr.
Woodward and Sande were surrounded, the former driving a way through
to the scales for Sande, who had yet to have his tack weighed. Out on the
porch of the pagoda viewing it all was Lord Derby, smiling on the crowd
and belittling admonitions to remember that he had been confined to his
bed the past two days with a cold.

The lawn before the long stands which a few moments before had been
packed with thousands was now swept almost clear by the driving rain. Lord
Derby stood it all. He watched Gallant Fox led off to the stable and the flo-
ral horseshoe lifted from around his neck. Sande and Mr. Woodward trotted
from the scales to the pagoda, and there was more hand-shaking all around.

The National Broadcasting men rushed their microphones into position and Lord Derby began to speak. The rain kept driving, but he disdained the joggles at his elbow to go inside. Mr. Woodward stepped into the shelter of the booth and William Burke Miller, holding the microphone, watched his clothes losing shape under the pelting drops.

Then came the presentations of the gold trophy, symbolic of triumph in what without question is America's greatest horse race and spectacle. When it was all over, Lord Derby went off with a wave of his hand to the hundreds who still clung to their places to be near and hear him.

The ranks of the special policemen opened up and Lord Derby, Mr. Woodward and Joseph E. Widener and the others passed under the stands and out of sight. The first visit to the Kentucky Derby of an Earl of Derby was over. The Kentucky race first was run in 1875, following a trip abroad in 1872 of Colonel M. Lewis Clark, who was one of the organizers of Churchill Downs. Colonel Clark modeled the race after the Epsom Derby, first run in 1780 and named after the House of Derby, of which the man who braved the weather at Churchill Downs today is now the head.

The Epsom Derby is at a mile and 881 yards and its Kentucky counterpart was the same length from its inception to 1896, when it was shortened to a mile and a quarter.

It was a mile and a quarter which Gallant Fox ran today and he ran it in a manner to indicate that every 3-year-old fixture of the year lies at his mercy.

Gallant Fox was making turf history by his victory. No other horse has won the Preakness and come on to take the Derby. Only one other horse, Sir Barton, has won both events, but he won the Derby first and then went on to Maryland for the lesser test. That was in 1919, when the dates were reversed.

GALLANT FOX BEATS WHICHONE 4 LENGTHS IN $81,340 BELMONT

BY BRYAN FIELD

ELMONT, N.Y., JUNE 8, 1930 — There no longer exists any doubt about William Woodward's Gallant Fox being the greatest 3-year-old of the year.

At Belmont Park before 40,000 persons, many of whom stood in a drizzling rain, the winner of the Wood Memorial, Preakness and Kentucky Derby added the historic Belmont Stakes to his list of triumphs, soundly beating Harry Payne Whitney's Whichone, considered by many before the race as the best horse since Man o' War.

The race had a gross value of $81,340—the richest of its kind anywhere in the world—and $66,040 of this went to the winner, bringing the earnings of the 3-year-old son of Sir Gallahad III and Marguerite to $198,730.

The end of the mile and a half test saw Gallant Fox four lengths in front of Whichone and going away further with each jump. James Butler's Questionnaire was four lengths, to be third, and Walter J. Salmon's Swinfield brought up the rear. Gallant Fox finished in 2:31 ⅗, the fastest time for the race since it was increased to a mile and a half in 1926.

While Gallant Fox set a record for the Belmont over the mile and a half route, the track record for that distance is held by Man o' War, 2:28 ⅘, established in 1920. The previous best time for the mile and half was made by Crusader in 1926 when he was clocked in 2:32 ⅗.

Earl Sande rode the winner, kept him in front from start to finish, and grinned through the patches of adhesive tape which marked a motor accident. He gave all the credit to his mount, which by winning the Preakness, Kentucky Derby and Belmont has equaled the feat of Sir Barton.

These two horses are the only ones to win the "triple crown," but Sir Barton's star later was dimmed by a defeat by the great Man o' War. There seems little likelihood of any horse stopping Gallant Fox, and if he goes on to the American Derby and American Classic in Chicago those races apparently will be at his mercy.

Great as he is now, he seems headed for greater glory. Mr. Woodward was warmly congratulated by Joseph E. Widener, president of the Westchester Racing Association, and others of the fashionable throng.

Mr. Woodward led his horse in from the racing strip to a roped off enclosure alongside the stewards' stand so that the spectators might get a good look at the 3-year-old champion. Mr. Woodward was indeed a proud man.

Gallant Fox was a fractious youngster and very nearly stepped on the foot of his owner, but Mr. Woodward held on to his bridle and managed the colt until Jim Fitzsimmons, trainer of Gallant Fox, stepped up and took him in hand. Fitzsimmons was congratulated right and left also, for he has done a great job of keeping the horse in tip top racing condition to beat the best of the East and the West.

Much of the sparkle and glamour was taken from the throng by the rain, but everyone went about the business of supporting his choice with vigor and enthusiasm. Despite the prowess of Gallant Fox, the Whitney horse was made the 3-to-5 public choice, while Gallant Fox was as good as 8 to 5.

Therefore, Gallant Fox was beating a very heavily backed favorite when he came down to the line first, but his reception and the roar of welcome were as virile as those in Maryland and Kentucky when he won the greatest classics in those states.

Few races have caused greater excitement in the East or for that matter, in the country, than the meeting between Gallant Fox and Whichone. The Belmont first was run in 1867 at old Jerome Park, but none of the great duels in its long history aroused as much interest as this one.

And when it came right down to the running, it was not a duel at all because Gallant Fox made a procession of it and never gave the others a chance. To stand off three challenges, from each of the horses running against him, and still have left enough speed to come away in fast time under a drizzling rain, is high testimony to his ability.

50,000 SEE OMAHA WIN DERBY
BY 1½ LENGTHS

BY BRYAN FIELD

LOUISVILLE, MAY 4, 1935 — Charging into the lead at the far turn, and never thereafter leaving the result in doubt, William Woodward's Omaha won the sixty-first Kentucky Derby in far easier fashion than his famous sire, Gallant Fox, also owned by Mr. Woodward. It was the third time the father and son double was completed in this classic mile and a quarter test, which was run in the rain before 50,000 persons.

At the finish Omaha was first by a length and a half, while Sachseamaler and Reuter's Texas Derby winner Roman Soldier was second, four lengths before Mrs. Ethel Mara's Whiskolo, which was second in the Texas Derby. Then came Nellie Flag, lone filly in the race.

Far back finished such highly fancied stars as Mrs. Payne Whitney's Plat Eye, Colonel E. R. Bradleys's Boxthom, C. V. Whitney's Today and Mrs. Walter M. Jefford's Commonwealth.

The time of the race was 2:05, which compares with Twenty Grand's track record of 2:01 ⅘ and Gallant Fox's 2:07 ⅗. Whether Omaha is better than his sire few will be bold enough to assert, at least until more has been shown, but the chestnut colt out of Flambino ran this afternoon in the manner of a champion.

The race had a gross value of $49,950, of which $39,925 went to the winning owner. Mr. Woodward bred both his Kentucky Derby winners and was the recipient of many congratulations from leading figures in society, business and politics who crowded these historic stands today.

The victory of Omaha was no surprise as he had been considered one of the best prospects for 3-year-old honors since his juvenile year. The colt, which paid 4 to 1, responded beautifully to Jockey Willie Saunders, gained a better early position in the first quarter-mile than had been expected, moved up swiftly in the backstretch and jumped his field at the far turn. From there home it was easy and he won with plenty to spare. In common with all but Nellie Flag, Omaha shouldered scale weight of 126 pounds.

There have been few Kentucky Derbies which have been as open as this one, and there have been few which saw such sharp changes and reversals. St. Bernard was first to break, but in the run for position past the stands Plat Eye forged to the front. As the field went around the first turn there was the inevitable crowding, in which Nellie Flag suffered. Whether this accounted for her defeat is impossible to say, but it certainly did not help her. Omaha was right behind Today, which was the betting choice following his victory over Plat Eye and Omaha in the Wood Memorial. It seemed that Saunders was watching Raymond Workman aboard Today, which moved strongly and went to the leaders. It was Omaha, however, which caught Plat Eye and at the far turn moved into a lead he did not relinquish.

Omaha is to be shipped East promptly and is an eligible for the Preakness, to be run next Saturday at Pimlico. His sire won the Preakness before the Derby in 1930, the order of running of these big 3-year-old specials having been reversed that year. Later he will run in the big stakes in New York.

There was considerable of a parallel between the weather on Gallant Fox's winning day and that of his son. It drizzled and misted all afternoon on Derby Day in 1930 until finally the track went off and could not be rated better than good. That happened this afternoon. A good track here is a none too trustworthy surface because of the heavy clay content of the soil.

Racegoers were surprised upon arrival at the track to see the famous old plant with many of the earmarks of an armed camp. Heavy wire barriers had been erected on the inside rail between various sections of the grandstand and at strategic points on the backstretch. In addition soldiers appeared to be everywhere.

This was due to the assignment of several hundred men from the National Guard. They were stationed all the way along both rails up and down the homestretch. The infield crowd was kept rather definitely under control by the adroit use of clubs as this or that group became obstreperous.

There also were policemen about by the score. In the far reaches of the backstretch mounted police patrolled every point. In addition, a group of

130 nattily garbed ushers came down from Chicago under the direction of Andrews Frain to augment the local talent.

Motorcycle escorts screeched notables through the streets and there was a distinct rush as each new celebrity arrived. Many of these gatherings of the curious dwindled away as a mere Governor or Cabinet officer stepped out. But when Jack Dempsey arrived he had to push his way through the crowd.

The altercations between the National Guardsmen and the crowd in the infield became more enthusiastic as the races passed and the rain continued to patter down. The thud of clubs began to be so frequent that many were heard to say that it would have been better to let a few hundred gate crashers crash the gate.

At last a chair was thrown from the infield through one of the portals at the National Guardsmen, who were mostly young men. The chair was promptly thrown back by the soldiers. Shortly thereafter half a dozen riflemen were brought along at the double and waved their guns menacingly at the crowd. But this time jeers and catcalls were making a constant chorus, with the gate crashers winning this verbal battle, at last.

OMAHA TAKES PREAKNESS BY SIX-LENGTH MARGIN

BY BRYAN FIELD

BALTIMORE, MAY 11, 1935 — Coming through the stretch by himself, William Woodward's Omaha won the historic Preakness Stakes, scoring the easiest victory in this famous test since Man o' War won in 1930. A cheering, surging throng of 45,000, the biggest ever to see a race at old Pimlico, yelled itself hoarse as Jockey Willie Saunders clucked to his mount on the far turn and put his opposition away.

Many members of Congress, the governor of the state, society folk, distinguished visitors, widely known politicians and plain everyday lovers of the thoroughbred made the chestnut son of Gallant Fox an odds-on favorite for the $28,825 mile and three-sixteenths test in which the winning owner's share was $25,325.

Omaha won by six lengths from Walter M. Jefford's Firethorn, which led Mrs. Dodge Sloane's Psychic Bid by the same margin. Strung out behind these were Mantagna, Commonwealth, stablemate of Firethorn, Brannon, Nellie Flag and Boxthorn.

Omaha duplicated the feat of his sire in winning both the Kentucky Derby and the Preakness, and he now will be shipped to New York to be prepared for the Belmont Stakes. He is the fourth horse to win both the Derby and the Preakness, the others being Sir Barton, Burgo King and Gallant Fox. If he wins the Belmont he will be the third thoroughbred to gain that triple crown. Sir Barton and his sire are the two which have done it so far.

Omaha won so easily under his scale weight of 126 pounds that few were prepared for the time of 1:58 $\frac{2}{5}$ which was hung out. This is one-fifth of a second slower than High Quest's record, set last year when he was forced to the last ounce by his stablemate, Cavalcade.

The winning time was two-fifths of a second slower than Gallant Knight's great track record of 1:58. The track was fast today as it was last year and for Gallant Knight.

Jockey Saunders, who had the leg up on Omaha both in Kentucky and this afternoon, rode the most confident kind of race. He was entirely cold as he scientifically cut down those in front and coasted through the stretch as he pleased. It is not too much to say that Omaha could have done much better and that Saunders was supremely confident of the outcome.

The strategy in the Woodward camp was to let the speed horses run themselves dull and then cut them down in the closing stages.

Saunders did precisely this, except that Omaha swallowed them up in a burning quarter of a mile at the far turn, which left the stretch run merely a gallop. This was like Gallant Fox in the Preakness of 1930, when he got away in a tangle and made a great spurt in the back stretch run to bring himself to contention and later to win a hard drive over Crack Brigade. Veterans had to go back to Man o' War's year to find as easy a victory, and many good horses have won the Preakness between that day and this.

OMAHA, 7-10, FIRST HOME IN THE $43,980 BELMONT

BY BRYAN FIELD

ELMONT, N. Y., JUNE 8, 1935 — Slashing through a drenching rain and slippery footing, Omaha won the historic Belmont Stakes before 25,000 persons in a manner definitely to establish himself as the champion 3-year-old of 1935. He brought to his owner, William Woodward, the distinction of being the one man to have bred and owned two triple crown winners.

To his Kentucky Derby and Preakness victories the son of Gallant Fox now has added the grueling Belmont to duplicate the feat of his sire. It was an easy finish after a testing race. Coming to the line in 2:30 ⅗ for the mile and a half, Omaha had Firethorn floundering behind him, only a length and a half back, but as badly beaten as if he were in the ruck.

Firethorn was second in the Preakness. The sloppy footing yesterday favored him, and he gallantly charged at Omaha from the head of the stretch to the sixteenth pole. There his strength was spent and he almost went to pieces, to finish soundly defeated. Eight or ten lengths further back Rosemont came in a tired third, after he had momentarily been in front only to collapse suddenly. Then finished Cold Shoulder and Sir Beverley, stable-mate to Omaha.

Once again admirers are prone to say that Omaha is greater than his sire, Gallant Fox, but Mr. Woodward has yet to join the number, even though time and performance may cause him to do so.

Omaha was a 7-to-10 shot with the big Belmont Park crowd which braved one of the wettest, rawest days of the year. He had Willie Saunders

52

in the saddle and once more the Montana lad was as cold as ice and turned in a faultless performance.

Saunders waited so long and he waited so well that some thought Omaha beaten at the top of the stretch. But at the finish the only horse forging on with any show of strength and power was the winner. How much "horse" Saunders had left for the stretch run is shown by the seasonal final quarter-mile in 0:25 ⅗. This blazing two-furlong effort, after a mile and a quarter had been put behind, was what brought disaster to the others.

Only Firethorn had anything to run against it, and his gallant best was far short of what was necessary. They ran head and head for a furlong, with Omaha slowly wearing the other down and slowly drawing off from him. At the sixteenth pole it was all Omaha. Firethorn could do no more. Omaha finished out bull-like, as if he could go on and on, while Firethorn was dead tired.

VICTORY IN DERBY TO WAR ADMIRAL

BY BRYAN FIELD

LOUISVILLE, MAY 8, 1937 — While his venerable owner lay seriously ill a thousand miles from the scene of action, War Admiral's flying heels drummed out a conquering answer to the challenge that he could not stay a mile and a quarter. Before 60,000 persons who jammed Churchill Downs, the son of Man o' War ripped off the second fastest performance in the history of the Kentucky Derby, which goes back to 1875.

At the end he was a length and three-quarters clear of Pompoon in a test that attracted twenty starters and grossed $62,575, with $52,050 going to Samuel D. Riddle, owner of the winner.

Mr. Riddle could not see the race because of his illness, but it was the first time the famous Glen Riddle silks have been seen in the Derby. War Admiral was the favorite. He led practically from end to end and stamped himself a worthy son of his famous sire, who stands at stud only a few miles away in the nearby blue grass.

Charley Kurtsinger, who piloted Twenty Grand to victory in 1931 when the track record of 2:01 4/5 was set, had the leg up on the brown son of Man o' War and Brushup and piloted his mount home in 2:03 1/5.

To a direct query, he had this answer: "There was nothing to it." Harry Richards, rider of Pompoon, gave just as pithy a retort. He said: "We went to him at the top of the stretch. Then he (War Admiral) went away as if we were tied."

Kurtsinger laid his whip on War Admiral but once, and that was turning into the final straightaway when he saw Pompoon looming over his shoulder. The flick of the bat sent War Admiral scampering along. To boot, he carried Pompoon a bit wide but could have won without that advantage.

The East got the first two places. The hope of the West was dimmed when Mrs. Ethel V. Mara's Reaping Reward could do no better than third, eight lengths back of Pompoon. Then came Melodist, the Wood Memorial winner, who forged up strongly after a slow start.

War Admiral always ruled the favorite and returned $5.20, $4.20 and $3.40 across the board. Pompoon was the third choice in the betting, returning $9.40 and $6. The return on Reaping Reward was $3.80, the entry of this fellow and Military being the second choice.

War Admiral now has started three times this year and won three times. In all, he has made nine racing starts, winning six, being second twice and third once. So far as could be seen, War Admiral came out of his race sound and easy, and it remains only for him to hold his form to make this a famous year of 3-year-old competition.

To Kurtsinger must go much of the credit of winning. He was aboard an obstreperous horse that contributed largely to an eight-and-a-half-minute delay. Getting War Admiral off at all was difficult enough, but getting him off well from post position No. 1 required that extra bit of skill which a good jockey has. The No. 1 post position is slightly around the bend in the track, and if Kurtsinger did not have War Admiral off winging he might have been bottled in there and never got to running.

But he did get away flying and the race was decided then and there, as matters turned out. When Kurtsinger had War Admiral settled into stride it was a question of who could catch him. None could.

In the stretch Pompoon got to within part of a length of him but Kurtsinger took the corner with all the skill of a veteran. He swished War Admiral's hindquarters at Pompoon and forced Richards to snatch on the right-handed rein to keep clear of the threat.

But there was no interference. It merely was the gesture of a canny veteran giving his mount all the best of it, and the rival horse all the worst of it. At the same time Kurtsinger whacked once with the whip. War Admiral went away from there.

Kurtsinger was warmly congratulated after the finish by his family, all of whom were present as he is a Louisville boy. He learned to ride only a few miles from the gates of Churchill Downs.

The saddle which was used on Man o' War when the super horse defeated Sir Barton in the famous match race in Canada was offered to Kurtsinger for use aboard War Admiral. He declined the offer with thanks. Asked why, he said: "Well, that saddle must be almost twenty years old and I'd hate to have any leather break in the Derby. Besides, I've got my own lucky saddle that brought Twenty Grand home."

WAR ADMIRAL WINS BELMONT STAKES FOR TRIPLE CROWN

BY BRYAN FIELD

ELMONT, N.Y., JUNE 5, 1937 — Running with a torn heel, but as easily as if he had wings, War Admiral clinched the 3-year-old championship before 35,000 persons by winning the sixty-ninth Belmont in time that shattered Man o' War's track record set seventeen years ago.

One of the greatest crowds ever to see a horse race at Belmont Park applauded the chestnut son of Man o' War as he coasted through the stretch to win by four lengths at the end of a mile and a half in 2:28 ⅗ over a fast track.

The triumph made War Admiral the fourth horse to win the triple crown of Kentucky Derby, Preakness and Belmont. The earlier three were Sir Barton, Gallant Fox and Omaha.

It was not until after the finish that War Admiral's torn heel was iced, the blood of the champion staining the tanbark saddling closure as the venerable Samuel Riddle defied his illness and weakness to come from the roof of the stand to the track level. He wished to lead his champion as has been traditional in this greatest of all 3-year-old tests since the inaugural running in 1867.

But that other veteran, Trainer George Conway, mindful of his employer as well of War Admiral, took the lead chain, and himself walked War Admiral in amid the applause of the thousands. Conway feared that War Admiral might be too much for his septuagenarian owner to handle, but, as things turned out, the son of Man o' War was as quiet as a mouse and was not blowing enough to douse a candle.

All this was a few minutes after the finish of the $50,020 race in which Maxwell Howard's Sceneshifter was second and the Falaise Stable's 60-to-1 shot Vamoose third.

After that the order was Brooklyn, Flying Scot, Pompoon and Melodist. The winner was a 9-to-10 favorite after once having been as high as even money and he carried scale weight of 126 pounds to earn $38,020 of the total purse.

But it may be many weeks, and perhaps months, before War Admiral runs again. In the stall after the finish last night Conway, his groom, and a veterinarian worked over the sliced heel. Jockey Charley Kurtsinger said:

"It occurred right at the break. He (War Admiral) was so anxious to get away that he reached too far under with his hind feet, and he clipped his front heels. The steel shoe sheared away a piece of his heel on the back part of the front hoof. The piece was almost as big as a half dollar."

In the heat of battle War Admiral never noticed the injury. And to see him run none would have supposed he was out for more than a gallop. The only time he had to put in any hard licks was in the three-eighths of a mile immediately after the start. Since War Admiral broke from the No. 7 post position on the extreme outside he had to get far enough in front so that he could cross over on his field.

Flying Scot, with Johnny Gilbert up, was sent out with a rush to try to prevent War Admiral from getting the lead. Despite the early speed of the Withers winner, he could not outfoot War Admiral even with that fellow's disadvantage of the outside post position. After a brief brush, the race was a procession. It may have been this early bit of dash that accounted for the amazing time which also was equal to the American record set by Handy Mandy under the feather of 109 pounds.

At the post War Admiral was his usual obstreperous self. Vamoose was also badly behaved, and Melodist was no angel. The break was an even one with Flying Scot trying to get the lead. But War Admiral was so fleet that he was in front going around the first turn. Flying Scot was second and Sceneshifter and Vamoose close up.

Once straightened away in the backstretch, there was nothing to the race. The leader kept on coasting along and never had to take a challenge from those in back of him.

70,000 WATCH WHIRLAWAY TAKE DERBY IN RECORD TIME

BY BRYAN FIELD

LOUISVILLE, MAY 3, 1941 — The Bluegrass-bred colt Whirlaway came into his own on the home heath before 70,000 persons by smashing the Kentucky Derby track record and winning sensationally by eight lengths in the $87,775 test, the richest 3-year-old race the world over.

Kentuckians had made this chestnut the favorite, despite his head-strong trick of running wide and practically bounding off both fences, and they screamed with delight when his course was straight and true this bright and sunny afternoon. His record time was 2:01 ⅖, over a fast track, reducing Twenty Grand's old mark by two-fifths of a second.

Warren Wright, breeder and owner of the son of Blenheim II who carried the devil's red silks of Calumet Farm, was the heart of a triumphal procession, going and coming to the presentation stand in the infield.

In the yells of delight that came to Mr. Wright's ears from all sides, there was a note of relief. Until he did so handsomely and well what all thought he could do, the thought and fear was in the back of every mind that Whirlaway again would be up to mischief and would toss off the glory that was rightfully his.

But Eddie Arcaro was aboard the Wright power horse, and he cannily steered between the contenders at the head of the stretch. No one can know whether Whirlaway was or wasn't going to run out, but with Arcaro handling things as skillfully as that, there just was no chance for trouble.

From that point on he came, opening up more and more distance, until at the last it was a romp with the flaunting banner of red jaunty and powerful in the last dash for home and victory. The distant second horse was Hugh S. Nesbitt's Staretor, who ran a fine race to save the place by a neck from the last rush of Louis Tufano's Market Wins.

Whirlaway now has run twenty-four times and earned $145,226 in his two seasons of racing. Only three times has he been out of the money and eleven times he has won. His admirers feel that he would have won many more of the races if he had not run wide at the turns.

The most telling impression left by the mile-and-a-quarter race was one of force and power. When the field came to the top of the stretch, Whirlaway already had made up half a dozen lengths from a rearguard position. There were five horses within shouting distance of the prize, and it looked like a tight stretch run among the lot.

It was like that when Whirlaway shot off from the others. He suddenly was a dash of color well in advance of the blotch of silks that was the contention. As the tense seconds that mark the stretch run ticked off, Whirlaway drove on faster and farther. There was no holding him or stopping him.

Of course, Arcaro wasn't trying to do any stopping. All he needed to do was sit still. Not the faintest bit of urging did the boy need do. And yet on Whirlaway came until he was eight lengths in the good at the finish.

There have been many races and many Derbies when complaint of crowding and interference could be made and was made. This was feared today and all because of Whirlaway and his run-out habit. Yet it is doubtful if any trainer has a complaint tonight now that the race is history.

Arcaro set sail midway of the backstretch. He skimmed the far turn on the inside of the tiring Our Boots, who could not keep up. Thus there was no runout there. In the meantime, Porter's Cap had turned on in earnest and was up abreast of Dispose. This is when they were coming to the head of the stretch. Staretor kept plugging along. And Whirlaway kept coming closer.

So the swing was made into the home lane with Dispose, Porter's Cap, Staretor and Our Boots all apparently with some kind of chance. Between them Arcaro lanced Whirlaway. There may have been a little thump or a bump as the Blenheim II colt came through, but if so it was nothing to cavil about even had the result been close.

But the result was going to be just as far from close as any Derby has been. All of Whirlaway's gaining in the backstretch and around the bend must have been made with the throttle only half open. Hence the five horses all in a knot at the head of the stretch were broken up in a twinkling. Whirlaway just went off and left the others when Arcaro gave him his head and opened up. It was a straight run to the wire then, no more turns, no more runouts, no more headaches, only gold and glory and the roar of the crowd in front and the new track record although, of course, none could know that instantaneously as the colt swept victorious past the finish line.

Jockey Arcaro came in for a full share of the credit, and not a few recalled that he was "born and raised" as they say out here, in Covington, Ky. His mother lives there now.

After the finish, Arcaro was all agrin and said: "He's the runnin'est horse I ever handled—you have to watch him awful close—but he's certainly the runnin'est horse I ever was up on. I tried to lay back, but when he saw those horses in front, he wanted to run. At that, he had everything left in the stretch."

Perhaps the best illustration of this is the fractional time of the race. Here are the fractions: 0:23 2/5, 0:48 3/5, 1:11 3/5, 1:37 3/5 and 2:01 2/5. The remarkable thing about this is the last quarter in 0:24 flat. A search of the Derby records so far as they were able here this afternoon indicates that no other horse in Derby history ever has run the last quarter this fast.

Owner Wright went down to the jockey quarters to congratulate Arcaro, and Colonel Matt Winn came in and proposed a drink. Arcaro piped up and said, "May I come too? I could stand one."

WHIRLAWAY, ARCARO UP, TAKES PREAKNESS BY 5 LENGTHS

BY BRYAN FIELD

BALTIMORE, MAY 10, 1941 — The same combination—Whirlaway and Jockey Arcaro—won the same way, on this bright Maryland afternoon when Warren Wright's Calumet Farm racer dashed blithely past 30,000 spectators to a $49,365 victory in Pimlico's fifty-first Preakness.

The first time past the stands, Whirlaway was five lengths behind the field. The second time past the stands he was five lengths ahead. In between was as decisive a performance as any Preakness winner has brought off.

The victory in this $69,500 Preakness was almost an anti-climax. The big roar from the thousands came a few moments after the break, up in the mile and three-sixteenths chute. Eddie Arcaro practically allowed Whirl-away to walk away from the gate.

This leisurely start may have been the strategy of trainer Ben Jones and Arcaro, since Whirlaway isn't a fast breaker anyway, but to many in the crowd it must have looked like a mistake, or a racing mishap. The result was seven horses running in a knot, and Whirlaway trailing far behind. It was a shout of consternation, for Whirlaway had been backed to even money over the good track, and eventually paid off at $4.40, $4.30 and $3.30.

Around into the backstretch the race remained the same. All eyes were on the bobbing dot, so far behind. And the trailing Whirlaway was very easy to see, dead last.

Then came the motion picture sequence. Whirlaway just began to gain and gain and gain. At the far turn he was up to the knot. Midway of the bend he had disappeared into it. Turning for home he emerged from it. Through the stretch he just galloped. More and more daylight opened behind him.

The big crowd yelled the second time when it saw Whirlaway, last Saturday's Kentucky Derby winner, come out of the pack, but it just leaned back with a sigh of relief as the colt went on with the stretch run to be timed in 1:58 ⅖, not particularly fast, but good enough considering that the track was off a bit.

Second in line was Ogden Phipps' King Cole, running his best race and finishing two lengths ahead of Woodvale Farm's Our Boots. After that the order of finish was Porter's Cap, Kansas, Dispose, Curious Coin and Ocean Blue.

All the starters shouldered 126 pounds and now Whirlaway is off to the Belmont in New York.

Jockeys have their own way of talking, and this exchange in the jocks' room was indicative of how easy the race was:

ARCARO: "Hey, Johnny, come here and wipe this jam off my mouth."
GILBERT: "What's the matter, what're you talking about?"
ARCARO (with a laugh): "That was just a picnic out there—just a picnic."

For publication, Arcaro was a touch more routine in his choice of words, but more emphatic than ever in making his point. He said: "There are no other 3-year-olds—just Whirlaway. I was practically left, but knew that he could go to the others when I clucked to him. So I clucked to him. And that's what he did."

Owner Wright and Trainer Jones had an echo in reply to requests for a statement.

WRIGHT: "He ran just the kind of race we expected. He'll win the Belmont the same way."
JONES: "That's just what we expected. That's just what he'll do in the Belmont."

WHIRLAWAY FIRST IN
$52,270 BELMONT

BY BRYAN FIELD

ELMONT, N. Y., JUNE 8, 1941—Whirlaway did the expected in his own proud manner when he won the seventy-third Belmont Stakes before 30,801 persons on the final afternoon of a record-breaking Belmont Park meeting. The chestnut colt from the Calumet Farm raced through the stretch so easily that he had his ears pricking, and he also had that mightiest triple crown tilted jauntily on his handsome forelock.

When he finished the historic mile and a half run that grossed $52,270 in 2:31 flat over a fast track, the son of Blenheim II and Dustwhirl became the fifth horse in American racing history to capture the Kentucky Derby, Preakness and Belmont Stakes.

Whirlaway was so good that he made ducks and drakes of his opposition. Robert Morris was second, beaten three lengths, and five lengths before Yankee Chance. Itabo trailed. The winner was a standout 1-to-4 favorite and returned only $2.50 and $2.10, there being no show betting.

Perhaps the best way to describe the manner in which Whirlaway dominated the field is to tell what Eddie Arcaro, the winning jockey, did in the race, and what he said about it. Before a half mile had been run Arcaro startled thousands by suddenly sending Whirlaway dashing to the front, a reversal of riding tactics from all of Whirlaway's previous races. It looked revolutionary from the stands, and indeed it was, for subsequently it was learned that the boy had had waiting orders from Trainer Ben Jones.

But this is what happened, as Arcaro tells it: "I was last with Whirlaway going away and I was going to stay last for awhile. But at the mile post (a mile to go), there was no pace. It was very slow. So I yelled to those other jocks: 'I'm leaving.'"

It was then that the watchers in the stand saw Whirlaway shoot to the front. He dashed far ahead in a twinkling.

Through the backstretch Whirlaway opened six or eight lengths. Robert Morris, Itabo and Yankee Chance followed in Indian file.

Would Whirlaway shoot his bolt? Had he got away from Arcaro? Was his headstrong trait coming out in a different way? All of these questions were asked and unanswered as the race went on.

The big challenge, and the only one of the race, came from the far turn to the head of the stretch. There Alfred Robertson moved forward with Robert Morris. Robert Morris cut that big lead, but he never made Arcaro go to a drive nor did Eddie ever make use of the whip.

Meanwhile Whirlaway was safely home with the triple crown safely his. Before him only Sir Barton, Gallant Fox, Omaha and War Admiral completed the sweep of Derby, Preakness and Belmont.

THE FLEET IS IN

BY ARTHUR DALEY

LOUISVILLE, MAY 1, 1943—Count Fleet will win the Kentucky Derby by either a length or a mile at Churchill Downs today. The Count is a cinch. The Count can't miss. If he does fail to capture the classic there undoubtedly will be mass suicide by those lovers of horseflesh whose only interest in the sport is the improving of the breed—and the collecting of winning pari-mutuel tickets.

The son of Reigh Count is a tremendous favorite to triumph, but that doesn't mean a thing. So many strange things can and do happen in racing that there never is a certainty until the numbers go up on the board and the lights flash the confirmation by adding the word "Official."

Of course, more persons would rather bet on Count Fleet than bet against him. He has the power, the speed and the class. He loves to run and he can go at breathless pace. He has beaten Ocean Wave and Blue Swords, the chief contenders, and the distance of a mile and a quarter is to his liking. Mrs. John D. Hertz's colt has enough room at that route to stretch out in his pace-eating strides and overcome the disadvantages inherent in a possible bad getaway.

The experts at Jamaica like Blue Swords better than Ocean Wave as an outside choice, and Trainer Don Cameron, who is closest to the Fleet, agrees. But the Kentucky folk have taken a fancy to Ocean Wave after his fast mile the other day at Churchill Downs. Even with a pair of high-powered binoculars, however, few can see any one outracing the Count.

Comparisons are odious, naturally enough, but there was a horse in the 1889 Derby who was as red hot a choice that year as the Count is today. His name was Proctor Knott, a strong, self-willed colt who had been the 2-year-old champion the campaign before.

The Kentuckians went for him hook, line and sinker. He couldn't lose, either.

Astride him was a tiny jockey, Pike Barnes. At the start Proctor Knott broke away as though he were going to a three-alarm fire. In those days the practice was to lay off the pace and make the last three-eighths or so a sprint. But Proctor Knott went catapulting out so fast that Barnes had all he could do to hold him in.

He tugged at the reins and used every ounce of strength in his little body in the futile restraint. Still Proctor Knott kept opening a wider and wider margin on the field. Around the last turn the colt gave the race a Whirlaway touch by swinging out wide to the outside rail, almost as though he were going to do a tight-rope dance along the rail to the wire.

Barnes strove manfully to control him, but to no avail. He was tired from his violent exertions and the horse was tired from his harum-scarum race. Meanwhile, the lesser-regarded Spokane stuck to his knitting and the inside pole to nail the seemingly invincible Proctor Knott right on the finish line.

Anguished Kentuckians stared unbelievingly at this astounding upset. One of them remarked mournfully, as he strode away into the night: "The tobacco crop can't be big enough this year to save the state."

Count Fleet is the Winter Book favorite. But so was Sun Briar in 1918, the 2-year-old champion of the season before. Willis Sharpe Kilmer thought he had another of those certain winners in him. Trainer Henry McDaniel traded four fillies for a rangy, fleshless colt who was to serve as Sun Briar's training partner.

Just before the Derby things happened. Sun Briar first had a poor trial and then a poor preparatory race. McDaniel shook his head sadly. His prized colt clearly was not in shape and Kilmer was driven to distraction at the idea of his wonder horse failing to win for him. His hopes were low as he watched the race. But then he perked up. The equine bag of bones who had been bought as a training companion plowed through the Churchill Downs mud to victory at odds in the vicinity of 30 to 1. He was—and is— the great Exterminator.

Grey Lag looked like another of those many certainties for the 1921 Derby and was deemed so fast a horse that he couldn't lose. But he went wrong before the race that finished him. However, Colonel E. R. Bradley had two colts ready for the run for the roses. He liked Black Servant far better than Behave Yourself, his other entry.

The Bradley future-book wagers went down on Black Servant and, the rumor is, he put not a plugged nickel on Behave Yourself. Into the home-stretch pounded Black Servant at the head of the procession. Then Behave Yourself, who did not behave himself very well considering that the cash was on the nose of his stablemate, roared up on the inside to win the Derby.

If Count Fleet triumphs Colonel Matt Winn can make a deep obei-sance to Secretary Cliff McCartney of the Metropolitan Jockey Club for staging the Wood Memorial a fortnight ahead of the Derby this year in-stead of the usual week ahead. Had this race adhered to its customary schedule the Count might have remained in New York instead of going to Kentucky, and those who bet on the son of Reigh Count in the winter book would never even have had a run for their money. Horse players def-initely don't like that.

COUNT FLEET TAKES PREAKNESS

BY ROBERT F. KELLEY

BALTIMORE, MAY 8, 1943— With the serenity of an old gentleman in his rocking chair on a front veranda, Johnny Longden sat down on the famous back of Count Fleet and rode a mile and three-sixteenths to fame and glory in the fifty-third running of the historic Preakness Stakes.

For one fleeting moment after the starting gates had been sprung New Moon, destined to finish in the ruck, led the way, but by the time the four-horse field was in front of the famed Pimlico grandstand, the Count was on top and he stayed there to win by eight lengths, as virtually everybody in the crowd of 29,381 had expected.

Blue Swords for the sixth time chased Mrs. John D. Hertz's great 3-year-old home to finish four and one-half lengths in front of Vincentive. Almost pulled up, New Moon completed the parade.

Count Fleet was the shortest-priced winner in the modern history of the stake, going off at 3 to 20 and returning $2.30 and $2.10 for $2. His backers sent $68,248 through the pari-mutuel machines on him in a race which saw $147,356 bet despite the fact there was no show pool.

There was no contest at any stage. Once the opening flurry had settled down Longden was in front, with Johnny Adams and Blue Swords to second-place, a retake of the Kentucky Derby.

Grim-faced and unemotional, Longden sat still. Once, rounding the turn into the stretch, he looked back over his shoulder to see what the rest of the world was doing, turned around again, sat down and came on home. He never touched his whip and never seemed even to use his heels.

A quarter of the way down the backstretch Blue Swords was apparently completely in control of second place. Vincentive made a run at him at the head of the stretch but he hadn't the stuff to bring him back. The pair had closed a little on the Count, who led by five lengths at the three-quarter mark, but turning into the stretch the champion simply let out a notch and drew away again.

The time of 1:57 ⅗ didn't threaten the Pimlico record of 1:56 ⅗ made by Riverland in the Dixie Handicap last week, but the track was only good.

Most of the racegoers came out in the late morning on the trolley cars and picnicked at the track.

Halfway through the big race it was apparent what the result would be. From there to the finish the roar of this horse-minded crowd was simply the tribute to a brown colt taking his place among the great horses of the past.

When the outrider led him back to the unsaddling enclosure, Longden's face for the first time relaxed. He took the wreath of black-eyed Susans in his lap for the photos with a grin from ear to ear.

Quietly pleased with the effort of his charge, Trainer Cameron said he would ship to Belmont Park, where the Count will aim for the triple crown in the Belmont Stakes on June 5.

Longden, cooling out afterward, had no comment except: "I'll say it's hot. The Count is a great horse. I was never worried for a minute." Adams, on Blue Swords, ruefully said, "He's too much horse for Blue Swords." Perhaps the best comment, though, was that of Wayne Wright on New Moon, who complained, "I couldn't even see the race."

COUNT FLEET FIRST BY THIRTY LENGTHS IN $50,090 BELMONT

BY BRYAN FIELD

ELMONT, N. Y., JUNE 6, 1943— Count Fleet achieved 21 yesterday— twenty-one races, the number run by Man o' War in his entire career, but a figure which only seems to be a milestone for Count Fleet on his way to further greatness.

Leading from end to end of the mile and a half of the seventy-fifth Belmont Stakes, Mrs. John D. Hertz's son of her own Reigh Count scored by thirty lengths, hard held, in 2:28 ⅕, three-fifths of a second faster than the superhorse had run the same twelve furlongs in the Jockey Club Gold Cup back in 1920.

One need not compare Man o' War and Count Fleet from the standpoint of greatness, for it is a question which never can be settled. But there was a disposition among some in Belmont Park's crowd of 19,290 to take notice of the fact that this country could and did produce a champion for each World War and that the links binding the interest of men and women in thoroughbreds and patriotism were as strong as a generation ago.

The sale for war bonds of the silks of Count Fleet in the unsaddling enclosure before Mrs. Hertz led in her champion brought $50,000. The sale for the day was estimated by Stanley Gould of the War Activities Committee to exceed $100,000, and the sale during the meeting to be beyond $500,000. Mr. Gould, congratulated for his auctions, in turn congratulated the officials of Belmont Park for having made them possible.

The victory was Count Fleet's sixteenth, to raise his total earnings to

$250,300, slightly more than Man o' War garnered when purses were so much smaller. Man o' War was defeated only once, and then a story went with it. Count Fleet has been second four times and third once, but never out of the money.

The way he ran to earn $35,340 of the Belmont's gross purse of $50,000 made one think that he never was going to be out of the money. There was nothing to the race, the riders of Fairy Manhurst and Deseronto giving up so far as winning was concerned after about six furlongs, even though they battled tooth and nail for the place money of $5,000. Fairy Manhurst, son of Man o' War, got that by a length.

The track record at Belmont is Bolingbroke's 2:27 ⅗, made on the Teletimer. That time smashed Sorteado's mark of 2:28 ⅖, which in turn had bettered Man o' War's 2:28 ⅘.

However, Count Fleet's clocking did break by two-fifths of a second the record for the Belmont Stakes. The previous test time for this classic since the distance was increased to a mile and a half was 2:28 ⅗, set by War Admiral, a son of Man o' War, in 1937.

After the finish someone asked Jockey Johnny Longden how it was Count Fleet hadn't broken Bolingbroke's record. The lad replied: "It's a long summer. We're trying to beat horses. Why run against the clock and risk injury, when the colt can breeze and sweep all before him?"

That's about all Count Fleet had to do—breeze. It was his sixth start of 1943 and his sixth victory, making the brown colt the first horse in history to win the five Spring specials of Wood Memorial, Kentucky Derby, Preakness Stakes, Withers Mile and Belmont.

The triple crown of Derby, Preakness and Belmont has become commonplace, a dozen horses having brought that off since Sir Barton did it first back in Man o' War's day. It doubtless will be a long time, though, before another 3-year-old will take all five of the big Spring stakes that now feature American Spring racing.

PART III

———————— ◆◆◆ ————————

"A great racehorse is born, but he is made as well . . ."
—ROBERT J. KLEBERG, OWNER AND BREEDER OF 1946
TRIPLE CROWN WINNER ASSAULT

Belmont Park Winner's Circle: 1946 Triple Crown champion Assault with jockey Warren Mehrtens and Helenita Kleberg, daughter of King Ranch owner, Robert J. Kleberg. NEW YORK RACING ASSOCIATION

IN 1946, on the strength of its six previous champions, the Triple Crown was recognized not only as a legitimate achievement but a transcendent one for horses. America was no longer distracted by war. It was ready for what the contemporary Hall of Fame trainer D. Wayne Lukas calls "Box Office Horses," animals whose personality and back-story matched their talent.

They got Assault, a well-bred but injury-prone colt that had stepped on a surveyor's stake as a foal, caught an infection and ended up wearing a special shoe on that foot for the rest of his life. Assault limped when he walked or trotted, and earned the nickname "Club-Footed Comet." As a two-year-old, he was just an average runner, winning just two of his nine starts.

When he entered the gate of the 72nd running of the Kentucky Derby, bettors sent him off at a very tepid 8-1. When he galloped off to an eight-length victory, a star was born. Assault's box office appeal was also greatly enhanced by the people around him. His owner, Robert J. Kleberg, was the lord of the nearly one-million acre King Ranch in Texas, and was a voluble sort who liked to pass on his breeding theories. The colt's trainer, Max Hirsch, was also a salty Texan. The jockey, Warren Mehrtens, was hardly a superstar rider, but rather a solid journeyman from Brooklyn who rewarded Kleberg and Hirsch's loyalty by treating Assault as a pet.

In 1947, Citation debuted in Maryland and quickly established himself as the best two-year-old in the nation after winning eight of nine races. But "Big Cy" became a star the next year when he swept the Triple Crown virtually unchallenged. He won the Derby by 3½ lengths from his stable mate Coaltown; the Preakness by 5½ lengths over Vulcan's Forge; and the Belmont Stakes 8 lengths ahead of Better Self. He was so dominant that his trainer Jimmy Jones raced him against older horses, which he also easily galloped away from. Citation won 19 of his 20 events that year and was named not only the best three-year-old in the country, but Horse of the Year. When he was retired as a six-year-old, Citation had a record 45 starts, 32 wins, 10 seconds, 2 thirds, and the distinction of the becoming the first horse ever to top a million dollars ($1,085,760) in purse earnings.

With Assault and Citation, the 1948 Triple Crown Champion, the coverage in *The Times* became less reverent toward the titans of the sport and more focused on the quirks and character of the horses. There was a greater willingness, too, to examine the role of pedigrees and bloodlines.

CRIME SOMETIMES PAYS

BY ARTHUR DALEY

BALTIMORE, MAY 10, 1946—Although he was responsible for a bold-faced Assault before some 100,000 eyewitnesses while purloining the Kentucky Derby last week, the shameless Max Hirsch will attempt to get away with Assault once again tomorrow in the fifth-fifth running of the Preakness Stakes at Pimlico. His victims received ample warning of his methods at Louisville and they are out to balk him in his depredations on nobility and commoner alike.

The Texas-born trainer of Texas-born Assault is fully determined to waylay Lord Boswell once again, as well as His Lordship's burly bodyguard, Knockdown. Another to be taken unawares last week was Hampden. They and sundry others are on the alert that such things don't happen again.

So magnificent was Assault in the Run for the Roses that the son of Bold Venture almost looks to be a lead-pipe cinch to repeat his triumph just as his daddy did before him. Having won $96,400 at Churchill Downs, the chestnut colt would not be at all a surprise if he added to it the major part of the $141,620 financial prize at stake in Baltimore. If that's accomplished, then the $100,000 Belmont, third diadem in the famed Triple Crown, will be dangling invitingly before him.

That's a large amount of loot for a horse to be shooting for and there will be glory as well as cash if he can accomplish it. As far as the glory part of it is concerned, only six colts ever contrived to achieve the triple in the long history of the turf—Sir Barton, Gallant Fox, Omaha, War Admiral, Whirlaway and Count Fleet.

Is Assault quite in their class as another equine version of superman? No one knows. He hardly could have given a more convincing performance than he did at the Derby, winning by eight lengths, a margin equaled only by Whirlaway, Johnstown and Old Rosebud. Past history proves not a thing. Old Rosebud didn't start in the Preakness. Whirlaway did and, with one of his typical whirlwind rushes in the stretch, won handsomely by five and a half lengths. Yet Johnstown was mired in the Pimlico mud in 1939 and finished far out of the money as Challedon triumphed pretty much has he pleased.

So that smashing Kentucky victory of Assault doesn't mean a thing. This is a different state, a different race and the Texas steed starts off again at scratch. The day of the Preakness often has been called Redemption Day because it has afforded the opportunity to some of the beaten nags to redeem their showings at Louisville. Alsab got even with Shut Out for the Churchill Downs upset by winning at Pimlico, while Bimelech, Col. E. R. Bradley's pride and joy, displayed at the Baltimore course the class he failed to demonstrate when Gallahadion put the crusher on him in the Derby.

Since Assault was something of a surprise victor last week, he won't be the odds-on favorite that Count Fleet was a few years back. He still hasn't convinced enough customers of his greatness and there's still plenty of room for speculation. What makes this particularly true is the fact that the racing strip at Col. Matt Winn's hoss emporium was far from fast for the richest Derby of them all.

Then, too, this will be a smaller field, which figures to aid a stretch runner like Lord Boswell. A dry track will also enable the huge Knockdown to lumber along with high speed without the mental hazards of puddles and holes, each of which the big fellow persistently jumped over with extreme fastidiousness at Louisville. Last but not least, there is Hampden with a new rider aboard.

This, perhaps, is the most intriguing tidbit of them all. Eddie Arcaro has abandoned Lord Boswell in favor of William du Pont's charger from Foxcatcher Farms. Job Dean Jessop was aboard the Delaware mount in the Derby and, despite his admitted class as a jockey, the Utah lad kicked away a certain second place by misjudging the finish line and pulling up his oatburner short of the wire, a most grievous social error. Arcaro won't need a compass or direction-finder to locate the terminal point of the race. He'll draw a bead on it from the very start.

The official announcement by little Eddie was that he expected to ride His Lordship in the Preakness, but that his agent had booked him for Hampden instead, all these manipulations surprising him no end—or so he claims. That may be so, of course. Yet an outsider can't help but wonder whether the clever jockey developed a preference for Hampden after riding both colts. Could be, you know.

Lord B. was pretty much of the favorite in the Derby and the best he could do was take fourth. He did run into one traffic jam when the field fanned out ahead of him at the upper turn, thus forcing him to drop behind and take to the overland route, a decidedly time-wasting process. Now Doug Dodson will have the leg up on His Lordship, a circumstance which hardly figures to plunge him into gloom.

There have undoubtedly been instances in previous Preaknesses where jockeys have fumbled the ball by picking the wrong horse just as Arcaro did in the Kentucky Derby of 1942, when he chose Devil Diver over winning Shut Out. But none of them come as readily to mind as the other classic example.

However, the Run for the Black-Eyed Susans (almost an infringement on the Run for the Roses copyright) did produce one famous case when the trainer guessed wrong. It was a dozen years ago that Bob Smith elected to shoot for the Triple Crown with Cavalcade, the Derby winner. So he sent High Quest out to set the pace for his better charger. The jockey, a certain Bobby Jones, saw a chance to win and took it, thus stealing the race from his illustrious stablemate. Rather than risk seeing the irate trainer, he wisely caught the next train out of Baltimore.

There may be more robbery at Pimlico tomorrow, but Max Hirsch already has made crime pay with Assault.

HIGH PAY AND SHORT HOURS

BY ARTHUR DALEY

ELMONT, N.Y., JUNE 1, 1946— It's nice work—if you can get it. How would you like to earn $950,520 for toiling exactly four minutes and eight seconds? But don't crowd, pal. You won't find a job of that nature in the "Help Wanted" columns. The field is an exclusive one, limited to the oat-munching creatures who run on the racetracks. In fact, the only one to fill the above description is Assault, winner of the Kentucky Derby, the Preakness and $195,520.

This afternoon the Texas-bred son of Bold Venture will be shooting for another large wad of folding money when he dashes the mile-and-a-half distance in the unprecedentedly rich $100,000 Belmont Stakes, third and last diadem in turfdom's famous Triple Crown. They have been conducting this race since 1867 and only six colts ever have achieved the triple in all that time—Sir Barton, Gallant Fox, Omaha, War Admiral, Whirlaway and Count Fleet.

So it's quite obvious what an exclusive group this is. Perhaps Assault belongs in their class, but he'll have to prove his right to greatness by triumphing today at beautiful Belmont, because this is the most searching test of the three. The distance is the longest, for one thing, and racing luck will have less to do with it than in either of the others. A horse beaten in the Belmont can have no excuses.

Up to two years ago it was axiomatic that every colt who sought to gain the last leg of the Triple made it. Both Burgoo King and Bold Venture had won both Derby and Preakness, but broke down before they even had a chance to take a whack at the third classic. But along came Pensive in 1944, a surprise winner at both Churchill Downs and Pimlico, and was thoughtless enough to lose to Bounding Home at beautiful Belmont. That broke the string.

Often in the past the "big" horse of the year had so demonstrated his class that rivals virtually gave him the race by default. The last of these came in 1920, when a powerfully built chestnut with a mane of flaming red hair found only one nag with the temerity to challenge him. The test was almost ludicrous. Donncona was the stooge or patsy and trailed by a mere six lengths two furlongs from the finish. But then Jockey Clarence Kummer shifted into high gear and gave out with the jet propulsion a quarter of a century before it even was invented. Not until then did Man o' War decide to run. He won by the trifling margin of twenty-five lengths in world record time that endures to this very day.

Assault won't win by any margin that great—if he wins at all. Matching strides with him will be Lord Boswell and Hampden, two most valiant and consistent pursuers. His Lordship, never a real contender in the Derby, was climbing up the back of the pride of Texas in the Preakness and lost out by the picayune margin of a neck, gaining so rapidly at the end that he'd undoubtedly have won had the race been just a few steps longer.

But Lord B. will have a new rider this time. Mrs. Elizabeth Arden Graham apparently changes jockeys faster than she changes shades of lipstick. She had Eddie Arcaro on His Lordship in the Derby and Doug Dodson on him in the Preakness. Now she's trying with Eddie Guerin. Maybe she's mad at Dodson because he was not the most obedient lad in the world at Pimlico and yet almost triumphed with him. The tender-hearted Mrs. Graham always instructs her jockeys: "Don't you dare beat my little horse."

Arcaro tried to cajole the obstreperous Lord Boswell at Churchill Downs and was sparing with his whip. But Dodson is more old-fashioned, it seems. As a firm adherent of the principle: "Spare the rod and spoil the child," he whaled the daylights out of Boswell at Pimlico and almost won with him. Maybe newcomer Guerin will try the flattery method on the Maine Chance steed. It remains to be seen, however, whether he can reap success with that method.

Jockey Warren Mehrtens, the cowboy from Brooklyn, probably will be a mite timid about using the bat on Assault. He gave him a lusty wallop with his whip halfway down the Preakness homestretch and this maneuver startled his mount so greatly that Assault almost jumped out of his skin. He veered skittishly to the rail and thus gave Lord Boswell his opportunity. But the son of Bold Venture is an eminently sound animal and undoubtedly will be the favorite.

That's one thing about the Belmont. It probably has fewer upsets than any of the other classics. There have been some close calls, of course, but they have been more of an exception than a rule. Perhaps none was closer than the 1908 race, when Colin beat Fair Play, the pappy of Man o' War, by a thin red whisker. Down through the years Colin has become something of an equine god because he was that rarity of rarities, a horse who never was defeated in his life.

He never came nearer to defeat, however, than he did on that foggy afternoon almost forty years ago. The fog hung over the course like a clammy curtain, blotting out a view of the start and veiling every turn. Then out of the shadows around the final bend came a misty figure, Colin. He was running effortlessly, loping along in front of Fair Play.

But there had been a change made in the position of the finish pole. It had been moved down the track some thirty yards from its usual spot and Jockey Joe Notter, a forgetful soul, pulled up his charger as soon as he passed the old finish line. Then he remembered—and barely got Colin over the real finish line to victory.

Down through the years this has been one of the most historic of all races on the American turf. It even contributed a phrase to our language. One account of the 1891 event related: "Montana appeared to have the race in hand Garrison brought Foxford up with a rush and won by a neck." The jockey was Snapper Garrison and he's the lad responsible for that catch-line "A Garrison finish."

The winner today will move into mighty select company.

ASSAULT, 7-5, WINS BELMONT STAKES FOR TRIPLE CROWN

BY JAMES ROACH

ELMONT, N. Y., JUNE 2, 1946 — Completing brilliantly a job started in the Kentucky Derby and continued in the Preakness, Assault slammed down on the stretch to win the seventy-eighth and richest Belmont Stakes, convince the last remaining doubters of his greatness and take his place with the six other big ones of the turf who have captured the mythical triple crown.

It was a magnificent performance and a crowd of 43,599 at old—and surprisingly chilly—Belmont Park cheered lustily as the King Ranch's chocolate-colored prize package poked his nose in front just before the eighth pole and drew away from the pack. He was three lengths to the good by the time he coasted under the wire at the end of the mile-and-a-half run.

There were still many doubters when the Texas-bred colt went to the post with six others. Despite his triumphs at Churchill Downs and Pimlico, the customers made him the 7-5 second choice—by a few hundred dollars in a $640,495 mutuel pool—to Lord Boswell, but at the end Lord B. was no better than fifth, and the gold and the glory were Assault's.

Second was Mrs. Walter M. Jeffords' Natchez, in that spot most of the way and in front early in the stretch. The third was Mrs. Aksel Wichfield's 45-1 shot Cable and fourth was Foxcatcher Farms' Hampden, a gallant pace-setter as far as he went, who found twelve furlongs about two too many.

Natchez had a length and a half advantage over Cable, whose margin was a head over Hampden. Another equine head separated Hampden and the Maine Chance Farm's thoroughly beaten Lord B., and then came Mrs. Jeffords' Mahout and Mrs. Alfred Roberts' War Watch to complete the parade.

At the end of the line was $77,400 in prize money for Assault, including a $2,000 nominating award for Robert Kleberg, owner of the vast King Ranch. This pay-off raised to $316,270 the earnings of Assault, who has taken five out of six for a 1946 total of $299,020 and hasn't far to go to surpass Gallant Fox's single-season mark of $308,275.

It was a joyous day for Owner Kleberg, for trainer Max Hirsch and particularly for Jockey Warren Mehrtens, the youngster from Jamaica High School, who has ridden Assault to every one of his victories.

Admiral Marc A. Mitscher, veteran of the Pacific War and commander of the Eighth Fleet, and Mayor William O'Dwyer were among those present for the handshaking and back-slapping in the winner's circle after the race. The Admiral presented the August Belmont Memorial Cup to Kleberg and the Mayor had a big handshake for pint-sized Mehrtens.

Mehrtens was beaming. Said he: "The only time I was worried was coming out of the gate when Assault stumbled. He recovered at once and we were never in difficulty again. I had more confidence this time than in either the Derby or Preakness, but I still can't believe we've won the triple crown."

Said Kleberg: "We're deeply happy and we feel others will agree with us now that Assault is a great horse. I want particularly to compliment Max Hirsch on a great training job."

In the jockeys' quarters the others weren't so gay. Eric Guerin, who had ridden Lord Boswell, summed up best what had happened to the favorite when he remarked: "He didn't have it when I asked for it."

Eddie Arcaro, who had been hoping for his fourth Belmont Stakes success aboard Hampden, said: "The winner bumped us in the stretch, but Hampden was a tired horse and it made no difference in the result."

Getting his name on the triple-crown list, along with those of Sir Barton, Gallant Fox, Omaha, War Admiral, Whirlaway and Count Fleet—and hopping up to twelfth position on the roster of leading American moneywinners—Assault was rated smartly by Master Mehrtens.

After that stumble at the start, which brought a gasp from the crowd, Assault got going in a hurry and was third behind Natchez and Hampden, the two that had been expected to set the pace, at the first turn. Then he went to fourth and he held that spot behind Hampden, Natchez and War Watch down the backstretch.

On the turn for home Assault, in his best Derby and Preakness style, was moving in high. Mehrtens had taken his time; he knew he had plenty of horse under him. Hampden and Natchez, and then Natchez alone, were still out there, but Assault was fairly flying—and the rest was easy. Just short of the eighth pole every last customer knew he had the race won, and it was a triumphal charge the rest of the way.

Natchez held on to the second position—it was worth $20,000—without too much trouble, but the next three had considerable of a fight for third before Cable, Hampden and Lord B. finished in that order.

The time didn't threaten Count Fleet's 2:28 ⅕, but it was a sound 2:30 ⅘ after fractions of 0:24 ⅘, 0:49 ⅗, 1:14 ⅕ and 1:39 ⅖. Those who had backed Assault thought that the pay-off of $4.80 for $2 was pretty sound, too.

Assault was at even money on the opening line with Lord Boswell 7 to 5, but the bettors couldn't see it that way. At the end the two were almost joint choices, with $147,409 having gone in on His Lordship and $146,587 on Assault. Hampden was the third choice at close to 4 to 1, and after that came Mrs. Jeffords' Natchez-Mahout entry at better than 8½ to 1.

Picketing of the horse park, which had begun May 22, and the return to the job of an assortment of employees ended with a minimum of official word as to what had gone on behind the scenes. A track spokesman simply reported that the men were back at work—or would be as soon as they got the word.

Teamsters' representatives, according to track officials, had demanded that the track direct all workers not affiliated with the American Federation of Labor to join that organization. Refusal on the ground that such a move would be illegal resulted in picketing, and among those who became non-workers in addition to van drivers were bartenders, admission-ticket sellers, electricians, carpenters, movie camera operators and, on Thursday and Friday, program printers.

First indication that all was serene again at beautiful Belmont came when the programs went on sale at the entrances. After the mimeographed sheets of the previous two days, racegoers gladly got up their dimes for the neat, pocket-sized jobs.

THE STUFF THAT MAKES
A GREAT HORSE

BY H. I. BROCK

JULY 7, 1946—Poets, they tell us, are born, not made. A great racehorse is born, but he is made as well. At least that is what you get from Robert J. Kleberg, owner and breeder of Assault, the great horse of the moment.

The chestnut colt, born and bred in Texas, is not a big horse. His height in equine terms is fifteen hands one inch and a half. He is not magnificent like Man o' War. He has not, perhaps, the grace and distinction of Gallant Fox. But he has a fine head and straight legs. When he moves his muscles seem to flow like a cat's. As he runs he gives an exhilarating effect of ease and efficiency. He is a great horse because he has proved his right to the title in the only test of a thoroughbred—which is to race him against his peers. If he wins, he is it. If he keeps on winning, he is It with a capital I.

Assault's name is the latest in the list of seven horses who have passed our top test for 3-year-olds, coming in ahead of all the rest in the Kentucky Derby, in the Preakness and in the Belmont Stakes at Belmont Park. On top of that, by winning the Dwyer Stakes at Aqueduct he has won more money in a single season than any other horse in the history of racing. He has $339,720 to his credit on that score, against $308,275, the previous high record, made by Gallant Fox sixteen years ago.

The money is important. Racing is big business today. But it isn't the money that makes the great horse. And the question is where the colt from way down in the Lone Star State got the stuff that ranks him with these other great horses, the other wearers of the triple crown, Sir Barton, back

83

in 1919, and after him, Gallant Fox, Omaha, War Admiral, Whirlaway and Count Fleet.

The greatest of all great horses, by general consent, Man o' War, is not in this list, because, though born and bred in the Blue Grass, he wasn't even entered in the Kentucky Derby in his year, 1920. But the Preakness, the Belmont and the Dwyer were among the twenty races he did win, and he was beaten only once in his whole career. Assault, for his part, has won all but one of the races in which he started this season—six out of seven.

The first requirement in any racehorse is thoroughbred blood. You must begin with that—which means that his ancestry goes back to one or more of the Arab or Barb stallions brought to England around the beginning of the eighteenth century, the horses who started the breed known in the old days as the "English Horse." This is the racing stock recognized by all the world's Jockey Clubs.

Among these thoroughbreds the ambitious breeder's concern is to select the lines that have produced the horses with outstanding records on the track and in the stud, lines known for special qualities which contribute to the winning of races—among which speed comes first. It must come there, since all the others, including spirit and endurance, only serve to make speed tell.

In that respect, Mr. Kleberg (who has given the subject prayerful attention) saw to it that Assault was well furnished. In the chestnut colt's pedigree are assembled the lines which have produced Man o' War and Equipoise on our side of the ocean which the airplane has reduced to a ditch, and, on the other side, St. Germans, carrying the blood of many English Derby winners in his veins and, incidentally, bred by Lord Astor.

One of St. Germans' sons was Twenty Grand. Another, out of a Commando mare, was Bold Venture. And Bold Venture is Assault's sire. Igual, his dam, was sired by Equipoise (holder of the speed record for a mile), the dam in that case being daughter to the full sister of Man o' War (Fair Play-Mahuba).

These few details—terrifying to a layman—are produced just to give an idea of the factors which enter into the racehorse breeder's calculations. Taking stock of observed qualities in each of the strains involved, Mr. Kleberg figures that, on the blood count, so to speak, Assault is entitled to a top-notch combination of speed, endurance and racing spirit.

But blood, even the best blood, is not enough. Not all offspring of great sires are heirs of greatness. And short of a fluke of fortune equivalent to a miracle, the best-bred colt does not just grow up like Topsy into a great racehorse.

Experience and an added flair have given some men a keen eye for a horse. A great horse, even in the raw, is not merely a critter endowed with the capacity to make time on his feet. He has personality. And there is a watchful eye on the colt from the time he is foaled, while he is a playboy in the pasture and later when he is a yearling and can carry a boy on his back and be galloped and "breezed" over short distances along with other colts.

To be sure, the evidences of special quality do not always appear in the early stages—some horses develop slowly. The story is that only a stable boy discerned the budding seeds of greatness in the gawky yearling who was Count Fleet, winner of the triple crown before Assault.

Also, there are various schools of thought about what should be done with a young horse to bring out his latent promise—whether, for example, to keep him up or turn him out. Kentucky, convinced that the art of raising horses is a Blue Grass specialty, has ideas of its own. But Mr. Kleberg, who can use for the job the great King Ranch of close to a million acres and has the Texas climate for ally, holds to the notion that the prospect (or candidate) for high racing honors is best off most of the time in the open, where, as the King Ranch's owner says, the young animal's feet—not the least important part of his equipment—take care of themselves, grow naturally, as they do not when he is pent up in a stall; it is enough to get him up when he is not taking proper care of himself in his grass lot and needs a bit of feeding or other attention.

Out in the open he gets his exercise naturally. Out there, too, the watchful eye can follow him and see how economically he moves his feet when he runs on his own.

It early appeared that Assault, though he has what Kleberg frankly calls a club foot, ran without lost motion. When later he was galloped with a boy on his back he showed that he had speed and a commendable native urge to get ahead of the other horse. With special and careful shoeing the deformed foot did not interfere with his performance.

When the colt was sent to Max Hirsch, the veteran trainer likewise recognized a horse of quality and promise. A racehorse, to make good, says Mr. Hirsch, must have brains, bone and nerve. He must have courage, persistence, bottom. This colt has all of these. He not only has speed but also the will to use it. More than that, he has a mind of his own—and confidence, a lot of confidence in himself.

The trainer plays a great part in making a great horse. And Kleberg says that Hirsch has what it takes for the job—knows how to bring out the best the colt has in him. The genial Texan adds that when "Max has brought the horse to top form he will try to force him to carry on beyond it."

A racehorse is a four-legged athlete. He has to be kept fit like a football player or a fighter. He must be brought to a keen edge for a contest, but follows a daily routine in training like any two-legged athlete. It begins when he is a yearling and takes on a regular pattern when he is a 2-year-old and first begins to race.

At the track, between his racing dates, you will find his hours of rest and exercise carefully regulated by the trainer, who knows his capacities, limitations and peculiarities. In the morning, before the racegoers arrive, he is out being "breezed" (run easily), "worked" (which means running harder) for short distances, galloped for longer distances or just walked. And after that you will find him in his stall, well groomed and fed—or feeding—with the trainer or owner, or both, looking him over with alert and practiced eyes to make sure he is in perfect condition. That's probably the end of his footwork for a non-racing day. As with other athletes, rest is a part of the routine, and the price of winning with a horse (as of liberty) is eternal vigilance. He has his vet and expert shoer.

Jimmy Fitzsimmons, who trained Gallant Fox for William Woodward, said that the Fox knew he was a racehorse, knew what was going on and ran his own races. Fitzsimmons added that about all he did was to help the Fox to educate himself—as, for instance, when he ran into difficulties about starting. That seems to be Max Hirsch's way with Assault, who likewise knows he is a racehorse and runs his own races.

The Fox, whose grace and distinction have been noted, was, nevertheless, a horse of moods, and "contemptuous" of training workouts. What was the use? Didn't he know his own business? And Hirsch says that Assault, often praised for his cooperative spirit, and usually kindly behaved in company, knows that he wants, and wants it when he wants it. He knows also what he does not want.

"If I stuck around in his stall when he did not want me there," says Hirsch, "either I'd get out or he'd kill me."

Earle Sande, the jockey who always rode Gallant Fox, used to sing to the Fox as he ran. Little Warren Mehrtens, the Brooklyn high school boy who has ridden Assault in all his races, has also an easy way with his mount. He waits until he senses that the horse is ready to get going—and then cooperates, as, for example, in the two taps with the whip which he gave the chestnut, "just for insurance," when they swung into the stretch in Dwyer.

"The boy has wonderful hands," says Kleberg. "He and the horse understand each other. Maybe Eddie Arcaro could win a race with him that Mehrtens couldn't, but it might spoil the horse for more races." In the Texan's opinion, Assault is not a horse to be forced. And he insists that more horses are spoiled than are made by people who try too hard to make them.

The reminder is not out of place at this point that Man o' War was a horse of tremendous personality—with terrific power behind it. He was a devil to break, a headache to handle as a raw colt in training, a catapult to ride on the track. There was no doubt that Big Red ran his own races. Jockey C. Kummer, who sat in the pilot seat in all the races he ran—except the one he lost by a nose—said that the boy on the big fellow's back was little more than a passenger.

Count Fleet was another sort, described as "a smart one." He was not nervous or temperamental. According to his trainer, Don Cameron, he was "placid and affectionate." But when he was on the track "the spirit of the chase came over him." And he, like the other great horses mentioned, was ridden by the same jockey in all his races—in this case Johnny Longden. It would seem, then, that having in the saddle a boy who really knows the horses is one of the things which counts toward enabling a great horse to deliver the goods that are in him.

These few examples tell more about what makes a great horse than could be conveyed by a catalogue of the qualities which add up to make the total sum. A great horse has character above and beyond the call of duty assigned to good performers on the track. He has courage and sticking power: you may call it "heart" if you will. He has personality—something in himself which distinguishes him from the horses that just run races and quite often win races. It is something that is born in a horse, something that horsemen are always looking for in their carefully bred racing stock.

And when those who do find it are wise enough to help the horse who has it—in Fitzsimmons' words—"to educate himself," that horse is equipped to use his God-given gift to the best advantage on the racetrack. It is then we have the horse that wins public acclaim as great. It helps if he has a name that sticks in the public mind and captures the imagination. Assault, like the other great horses mentioned here, has that as well.

CITATION, COALTOWN FINISH ONE, TWO IN KENTUCKY DERBY

BY JAMES ROACH

LOUISVILLE, MAY 1, 1948 — Eddie Arcaro and Ben Jones rolled that "4" today and it wasn't a hard point to make, after all.

Before a whooping crowd of close to 100,000 in the seventy-fourth edition of the Kentucky Derby at the old Churchill Downs, Calumet Farm's Citation was an easy first, Calumet Farm's Coaltown was second and the four other 3-year-olds in the line-up were nowhere in particular at the end of the mile and a quarter.

Arcaro, on Citation, became the first jockey to win the Julep Belt classic a fourth time, Ben Jones, with an assist from his son Jimmy, had program listing as the trainer of the Calumet pair for this race, and so he became the second trainer—the other was the late H. J. (Derby Deck) Thompson—to hit the jackpot on a fourth great occasion.

The field was the smallest in a Derby since 1907. With Citation beating his stablemate by three and a half lengths, this was the order of finish after the first two: Third was Ben F. Whitaker's My Request, beaten for the first time this year, three lengths astern of Coaltown; fourth was R. W. McIlvain's Billings, another length and a half away; fifth was Mrs. John Payson Adams' Grandpere, and last was William L. Brann's Escadru.

The big gap was between fourth and fifth, Grandpere nosed Escadru out of fifth place, but both were twenty lengths back of Billings. Thus the invaders of the Bluegrass State didn't do well at all; the first four are Kentucky-bred, Grandpere is a Californian and Escadru a Marylander.

Contrary to expectations in a race on which there was only straight betting, Calumet's mighty pair did not go to the post as the shortest-priced favorites in Derby history, but at 2 to 5 did equal the record as the shortest-priced choice since the pari-mutuels were put in use here. Bimelech, second in 1940, was a 40-cents-on-the-dollar proposition; so was Count Fleet, winner in 1943.

It was a Calumet Derby from flag-drop to photo-snapping. Coaltown, ridden by Newbold Leroy Pierson, was on top, winning the first eighth of a mile and Citation soon was his closest pursuer.

Coaltown, unbeaten in his four previous starts, was ahead by perhaps as many as eight lengths at one point in the backstretch, and it was the two in the devil's red silks side by side as the turn was made into the homestretch. Outside the three-sixteenths pole, with the race following the precise script so many racing folk had foreseen. Citation was in front—and from that point he went calmly about his business.

Arcaro whacked Citation at the eighth pole just for insurance. He finished in 2:05 ⅖, looking as if the task hadn't been particularly difficult.

The chart man wrote "handily" as his description of the victory, and "easily" as Coaltown's manner of taking runner-up honors. The chart man could hardly have picked two more appropriate words. But he might have written "they laughed home."

It was an off track into which the Derby horses dug their hoofs. Early morning rain led the management to post "track sloppy" on the infield boards. Under the conditions, the time was excellent and Coaltown's way-station clockings were remarkable: 0:46⅖ for the half, 0:59⅓ for five furlongs (only one-fifth of a second away from the track record), 1:11⅖ for six furlongs, 1:35⅗ for seven and 1:38 for the mile.

Arcaro, who had arranged for part of his winnings to go to Mrs. Al Snider, widow of the Calumet rider who lost his life on a fishing expedition in Florida during the winter, was the most jubilant little man in these United States when he returned to the jockeys' quarters.

Said he: "For once I picked the right horse. He's great. He'll win the triple crown."

It was Master Eddie's ninth Derby ride. He won with the Woolford Farm's Lawrin in 1938, Calumet's Whirlaway in a record 2:01 ⅖ in 1941, and with Fred W. Hooper Jr.'s Hoop Jr. in 1945. Last year and in 1946 he was unable to mark up No. 4.

Calumet also won with Pensive in 1944. Ben Jones trained that one, Lawrin and Whirlaway.

Two jinxes bit the dust on this gray day. No previous winner of the

Belmont Futurity had gone on to Derby fame: no previous winner of the Derby Trial had hit the derby double. Citation apparently never has been told about jinxes.

It was his fifteenth decision (nine in stakes) in seventeen starts and it increased his collection of racetrack swag to $331,830. He has earned $176,150 in compiling a seven-for-eight record as a 3-year-old.

Citation is a bay colt by Bull Lea and Hydroplane II. His dam was imported from England in 1941 by Warren Wright, who had purchased her from the late Lord Derby. Coaltown is by Bull Lea (that old boy was eighth in the 1939 Derby) and Easy Lass.

The customers here from all points of the compass were a wilted lot at the end of the day—more wilted than the four-legged principals in the main act of the show. It was a muggy day—hot and steamy for the first half of the afternoon and then a bit cooler. During the early races the sun burned through the clouds a few times, then called it quits. So it was grayish overhead and there was the threat of rain as post time neared for the big number.

The greatest crush in the infield—where seven bands were at work—was along the fence in the stretch between the quarter pole and the sixteenth pole. The red, blue, green and khaki uniforms of the oom-pah boys—and girls—helped to make it the usual splashed-with-color show. So did the beds of flowers in the infield. So did the spectators; some who hadn't been very colorful when they arrived were colorful indeed when they checked out.

Eddie Arcaro was late for dinner last night. He had to pay a visit to the local pokey. A friend was driving Arcaro and Kirkland to town from the track, and the friend honked his horn a couple of times more than a local gendarme thought necessary. This friend explained to the gentleman in blue that he was in a bit of a rush to get two Derby riders to dinner. The gendarme expressed great disinterest in jockeys, the Derby and racing in general, and proceeded to deliver a long pep talk. Arcaro, hungry and irate, spoke for the defense. He apparently did not speak wisely. He was hauled off to the jailhouse, where two minutes of explaining resulted in general handshaking, much laughter and a late dinner.

Three kids shinnied up a pipe, then dropped twenty feet from the top of the fence into the grounds. Nearby, watching with great interest was one of the track's policemen. Once they had made four-point landings, he turned his back. It happened shortly before noon. So add at least three to attendance figures.

CITATION WINS 1½-MILE BELMONT IN 2:28⅕ FOR TRIPLE CROWN

BY JAMES ROACH

ELMONT, N.Y., JUNE 13, 1948 — In a gallop, with his ears pricked and with apparently about as much expenditure of energy as in a midweek workout, Calumet Farm's magnificent Citation completed the business of winning American racing's triple crown in an astounding performance at Belmont Park yesterday.

It was astounding because Citation, despite the ease with which he took the eightieth running of the $117,300 Belmont Stakes by more than half a dozen lengths, equaled the stake record for the mile and a half classic.

Horsemen blinked a couple of times when 2:28 ⅕ flashed on the Teletimer board in the infield, the same figures that had gone up after Count Fleet's triumph in 1943.

For about half the way it looked like a contest. Then Citation began to open up on the other seven.

First he had three-quarters of a length advantage. Then it was one and a half at the far turn. In practically nothing flat on the final bend he was three or four to the good. Then it was a solo flight through the straightaway.

So it was that the Belmont, sternest of the tests for 3-year-olds, proved an even easier proposition for the Calumet colt than the Kentucky Derby and Preakness had been.

And so it was that he made his record eighteen victories in twenty starts, added $77,700 to his earnings, boosted them past the half-million mark and gave Jockey Eddie Arcaro and Warren Wright's Calumet Farm their second winner among the eight that have taken the three-deck crown. Calumet's first was Whirlaway in 1941.

Closest pursuer of the champion at the end of the line was King Ranch's Better Self, who closed in along the rail in the final furlong to take the $20,000 place money by half a length from William L. Brann's Escadru.

Fourth, after a gap of some five lengths, was C. V. Whitney's Vulcan's Forge. Then followed A. J. Sackett's Gasparilla, William Helis' Salmagundi, Belair Stud's Golden Light and Glen Riddle Farm's Faraway.

For the fourteenth time in his racing career Citation was an odds-on choice. Price makers had predicted that he would be 1 to 5, and 1 to 5 he was—despite the fact that his stable-mate Coaltown was a late scratch—after the 43,046 customers had completed their scrimmaging at the mutual windows. Citation was 3 to 20 to place and the legal minimum of 1 to 20 to show, the track having to put $3,041.80 into the show pool to make good on those nickel-on-the-dollar pay-offs to the "sure thing" gentry.

Faraway, 28 to 1-shot ridden by Ted Atkinson, thrilled the onlookers in the early stages. He went up to run with Citation, who stumbled a bit breaking out of the gate from the inside slot but nevertheless charged almost at once into the lead. They went head and head to the first curve, head and head around it and down the backstretch.

At about the seven-furlong pole there was a yell from the crowd as Arcaro let out half a wrap and jumped clearly ahead at once. Faraway stayed in the hunt for a while, then faded on the turn for home, a fade that dropped him all the way to last place.

On the bend Arnold Kirkland began his bid with Escadru, the pride of Maryland, and Warren Mehrtens cut loose from the middle of the pack with Better Self. They were second and third in that order to the stretch, but they hadn't the slightest chance of catching the flier up ahead. The fight for second place and the move-up to fourth of the late-running Vulcan's Forge provided the only excitement through the final yards. Arcaro's whip was excess baggage.

Arcaro, winning a Belmont for a fourth time—the only jockey still active to have accomplished that feat—sent the Bull Lea Hydroplane II colt along at an even pace. The quarters were clicked of in 0:24 ⅕, 0:24 ⅕, 0:24 ⅕, 0:25 ⅗ and 0:25 ⅗. Times were 0:48 ⅖ at the half, 1:12 ⅗ after six furlongs, 1:3 at the mile and 2:02 ⅗ after a mile and a quarter.

Said Arcaro: "He's the greatest horse I've ever seen. Maybe I shouldn't have let him win by so much, but I couldn't take any chances for that kind of money. I think he can run an eighth in 0:11 flat in any part of any race."

Said Trainer Horace Allyn (Jimmy) Jones: "Nice ride, Eddie." Jimmy's father, B. A., saddled Whirlaway in 1941 for the Derby-Preakness-Belmont three-bagger.

Owner Wright, the Chicagoan whose Calumet Farm is located at Lexington, Ky., did a job of backpatting on Master Eddie just prior to the presentation of August Belmont Memorial Cup and a permanent trophy in the winner's enclosure.

With a dozen stakes and $544,700 to his credit in two seasons, Citation has won $398,020 this year with nine victories in ten starts. He needs only one more big stake—and the Arlington Classic is his next major objective—to eclipse Assault's record of $424,195 for earnings during one year.

The customers—some 7,000 more of them had been expected—had a warm day at the horse park. For the first time this season there was a shirt-sleeved gathering.

A CITATION OF FACTS

BY ARTHUR DALEY

NOVEMBER 3, 1948 — There was a story floating around Baltimore last weekend that they didn't even bother to give Citation a rubdown after his walkover in the Pimlico Special on Friday but that Eddie Arcaro desperately needed a rubdown. He'd strained every muscle in his arms while trying to hold back the explosive Calumet Comet in his majestic solo flight around the historic old track. The tale was never confirmed but it sounds reasonable. Citation just happens to be that kind of horse.

The handsome bay concluded his labors for the year with that magnificent exhibition and now will have a couple of months to rest, doing nothing more arduous than munching red clover hay and counting his money. He has an awful lot of it to count, too. The earnings of this amazing 3-year-old colt have now reached $830,250 for two brief seasons of campaigning and he is rapidly overhauling Stymie as the top money winner of all time, trailing by merely $81,085 and destined to become the first equine millionaire next spring.

Since the element of competition is entirely lacking, a walkover could be a most dreary affair. But Citation can make even a walkover exciting. The Pimlico authorities wisely dressed up the occasion with the red-coated band, which always looks like a road company from *Rose Marie*. They introduced the colt with the booming words "Pimlico proudly presents." They hung a blanket of chrysanthemums around his neck in the winner's circle afterward and, in between, Citation put on a show.

For the Calumet colt this was a return engagement. Last May he won the Preakness at the Maryland track in 2:02 ⅖, running against horses. He won this one against ghosts in 1:59 ⅕, pulling Arcaro's arms out of their sockets as he fought to get the affair over in a hurry. Eddie held him in tow in the backstretch but finally let him go in the last straightaway.

Observers on the sports patrol learn to respect the opinions of horsemen more than any others. A football man will step overboard and hail a run-of-the-mill back as "greater than Jim Thorpe." A baseball operator will say that so-and-so will be better than Ty Cobb or Babe Ruth. But they never get effusive on the turf. Admissions are so grudging and superlatives are so scarce that even the mild term of "great" is withheld until the label is so clearly earned that there isn't the slightest doubt about it. And the horsemen are so enamored with Citation that they've lost all their restraint.

For the better part of three decades there has been only one "greatest." He was the immortal Man o' War, the norm of racing perfection. Yet Citation has already looked Big Red in the eye and said to him, "Move over, bud." The turf experts and the turf die-hards have raised the Bull Lea colt to the same pedestal that Man o' War has proudly held all alone for these many years. Many of them, surprisingly enough, even go that one unbelievable extra step and declare that Citation is better than Big Red, "the mostest horse."

Even as far back as last February trainers in Florida were beginning to mention out loud that perhaps Citation might become not just the horse of the year but the horse of the decade or the century. The unexcitable Ben Jones wouldn't comment for publication but he did make a confession to Bill Corum in these words, "Maybe he's the best we've ever had. Maybe he's the best I ever trained. Maybe he's the best I ever saw. Maybe he's the best there's ever been." He can say that again.

As a 2-year-old Citation lost only one race and that was to his stablemate, the filly Bewitch. He could have won but he was just being polite with a gesture that meant, "Ladies first." As a 3-year-old he lost one race.

That was to the sprinter Saggy on a bad track shortly before the Kentucy Derby. Arcaro was aboard him for the first time, didn't know his habits and didn't want to risk punishing him with the Run for the Roses in the offing.

As for Citation's habits, they've been so commendable that other jockeys drool enviously at the very sight of Master Eddie on the Calumet Cannonball. Most horses have what the railbirds call one "move." That means that they have to make their lone victory bid with a little something extra at either the start or the finish or at some intermediate strategic point. Once that bolt is shot, however, they're done. Rare is the horse which has two moves. They say that Man o' War had three. How about Citation? That question was once asked of Arcaro.

"He's the doggondest colt I ever rode in my life," he said admiringly. "I swear he has ten moves. He'll move for you at the start, around the turn, in the backstretch or any time you want." In the Preakness Doug Dodson on Vulcan's Forge drew up to Citation's shoulder and, boom, there suddenly was daylight between them. "I just put him into high gear," modestly explained Master Eddie.

That's why the Bull Lea colt is so great. He doesn't have to race in a certain pattern. He can take command of a test at the very start and blaze the trail. He can come from behind. He can break a race apart with a sudden spurt in the middle. His versatility in a sport which can produce versatility so infrequently is a most remarkable trait. Nor does he have to be contained with specific distances. He has won this season at six furlongs and also at two miles without being tested.

It was inevitable, of course, that he should be compared to Man o' War. The 3-year-old champion of 1948 didn't set records the way the 3-year-old champion of 1920 did. After all, Big Red turned in record clockings in eight of his eleven races and then retired to stud where he was to gain enduring fame as a sire. Citation set only two records this season and he's a long way from the stud.

His big test will come in the 1949 campaign when the handicappers load weight on his back as they are bound to do. And no one can scream louder or in deeper anguish at top weights on a horse than Messrs. Ben and Jimmy Jones. But this also could serve to prove Citations's greatness as it proved Exterminator's greatness. Even in a walkover he looks awesomely impressive. He's all horse and already is worth more than his weight in gold, an equine Fort Knox.

PART IV

◆◆◆

"He was a glorious creature, this copper-colored stallion,
and he has earned his wings."
—*TIMES* EDITORIAL ON SECRETARIAT

Secretariat in November 1973, after his Triple Crown season. AP IMAGES

IT HAD BEEN 25 years since Citation swept the Triple Crown when Secretariat nosed into the starting gate of the Belmont Stakes on June 9, 1973. In that time, six others had reached the doorstep of history, but got no further, unable to win over that last mile and a half. They were very good horses—Tim Tam, Carry Back, Northern Dancer, Kauai King, Majestic Prince and Canonero II. They just weren't great ones.

There was little doubt that Big Red, as Secretariat was known, was about to become the ninth Triple Crown winner. Bettors made him the 1 to 5 favorite, only slightly shorter than the odds they could have gotten after he was named Horse of the Year as a two-year-old. In his debut on the Fourth of July, Secretariat's odds were 3-1 (the highest they'd ever be) and he was bumped repeatedly coming out of the gate to finish fourth, the only time in 21 career starts that he ever finished off the board. He went on to win seven of nine starts as a juvenile and would have been a perfect six for six in stakes races if he had not been disqualified in the Champagne Stakes.

Secretariat wore the mantle of greatness even before he ran the fastest Kentucky Derby in history (1:59 and 2/5 seconds for a mile and a quarter), and easily won the Preakness. He was so well bred, so good looking and so accomplished that in February of 1973, months before the Triple Crown races, he was syndicated as a stud prospect for more than $6 million, at the time an unheard-of sum. "Even if he doesn't win the Triple Crown, he's

worth the money," said Seth Hancock of Claiborne Farm who put together the deal.

The breeders of the bluegrass were not the only ones who locked on to
the ripped chestnut. Red Smith practically took up residence in Secretariat's barn. He was transfixed by the powerful chestnut, and chronicled
his feats throughout the Triple Crown in his inimitable style.

Still, neither Smith, nor anyone else, could have imagined how Secretariat would rocket away from his four rivals and float around the Belmont
oval as if on a cloud. Chick Anderson, who called the race that day, put a
memorable soundtrack to this performance when, his voice summoning
awe, proclaimed: "Secretariat is moving like a *tremendous* machine. He's a
sixteenth of a mile ahead of the other horses!"

He won by a soul-stirring 31 lengths, set yet another record, and
locked up the title of the greatest of Triple Crown champions.

"At that moment he was not a horse but the archetype of the horse: big,
burnished and fresh from the hands of his maker," the *Times* wrote. "So
profound is beauty's grip on the imagination that millions of people fell in
love with Secretariat."

SECRETARIAT IS A BLUE CHIP IN THE RACEHORSE MARKET

BY STEVE CADY

FEBRUARY 28, 1973 — In the bullish world of horse breeding, buying Secretariat at $190,000 a share makes as much sense as buying I.B.M. at $431.

Supply and demand dictates the price and there's only one Secretariat. With the horse market so strong, Monday's world-record $6.08 million syndication of the 3-year-old colt has caused hardly a ripple of surprise.

"I'd say it wasn't really a gamble," Seth Hancock said yesterday from Claiborne Farm in Paris, Ky. "Even if he doesn't win the Triple Crown, he's worth the money. He's got all three things you want in a sire: pedigree, looks and performance."

Hancock, son of the late A. B. (Bull) Hancock, is managing the syndication for Mrs. John Tweedy, in whose Meadow Stable silks Secretariat will race this year. Mrs. Tweedy will retain four of the 32 shares in the breeding syndicate.

Hancock said the names of the 27 other syndicate members would be disclosed today, as soon as "the last share" in the 1972 Horse of the Year is sold.

"Some of the finest people in racing are in this group," he said. "All of them own good broodmares. If Secretariat wins the Derby or even the Triple Crown, the members could sell their shares. But I doubt if they would. They're looking for a good horse."

For his $190,000, each shareholder is entitled to send one mare a year to Secretariat—starting next winter, when the colt is retired to Claiborne Farm. The breeding season runs from mid-February to early June. Most top sires are bred to no more than 30 or 40 mares a year, a control measure that limits the supply and helps create multimillion-dollar breeding syndicates.

For commercial breeders in the syndicate, the goal is a series of foals that can be sold for six-figure sums at the yearling sales in Saratoga or Keeneland. If Secretariat continues to race well this season, a commercial breeder with one share in the syndicate could expect to "get out" (i.e., recover his initial investment) with three or four foals.

For most of the syndicate members, though, the goal is a long-range one: a son of Secretariat who might win the Triple Crown, a daughter of Secretariat who might foal a Triple Crown winner.

Meanwhile, Secretariat himself hasn't even made his racing debut as a 3-year-old. The chestnut son of Bold Ruler–Somethingroyal will take the New York route to the Kentucky Derby, arriving here from Florida on March 14 and making his first start of the season in the seven-furlong Bay Shore at Aqueduct on March 17.

"Yes, I think we might find a stall for him here," Kenny Noe Jr., racing secretary for the New York Racing Association, said yesterday.

Last season, en route to becoming the first 2-year-old Horse of the Year, Secretariat won seven of nine races and earned $456,404.

"You could say he looked like a million dollars," said Noe, "but I guess that'd be an understatement. He looks like six million."

ONE MORE, AND THEN
TO LOUISVILLE

BY RED SMITH

APRIL 9, 1973 — By the time the "official" sign went up there was a long line at the $100 win cashier's window waiting to collect $110 for each ticket. A few yards away the cashier at the $5 place and show window began paying off $5.25 for each bet on Secretariat, $6.50 and $5.25 on Champagne Charlie and $5.25 on Flush to show. "This is the breadline, Dave," the man at the $5 grill called across the room to the man behind the $100 wicket. He may not have known at the time that he was dipping into the New York Racing Association's pocket to make up a minus pool of $14,900, which is what happens to a racetrack when a successful favorite like Secretariat draws so much of the action that losing bettors don't lose enough to give the winners their legal minimum return.

The way business is these days in New York racing, even a minus pool of $14.90 would be a blow, but no complaints on that score were heard from management Saturday. That showy dude Secretariat had drawn the year's biggest crowd to Aqueduct and the act he put on for the 41,998 witnesses was worth every penny he cost.

Carrying 126 pounds, the same weight he will have in the Kentucky Derby, the Preakness and the Belmont Stakes if he gets to those Triple Crown events, he matched the 10-year-old track record of 1:08 ⅗ for six furlongs, took a deep breath and went on to equal the mile record of 1:33 ⅖, winning the Gotham Stakes by three widening lengths.

In his second start as a 3-year-old, the 1972 horse of the year gave 11 pounds to the 4-year-old that set the mile record five years ago and 14 pounds to the originator of the six-furlong mark. He set his own pace and required no more urging than a perfunctory tap of Ron Turcotte's whip:

This one is a smasher, and no mistake.

When the colt came back to the winner's circle, his coppery coat looked perfectly dry and he didn't appear to be puffing. Half an hour earlier, his most persistent pursuer of last year, Stop the Music, had come back the winner of a $15,000 allowance race, and the physical contrast was striking.

Stop the Music is a shifty little colt with a charming head and an air of jaunty eagerness. Secretariat is a great big athlete, calm and competent. He must have an unusually big stride, for he runs with so little show of effort that he does not seem to be hitting the speed the Teletimer registers.

In the Bay Shore Stakes two weeks before the Gotham, Secretariat had loitered amid flying slop for six of the seven furlongs, then bulled between Actuality and Impecunious and pulled away to beat Champagne Charlie by 4½ lengths. Turcotte, whose thread-needle tactics in that race had not been acclaimed universally, played safe in the Gotham by letting his mount go to the front inside the first half-mile.

With a quarter of a mile left, Turcotte let the colt catch his breath, enabling Champagne Charlie to move up in menacing fashion. Then the whip swung once, and they started putting the chairs on the tables.

Besides padding out a bankroll of $523,034, Secretariat proved in this race he could set the pace and win as convincingly as he does coming from behind. He had already shown utter disregard for track conditions. He has now finished in front 10 times in 10 starts since the first race of his life, when he was slammed leaving the gate. He finished fourth on that occasion, so he has never come back without a piece of the purse.

His impersonation of Bronko Nagurski in the Bay Shore wasn't his only contretemps in the homestretch. When he won the Champagne Stakes last fall, he and Stop the Music were moving between horses when Secretariat felt Turcotte's whip for the first time in his life. He ducked in and bumped Stop the Music. Secretariat won but the stewards put up Stop the Music's number and gave Secretariat second money.

There was another bumping in Secretariat's next race, the Garden State Stakes. On the stretch turn, Impecunious knocked Knightly Dawn into Secretariat, but the big horse kept right on going and won by himself. Jaime Areliano, Knightly Dawn's rider, claimed foul against both of the others. Impecunious was disqualified but Secretariat's number stayed up. Then after the colt's fullback rush in the Bay Shore, Jimmy Moseley on Impecunious entered a foul claim, which was disallowed.

That made it three claims in his last four races before the Gotham. On

Saturday, confident that he had committed no sins out front by himself, his owner, Mrs. John Tweedy, embraced Lucien Laurin, the trainer, without waiting for the stewards' approval. Her stomach must have done a barrel roll an instant later when the "inquiry" sign on the tote board brought hoots from the crowd. In a moment, though, blinking numbers indicated that it was Angel Santiago on Dawn Flight claiming foul against Champagne Charlie.

With one more race—the Wood Memorial on April 21—between him and the Kentucky Derby, the big story now is Secretariat's run at the Triple Crown. The only colts in the last quarter-century that were as impressive as Secretariat at this stage were Citation, Nashua and Native Dancer. It may be worth remembering that only Citation won the Triple Crown.

WORD FOR IT HAD TO BE CLOCKWORK

BY RED SMITH

LOUISVILLE, MAY 6, 1973—Secretariat was the first to get up in the barn at 4 o'clock this morning. He was the first to get home at 5:39 this afternoon in the 99th and richest Kentucky Derby. It was also the swiftest, the most lavishly supported by the betting public, and easily one of the most melodramatic as 1972's horse of the year rushed from last to first and ran the last quarter-mile in 23⅕ seconds.

When Edward Sweat, their groom, came out of the tackroom at 4 A. M., both Secretariat and Angle Light were on their feet and watching for him in the darkness. The favorite and his entrymate might not have known this was Derby Day, but their stomachs were on Daylight Saving Time and they knew breakfast should be coming. Sweat measured out two quarts of oats for each and retired to the tackroom, where he has a cot but seldom sleeps.

"In New York we have a night watchman," he said, "but here I'm the watchman. I might sleep half an hour, then I jump up and look around. Down here I want the job right, so I just as soon do it myself. Not that I don't trust 'em, but it's my horse and if anything went wrong it'd be my responsibility. It got chilly last night, so I closed the lower doors on the stalls and after that it was quiet."

When the horses were finished with breakfast, he swept and raked the stalls, carpeted them with new straw, brushed the colts and cleaned their hoofs, then waited for Lucien Laurin, the trainer he has served for 18 years. As soon as the boss arrived, Sweat led the horses out and turned them over to George Davis, the exercise rider, and Yann Houyevet, a young Frenchman who wants to be a trainer and is studying American methods.

Both colts were so full of themselves they dragged their hot-walkers around the barn at a half-run until the groom fitted Secretariat with a type of bit he calls a "shift" and put a chain bit in Angle Light's mouth. They were walked for 25 minutes, rubbed and tidied up again and put back in their stalls. At 10:30, after a blacksmith had made sure their shoes were fitted satisfactorily, each got a pint of oats for lunch. Sweat also hung a loose bundle of hay about the size of a basketball in a net inside each stall door.

"That lunch tells 'em something," he said. "If they wasn't racing they'd get four quarts of oats with a quart of sweet feed and I might let 'em have a few carrots. When they only get that little bitty lunch they know something's up, probably know they're going to race. They won't get nothing now till after the Derby."

"Secretariat heard you say that and laid his ears back," a visitor said. "He's mad at Edward Sweat."

"He tries to bully you once in a while," the groom said. "Gets a little tough and don't let me in the stall. I just wait till he changes his mind and then go in. Funny, with all the excitement this week, he's more relaxed here than in New York. Same with Riva Ridge last year. He just laid down and went to sleep. When they told us, 'Get your horses to the paddock,' I went in and he was lying there plumb out."

Now and then, strollers passed, but the presence of uniformed Clarence Coleman, a guard for Barricade Security, kept most of them at a distance. They cast sidewise glances toward the barns. For the first time in a week, the Churchill Downs stable area was peaceful. When the first race started a little after 11:30, the amplified voice of the track announcer came faintly across the barn roofs. As the horses reached the stretch, the roar of horseplayers sounded like distant surf.

By noon the infield crowd had grown hard to believe. Traffic still moved freely back of the grandstand and in the gardens behind the clubhouse—the seats at Churchill came clear down to the outside rail, so there is no "lawn"—but the center field was a half-mile oval of people held as if in aspic. Raising the $3 admission charge to $5 did not discourage the college kids, who once again made up a majority in the biggest, barest, most painfully sunburned horde ever funneled into this cavalry post.

They made a display of skin, nude of foot, back and abdomen. Now a dissident kid seeking to avoid attention climbed a tall flagpole and slid down to a reception committee of cops. There a pack of young men tossed their girls 15 to 20 feet aloft on a blanket. With faintly alcoholic but warmly courteous insistence, two tomentose knights persuaded strangers to drink from a two-quart carton of screwdrivers. Frisbees sailed and dipped like gulls on the beach.

Back in Barn 42, Angle Light lay snoozing in the straw, Secretariat gave up waiting for his groom to bring more oats and retired to the back of his stall, Edward Sweat cleaned tack and rolled bandages, Clarence Coleman drowsed on a camp chair in the sun.

Ron Turcotte, Secretariat's rider, arrived at 1:30 and pushed through the clubhouse gardens to the jockey's quarters, stopping occasionally to autograph a program. "I wouldn't trade him for any of them," he said when asked about his mount's chances.

After a late lunch, Laurin returned to the barn, and about 45 minutes before post-time for the ninth race the two colts were turned over to pony boys. Trainer, grooms, ponies and racehorses set off on foot, across the stable area, around the wrong way of the clubhouse turn, through the gap beneath the ancient stand and into the screened-in paddock, where Turcotte waited for Secretariat and John LeBlanc for Angle Light.

"I don't think he will disgrace himself," Laurin said.

"I think he will redeem himself."

The forecast remains operative.

SECRETARIAT "TOLD" JOCKEY HOW HE WANTED TO WIN IT

BY STEVE CADY

BALTIMORE, MAY 19, 1973 — Mrs. Penny Tweedy said it all in a few jubilant words at the champagne party in the pressbox after Secretariat's smashing success in today's 98th Preakness: "We got two down, and one to go."

The big, brash Meadow Stable colt managed by Mrs. Tweedy had easily added the second part of the Triple Crown to his Kentucky Derby victory of two weeks ago. Only the Belmont Stakes remains.

"Now," said Mrs. Tweedy, turning to Lucien Laurin, the horse's trainer, and Ron Turcotte, the jockey, "it's up to these two men to go back to work."

She didn't need to mention the horse, because winning classic races looks more like play than work for this $6.08-million 3-year-old. The way he ran today, it almost seemed as if he knows how to think, too.

"The pace was slow and he wanted to run," said Turcotte. "He was determined to run. I figured, if this is the way he wants to do it, I'll let him have his way."

Secretariat's "way" was to go three-wide on the clubhouse turn while rushing from last to first in the six-horse field. Asked how the winner let him know he wanted to run, Turcotte replied, "The horse and myself, I guess we talk a little bit."

When Turcotte sent his mount three-wide on the turn, some of the faint-hearted Secretariat backers groaned. "Oh, no, don't go around horses," yelled a man who hadn't noticed the slow time of 25 seconds for the first quarter on the tote board.

But the colt they call "Big Boy" went—to the lead early in the backstretch and then into the winner's circle. And as one admirer suggested with a shout of, "All the way this year, baby," he went a long way toward the first Triple Crown sweep in 25 years. It was so easy that Turcotte never had to touch his wonder horse's expensive hide with the whip.

So thoroughly did Secretariat crush second-place Sham and the others that some of the tribute-paying reporters found it hard to find an angle.

"It was so one-sided," said a man in the jockey room. "No big turning point, no head-to-head duel. What do you write about except to say he's a superhorse?"

If there was a turning point, it had to be Turcotte's decision to let his horse roll on the first turn even if it meant losing ground by going wide.

"It's always a concern when you go three-wide there," admitted the rider. "But my colt has been getting sharper and sharper. He almost ran off with me yesterday morning just galloping two miles. I had to turn him loose because they were really slowing it down up front."

Turcotte said that he had "turned my horse's head out a little" when he spotted some overly ambitious photographers at the head of the Pimlico stretch and that he had glanced over his right shoulder on the backstretch to check the progress of the other horses.

"I always check back whenever I hear a whip crack or a horse coming up," the rider said.

Most of the whip-cracking Turcotte heard today was done by Laffit Pincay Jr. aboard Sham. In the Derby, Sham had the lead turning for home, and Secretariat nailed him in the stretch. Today, it was Secretariat in front with a hand-ride through the stretch and Sham, under heavy left-handed whipping, trying unsuccessfully to catch him.

In the jockey room, Pincay reflected the kind of respectful frustration riders who challenge Secretariat must feel—not to mention the horses who challenge him.

"I kept waiting for Ronnie to hit him," said Pincay, shaking his head. "I don't think he ever hit him. He went by me flying, I didn't expect it that soon. In the stretch, my horse kept trying. I kept whipping and whipping, but we couldn't get close."

Asked if he thought Secretariat was a superhorse, Pincay nodded slowly. "He could be. My horse ran a powerful race, but he just couldn't gain no ground on that other one."

Ben Feliciano, rider of last-place Torsion, was more emphatic. "I always though he was a superhorse," said Feliciano. "Now maybe all the people who didn't believe will believe."

The 1, 2, 3 finish of Secretariat, Sham and Our Native, the same as in the Derby, was the first time this has happened.

Now comes the Belmont, three weeks from now, and speculation has already begun on the possible cast of equine characters.

"Whom do you expect to face in the Belmont?" Laurin was asked at the post-race champagne session.

"I don't have no idea," replied Secretariat's trainer.

The way Big Boy is going, maybe it doesn't make any difference.

SECRETARIAT SWEEPS TO TRIPLE CROWN BY 31 LENGTHS

BY JOE NICHOLS

ELMONT, N.Y., JUNE 10, 1973 — Secretariat won the Belmont Stakes yesterday with a finality that was incredible. The Meadow Stable star flashed to success in the 1½-mile event by the improbable margin of 31 lengths over Twice a Prince, his runner-up, and even with the big margin, he set a track record time of 2:24.

The performance was executed under a splendid ride by Ron Turcotte, and was most noteworthy in that it enabled Secretariat to become the ninth winner of the Triple Crown for 3-year-olds.

A quarter of a century ago Citation turned the trick, and Secretariat is the first since then to do so. He won the Kentucky Derby at 1¼ miles on May 5, and the Preakness at 1³⁄₁₆ miles on May 19.

A crowd of 69,138, the second largest turnout to see a Belmont Stakes, attended the 105th running of the race. It had five contestants, and the advance indications were that it would turn out to be a duel between Secretariat, whose payoff at the end was $2.20 for $2 to win and $2.40 to place, and Sham, who competes in the silks of Sigmund Sommer.

Sham was in there for a while, but he found the going too tough as the contest went on, and he wound up in the most unlikely spot—last place. The colt that finished back of Twice a Prince was Arthur Appleton's My Gallant, who was a half-length out of second place and 13 lengths ahead of C. V. Whitney's Pvt. Smiles. Sham trailed that one by three-quarters of a length.

The exacta of Secretariat and Twice a Prince returned $35.20 for $2. The OTB letters were A and E.

The race had a gross value of $150,200, with the five starters, and the share to the winner, who is trained by Lucien Laurin, was $90,120.

In the day or two preceding the Belmont, Sham's trainer, Frank (Pancho) Martin, had said he would send a "rabbit," Knightly Dawn, into the race, to test Secretariat with an early pace, but yesterday morning Martin changed his mind and withdrew Knightly Dawn.

The race, as regards tight competition, was hardly a tingler, considering the huge margin of victory. But it held continuous excitement because of the superequine achievement of Secretariat.

At the start he went to the front with Sham, who was ridden by Laffit Pincay, and for a spell the pair raced together, the others being "nowhere."

Approaching the three-quarter pole, Turcotte turned around to spot his pursuer who was two lengths behind. Assured that his margin was a comfortable one, Turcotte just sped away to the score, which had to be the easiest one of Secretariat's career, while Sham cracked completely under the fast pace.

Fractional times, most of them set by Secretariat, were 0:23 $\frac{4}{5}$, 0:46 $\frac{1}{5}$, 1:09 $\frac{4}{5}$ and 1:59. The mark that Secretariat shattered was 2:26 $\frac{3}{5}$, set by Gallant Man in the Belmont Stakes in 1957. Each horse in the Belmont carried scale weight of 126 pounds.

It was obvious through the going that Turcotte was out for the record with Secretariat, just as he did in the Kentucky Derby of 1$\frac{1}{4}$ miles. In that race Secretariat, in beating Sham by 2$\frac{1}{2}$ lengths, was timed in 1:59 $\frac{2}{5}$, beating the standard of 2:00.

In the Preakness of 1$\frac{3}{16}$ miles there was a misunderstanding about Secretariat's time, and the matter was finally resolved with a clocking of 1:54 $\frac{2}{5}$, as against the standard of 1:54. Some clockers caught Secretariat in 1:53 $\frac{2}{5}$. In that race Sham also was the runner-up, again by 2$\frac{1}{2}$ lengths.

When he returned to the winner's circle yesterday Turcotte corroborated the speculation that he was record-conscious. He said, "When we got to the stretch, and I saw those figures on the tote board, I knew that I was going to a record."

The world record for a mile and a half (on turf, and not on the dirt, like the Belmont) is 2:23, set by Fiddle Isle at Santa Anita in 1970. The American record on dirt, which was broken yesterday, was 2:26 ⅕, set by Going Abroad at Aqueduct in 1964.

The occasion of the Belmont Stakes was one of complete joy, glory and accomplishment for Mrs. John (Penny) Tweedy, who directs the activities of the Meadow interests founded by her late father, Christopher T. Chenery; for Turcotte, who has ridden Secretariat in all but the first two of the colt's 15 races, and for Laurin, who trains for the Meadow interests.

For this Belmont marked consecutive successes for these track notables. Riva Ridge of the Meadow Stable won the Belmont Stakes last year.

Secretariat is a Virginia-bred son of Bold Ruler and Somethingroyal, and now has a record of 12 victories in his 15 races. His share of yesterday's gross purse was $90,120. This sum raised his season's earnings to $438,838, and his career earnings, over the last two years total $895,242.

Gov. Nelson A. Rockefeller, along with Gov. Lynwood Holton of Virginia, presented the Triple Crown trophy to Mrs. Tweedy. Governor Rockefeller also presented the Belmont Trophy to Mrs. Margaret Chenery Carmichael, vice president of the Meadow Stable.

Secretariat entered the race with so formidable a record that he became the prohibitive favorite all through the betting, which was on win and place only. The place price on Twice a Prince was $4.60.

The Triple Crown has now been won nine times, starting with Sir Barton in 1919. He was followed by Gallant Fox in 1930, Omaha in 1935, War Admiral in 1937, Whirlaway in 1941, Count Fleet in 1943, Assault in 1946, and then Citation.

There were several instances following Citation in which horses won the first two legs only to falter on the third, that it was ventured in some quarters that the Triple was a modern impossibility. Secretariat now put that theory to rest.

Secretariat now figures quite highly in the economic scheme of things in the thoroughbred world. He has been syndicated for breeding purposes for $6,080,000, his career in that field to begin when his racing days are over, late this year.

Mrs. Tweedy, a-tingle over the victory for some time after it happened, said, "That horse is wonderful, and the reason he is, is because he has been trained magnificently."

Laurin, hearing this, gave credit to the breeding and the ownership, and to Turcotte, whose record-breaking ride pleased the trainer no end. Asked if Secretariat was the best horse in his recollection, Laurin said, "Positively."

Pincay, of Sham, said, "I was following the trainer's instructions in trying to go to the front, but I couldn't pass Secretariat. My horse just didn't run the first mile, and I never could get him started. I didn't use my horse in the stretch, as I was not going to abuse him. He was not the same horse that ran in the Kentucky Derby."

Commenting further on his ride on Secretariat, Turcotte said, "He's just the complete horse. I let him run a bit early to get position to the first turn. Once he got in front of Sham he wasn't about to give anything away."

Laurin's further comments were, "I wondered a bit when I saw those early figures, wondered if he was going too fast. But I told myself that Ronnie [Turcotte] knows the horse, and that made me feel better. And I felt better all through the stretch when he was drawing out and still running like a gem."

Baeza, of Twice a Prince, said, "My horse ran a better race than expected, but Secretariat is a superhorse."

Angel Cordero, who rode My Gallant, said, "That winner is a real runner. When he and Sham hooked up early I thought to myself that they would run each other into the ground and that I had a chance. But that all changed when Secretariat ran off by himself. He's the best I've ever seen."

A LITTLE GREEDY, AND
EXACTLY RIGHT

BY RED SMITH

JUNE 11, 1973 — The thing to remember is that the horse that finished last had broken the Kentucky Derby record. If there were no colt named Secretariat, then Sham would have gone into the Belmont Stakes Saturday honored as the finest 3-year-old in America, an eight-length winner of the Kentucky Derby where he went the mile and a quarter faster than any winner in 98 years and an eight-length winner of the Preakness. There is, however, a colt named Secretariat. In the Derby he overtook Sham and beat him by two and a half lengths. In the Preakness he held Sham off by two and a half lengths. This time he and Sham dueled for the lead, and he beat Sham by more than a 16th of a mile. There is no better way to measure the class of the gorgeous red colt that owns the Triple Crown. Turning into the homestretch at Belmont Park, Ron Turcotte glanced back under an arm to find his pursuit. He saw nothing, and while he peeked, his mount took off.

Secretariat had already run a mile in one minute, 34⅕ seconds. Up to three weeks ago, no horse in Belmont history had run a mile in less than 1:34⅖. He had run a mile and a quarter in 1:59, two-fifths of a second faster than the Derby record he had set five weeks earlier. Now he went after the Belmont record of 2:26⅗ for a mile and a half, which was also an American record when Gallant Man established it 16 years ago.

With no pursuit to urge him on, without a tap from Turcotte's whip, he smashed the track record by two and three-fifth seconds, cracked the American record by two and a fifth, and if Turcotte had asked him he could have broken the world record. If he had been running against Gallant Man, the fastest Belmont winner in 104 years, he would have won by 13 lengths. Unless the competition spurred him to greater speed.

"It seems a little greedy to win by 31 lengths," said Mrs. John Tweedy, the owner, and then repeated the rider's story of how he saw the fractional times blinking on the tote board, realized there was a record in the making, and went after it in the final 16th.

It is hard to imagine what a 31-length margin looks like, because you never see one, but Secretariat lacked eight panels of fence—80 feet—of beating Twice a Prince by a 16th of a mile. This was the classic case of "Eclipse first, the rest nowhere."

The colt was entitled to his margin and his record. At the Derby he drew a record crowd that broke all Churchill Downs betting records and he set a track record. He set attendance and betting records at the Preakness and may have broken the stakes record, but if he did discrepancies in the clocking denied him that credit. Last Saturday belonged to him.

Indeed, Belmont was kinder to the Meadow Stable than Pimlico had been, in more ways than one. On Preakness day, while the Tweedy party lunched in the Pimlico Hotel near the track, a parking lot attendant smashed up their car. They walked to the clubhouse gate, found they hadn't brought credentials, and paid their way in. While the horses were being saddled in the infield, somebody in the crowd accidentally pressed a lighted cigarette against Mrs. Tweedy's arm. On his way back to his seat, John Tweedy had his pocket picked.

"Boy," he said after that race, "we needed to win this one today, just to get even."

At Belmont there were the few scattered boos that most odds-on favorites receive here, but the prevailing attitude was close to idolatry. Well, perhaps that isn't the best word because it suggests a cathedral restraint. Idols are remotely chilly. This congregation was warm. Horse players passing the Tweedy box raised friendly voices:

"Mrs. Tweedy, good luck."

"Thank you."

The voices followed her to the paddock where her colt was cheered all around the walking ring. They followed as she returned to the clubhouse.

"Mrs. Tweedy, good luck."

"Thank you."

Secretariat was cheered in the post parade, cheered as he entered the gate, and when he caught and passed Sham on the backstretch the exultant thunders raised gooseflesh. At the finish the crowd surged toward the winner's circle, fists brandished high. After 25 years, America's racing fans had a sovereign to wear the Triple Crown.

Parallels are striking between this one and his predecessor, Citation. Both colts raced nine times as 2-year-olds and finished first eight times. At 3, each lost once en route to the Derby, Preakness and Belmont. Both made each event in the Triple Crown easier than the last. After the Belmont, Citation won his next 10 starts for a streak of 16 straight. Secretariat's stud duties won't permit that. Love will rear its pretty, tousled head.

EDITORIAL: THE END OF PEGASUS

OCTOBER 8, 1989 — Television has provided the world with many remarkable images over the years, but none more beautiful than that of a horse named Secretariat winning the Belmont Stakes. He had already won the Kentucky Derby, setting a still unbroken track record, and the Preakness; so much excitement had been stirred by the prospect of his winning racing's Triple Crown that some of those who tuned in that June afternoon of 1973 may have been watching a race for the first time. What they saw was Pegasus.

Secretariat won by 31 lengths, pounding down the stretch with his mane flying, running it seemed for the sheer joy of it. At that moment he was not a horse but the archetype of the horse: big, burnished and fresh from the hands of his maker. So profound is beauty's grip on the imagination that millions of people fell in love with Secretariat that day, and remain so after his death last week.

Even the least sentimental among us may wish for some kind of heavenly pasture for Secretariat. He was a glorious creature, this copper-colored stallion, and he has earned his wings.

PART V

◆◆◆

"This horse has a prayer."
—George Vecsey

Churchill Downs: Placing bets on the Kentucky Derby, 1996. KEVIN R. MORRIS/CORBIS

The New York Times has never been the first read for horseplayers looking for a daily winner or two at the racetrack. Over the years, however, our reporters and columnists have hardly been blind to the colorful milieu that surrounds America's three classic races. Nuns offering divine intervention and the prototypical "wise guys" touting the "horse right here" have been visited for journalistic and prognostication purposes. None ever took the position championed by famous muckraking journalist Nelly Bly who once damned Saratoga Springs—the sport's horse heaven—in a 1894 story in *The New York World* headlined: "Wild Vortex of Gambling and Betting by Men, Women and Children," and despaired over the fact that "gamblers, horse owners, jockeys, millionaires and actors mingle together promiscuously."

And the odds are good that more than a few of our ink-stained scribblers have made a modest wager on a horse, even though heaven forbid they admit it. Reporting on the Belmont Stakes undercard in 1941, the correspondent John Kieran described the disappointment of a pitiful $34 daily double payoff. "This innocent bystander," he wrote, "had been led to believe that anybody who hit the daily double had to hire a truck to carry off the returns on a $2 investment." Steven Crist, who covered horse racing for *The Times* in the 1980's and is now the editor and chairman of the *Daily Racing Form,* has gained well-deserved fame for his handicapping prowess. And Bill Barich has found another way to back a winner: just be in the right place at the right time.

A BIG DAY AT BELMONT

BY JOHN KIERAN

JUNE 8, 1941 — It was hot, sweltering. Outside the gates at Belmont the customary philanthropists were hawking their tip sheets, offering a future fortune for fifty cents in hand, or even a quarter in hand. Just buy their marked cards and a fortune was as good as ready for collection inside the gates, or so the philanthropic hawkers insisted, but the hurrying thousands scurried by, paying little attention to the loud-voiced philanthropists. Maybe the racegoers were not interested in making money.

Young Harry Stevens of the famous catering clan was encountered at the entrance to the clubhouse restaurant. "A big day," said young Harry, "but not as big as Decoration Day. There'll be more room to move around."

Even so, the lawn was thronged and traffic was difficult under the grandstand when the jumpers came out for the first race. The tote board showed $15,748 wagered on Naruna, the Hitchcock hedge hopper, to win. "They must think that horse is home free," said one awed onlooker. Well, those who thought so were a trifle mistaken. It was Chuckatuck of the Log Cabin Stud that won the race and paid $8.50. Naruna tried hard in the stretch, but just couldn't overhaul Chuckatuck.

The rail was lined six deep as the horses paraded for the second race. Word was passed that there was $60,952 in the daily double pool. When C. V. Whitney's Kingfisher won the second race, the daily double pay-off was $34.30. Shucks! This innocent bystander had been led to believe that anybody who hit the daily double had to hire a truck to carry off the returns on a $2 investment.

Along came Dave Woods, Alfred Gwynne Vanderbilt's number one boy at Pimlico and Belmont Park. It was remarked to Mr. Woods that it was a shame to have only four starters in a race like the Belmont, rich in tradition as well as money. It was suggested that he might have scampered around and hired a half dozen gallopers just to fill out the field. "What!" said Mr. Woods sharply, "and be accused of commercialism? They'd say we were just trying to stir up more betting on the race. As it is, with only four starters, we can't have any show pool on the race."

While most of the visitors at Belmont were studying form charts, looking over the horses in the paddock or investing at the mutual windows, this innocent bystander was gazing in awe at the big tote board in the infield. How those figures do mount up!

It was somewhat startling to see $31,000 bet on one horse in a minor race, practically all of it wagered by persons who wouldn't know that horse from a hundred others except for the number it wore. And there isn't always safety in numbers. Over $70,000 was wagered on Mioland in the Suburban and Mioland didn't bring back a nickel of it. He finished out of the money.

What else is happening in Sweden just now this observer wouldn't know, but a visitor at Belmont yesterday was Rolf Lamborn of Stockholm, recently arrived, who said that racing was going strong in Sweden and new records for mutual handles were being made week after week. The Swedish visitor said he was over here to pick the best of the photo finish cameras and take it back with him through the war zone for use on the Swedish turf.

There were five horses in the national Stallion Stakes, but two ran as an entry and thus there was no show betting allowed. With the Belmont, that made two races without show betting, and the biggest races on the card, one of them the big race of the meeting. This cut down the mutual handle on the day. However, that isn't going to put the Belmont Park stockholders on the bread line. They're still doing all right.

Another explanation offered for the comparatively modest mutual handle at Belmont yesterday was that the crowd was not entirely an aggregation of brisk bettors. One veteran estimated that some thousands came out just to see Whirlaway run and didn't expect or intend to make any money out of it.

Roughly $22,000,000 went through the mutual windows during the Belmont meeting. This is a hint to the worried officials in Washington, D. C., just in case they are wondering where there is loose money that might be raked in to build battleships and airplanes.

There was a stir through the crowd as the starting gate was pulled across the track near the lower end of the grandstand. It meant that the big race was coming up. Whirlaway was going to rush off and come back with high honors, winner of the triple crown of the turf, the Derby, the Preakness and the Belmont. Or could he fail and fall short? That was what many in the crowd came out to see.

Whirlaway was escorted by his own lead pony, a stylish-stout gray. That cost Warren Wright $10 extra, but, on what Whirlaway won at Churchill Downs and Pimlico, he could well afford it.

The lead pony took Whirlaway right up to the rear of the stall gate and there they had to part. Whirlaway was on his own to try conclusions with Itabo, Yankee Chance and Robert Morris.

Strange to say, Whirlaway wasn't last from the starting gate. Robert Morris had that doubtful honor. He seemed confused and looked as if he didn't know which way to run. Whirlaway went off in third position for a change. Robert Morris finally straightened out and went in pursuit of the hurrying trio up ahead.

But there really was nothing to it but a victory parade for Whirlaway. The Calumet colt took the lead after rounding the lower turn and went away out ahead, coasted most of the way and romped in a winner, the fifth horse in turf history to win the triple crown. In adding Belmont to the Derby and Preakness, Whirlaway won $39,770 and a blanket of flowers. The flowers were distributed among Whirlaway rooters in the crowd, but the money was kept intact.

HORSE AS SMART AS A HORSEPLAYER

BY RED SMITH

MAY 31, 1978 — Making small talk in Shea Stadium, Ralph Kiner of the Mets broadcast team said: "Who's going to win the Belmont?"

"Pay no attention to me," a guy said, "but I still have to give Alydar one more chance."

"If Affirmed beats him again," said Mike Shannon, who swapped his place in the St. Louis outfield for a seat behind a microphone, "it might just about finish Alydar. Wouldn't he get the idea that he can't win?"

"I don't think he knows Affirmed from any other horse," somebody else said. "And when he loses by a neck or a head, do you think he knows he was beaten?"

"I don't know," Kiner said, "but some horses are competitors. Take an athlete like Affirmed. He just won't let anything get past him."

"Did you ever hear of a horse named Sands of Pleasure?" a man asked. Nobody had.

Joe H. Palmer wrote about Sands of Pleasure ever so long ago in a discussion of the comparative intelligence of animals. The piece is in a book called *This Was Racing*, which may still be available from the Henry Clay Press of Lexington, Ky.

Joe respected horses but he conceded there were some tricks they couldn't be taught. He said a horse couldn't stack boxes on top of one another to reach a bunch of bananas on the ceiling because he had no hands to lift the boxes and he didn't like bananas, anyway. He said a horse couldn't be taught to sit up on his haunches and beg because it was difficult to support him that way and it was a damned undignified position, which horses realized and politicians didn't.

However, Joe suggested that the story of Sands of Pleasure might have some bearing on the argument that horses just ran because they were bred and trained to run and didn't have any idea of what the racetrack was all about.

Sands of Pleasure was by Fair Play, later the sire of Man o' War. He was a stakes racer in his youth but as he grew older he dropped down into the claiming ranks. One day he was beaten a nose on the post, or, at least, the placing judges said he was. This was in the days before the photo-finish camera, when the judges hung up three numbers and hoped for the best, like umpires.

When Sands of Pleasure cantered back to the finish line his jockey, seeing his number posted in second place, steered him to the outside rail to dismount. Sands of Pleasure raised holy hell, trying to throw the rider, rearing and kicking out at everybody and everything near him. This disturbed his trainer, for the Fair Plays were a headstrong lot and some grew moody as the years overtook them. When that happened, their racing days were just about over.

After a good deal of thought, the trainer put Sands of Pleasure in a race where the horse was clearly over his head. Beaten off by several lengths, Sands of Pleasure pulled up quietly and never even glanced toward the winner's circle when he was unsaddled out on the track.

"I think," the trainer said to himself, "this tells me something."

He waited until he found a race that he thought would fit his horse. Then he told the rider: "If you get off clean and nothing happens, I think you'll have a pretty fair shot. But if you do win, don't take him to the winner's circle. Ride him over to the outside rail and unsaddle there."

Sands of Pleasure broke on top, held his field and won eased up by a length or better. Pursuant to instructions, the jockey brought him back and pulled up facing the rail. Afterward he swore that the horse turned and looked him in the eye. Then Sands of Pleasure took the bit in his teeth and walked to the winner's circle.

So there it was, Joe Palmer said. In those days it was an article of faith with beaten horseplayers that placing judges were purblind incompetents or of low moral standing, and there was no photo-finish picture to change his view. It was obvious that Sands of Pleasure subscribed to this opinion after that nose finish, which proved him the intellectual equal of a $2 bettor. In the second race he accepted defeat philosophically. In the third he knew bloody well he was the winner and was having no nonsense about it.

"I'm not sure how much Alydar and Affirmed know about that rivalry of theirs," the man said at Shea, "but they are both racehorses."

THIS HORSE HAS A PRAYER

BY GEORGE VECSEY

JUNE 10, 1988 — At first they prayed only for the health of the horse named Risen Star, but lately the residents of an old-age home in New Orleans have been reassured there is nothing sacrilegious in rooting for the horse to finish first.

"The Bible tells us to pray for whatever we need," says Sister Mary

Vincent, the administrator of the Mary Joseph Residence, who has never been to the races, never made a bet, but knows a chance to fix the roof when she sees it.

Tomorrow, the Residence's 122 residents will gather in the auditorium, under a giant black-and-gold star with the word "hallelujah" printed underneath. They don't mind admitting they are rooting for Risen Star, winner of the Preakness, to win the Belmont and capture the $1 million bonus in the Triple Crown series.

The link between the home and the horse has been one of the most overlooked factors in racing this spring. While racing people studied bloodlines and the condition of the track and the recent workouts for guidance, the answer was as obvious as a black-and-gold star.

All the furor over whether mean old Woody really sent out Forty Niner to block out poor old Eugene's Winning Colors has obscured the fact that Louie Roussel 3d's Risen Star was carrying the hopes of The Little Sisters of the Poor.

The connection between the Mary Joseph Residence and Risen Star began when Sister Mary began calling upon wealthy New Orleans residents and asking for contributions.

"Our order has been in New Orleans for 120 years," said Sister Mary, who was transferred there from Latham, N.Y., four years ago. "We built this home 15 years ago and almost immediately the soil subsided and we had to rebuild it. We've been going through tough times in Louisiana because of the oil business. Medicare only pays for half the cost. We have to go out collecting for the rest."

One of the first persons she visited was Roussel, a young trainer from a wealthy family, who said he had attended Jesuit High, Louisiana State University and the University of Loyola Law School, and later donated $1 million to his old high school.

"I asked him for a donation and he said he would think about it," Sister Mary said. "He told me: 'Sister, I have a deal for you. Say a prayer for us and I'll give you a portion of what we win.' I said, 'You've got a deal.'"

The horse was named after the star of Bethlehem and the words of an angel at Jesus' tomb, "He has risen." The trainer has been described as a "born-again" Roman Catholic, but he declined to use that term to describe himself this week. Usually, it refers to somebody who had a sudden spiritual rebirth.

"I've never had a faith crisis," Roussel said. "I've always been a Catholic. One year I went to confession 71 times, which must have been a record, more than once a week. I believe that if you do wrong, it doesn't mean you're not a good Catholic."

Roussel said he was touched at hearing about the elderly, poor residents of the home. He said: "The sad thing about these people is that they have outlived their friends, and sometimes their sons and daughters don't have time for them. Society is geared to young people, but older people are a treasure."

After the meeting, Roussel promised Sister Mary a portion if Risen Star won the Sport of Kings Futurity. After the race, he called and said: "Sister, I've got bad news. We didn't win. But I'll give you a percentage anyway."

For a while, Roussel was happy just to think that the elderly people were rooting for his horse to "get on the board." When Risen Star won the Lafayette, Roussel sent another check. Then the horse was shipped north to the Kentucky Derby, where he finished third, and the Preakness, where he won.

"We all gathered in the auditorium in front of a big television," Sister Mary said. "Southern people know how to have a good time, and our residents are very much alive, well into their 80's."

Before the Preakness, they prayed for the horse to win.

"This is the way I think about it," Sister Mary said the other day. "Our reading for today was from First Kings, chapter 17, verses 1–6. It tells how the Prophet Elijah was fed through a raven." So he went and did according to the word of the Lord; he went and dwelt by the brook Cherith that is east of the Jordan. And the ravens brought him bread and meat in the morning, and bread and meat in the evening; and he drank from the brook.

"Christ asks us to pray for all the creatures of the world," Sister Mary said. "I wouldn't want the horse to be hurt by running, but I can pray for it to win.

"People ask me if I'm supporting gambling and I say, horse racing doesn't have to be only gambling. It is also a sport. As long as it doesn't drive people to neglect their children. And look how Louie is trying to help people through his horse." The residents of the home have never seen Risen Star except on television. They suffered when the New Orleans papers ran huge headlines that the horse was injured and might have to be scratched. But on Monday they rejoiced when he galloped two and a quarter miles with no sign of swelling.

"Risen Star has needed their prayers," Roussel said.

Win or lose tomorrow, Roussel said, he will bring Risen Star to the home when they return to New Orleans. "They've adopted a mascot," he said. "They're part of the team." Sister Mary talked to Roussel on a live television hookup yesterday, but they have not discussed exactly how much Roussel might donate from his Triple Crown winnings. The winning share tomorrow will be $303,720 and the horse could win as much as $1 million extra by outpointing Winning Colors in the Belmont.

"I have no idea how much he will give us," Sister Mary said the other day. "Somebody mentioned tithing, 10 percent, but that never came from me. He could do even better than that."

DERBY DAY CAN BE
A WINTER SPORT

BY STEVEN CRIST

LAS VEGAS, JANUARY 24, 1989 — If there were no such thing as a Kentucky Derby winter book, sportswriters might have to invent one. It is far more convenient and official sounding to refer to Easy Goer as "the winter-book favorite for the 115th Kentucky Derby" than as "the early choice of anyone but a dimwit."

But there really are winter books, and at least three are already open for business here in Las Vegas, a mere 14 ½ weeks before Derby Day.

You can walk into Caesars Palace, the Frontier or the Aladdin Hotel, stroll past the slot machines and blackjack tables into the race book, and bet on one or more horses to win the Derby.

Odds are listed for more than 200 candidates for the race, and the prices are much higher than you are likely to get if you wait until May 6 at Churchill Downs. These hotels are not charitable organizations, so of course there is a catch: If your horse does not run in the Derby, you do not get a refund.

Nor are the odds particularly generous. The majority of the 3-year-olds are listed at between 80-to-1 and 100-to-1, but they have chances only an owner could love.

In fact, much of the winter-book money comes from owners and trainers.

If you had a horse with even a prayer of making the Derby, wouldn't you feel almost obliged to bet a few dollars at 100-to-1? Such winning bets ensure the continuing romance of the winter books. Six years ago, Sunny's Halo paid just 7-to-2 winning the 109th Derby, but his trainer, David Cross, said he got better than 50-to-1 and cleared more than $100,000 in the winter book.

Jack Van Berg said he would have cleared $380,000 if Wheatly Hall had won the 1986 Derby, and he settled for a lot less betting Alysheba at 20-to-1 the next year. D. Wayne Lukas said that his stable help bet about $1,500 at 100-to-1 on Winning Colors last year.

Betting the winter-book favorite would have left a horseplayer with nothing but losing tickets the last nine years, since none have won since Spectacular Bid in 1979. Still, the favorite always seems an appealing play and does so again this year.

If Easy Goer wins his three preps for the Derby, he will be a heavy favorite, even-money or less on Derby Day. But last month, you could have gotten 6-to-1 on him. So many people did that he is now down to between 5-to-2 and 7-to-2, depending on where you bet.

The winter books provide a sort of rough early consensus of the order of the Derby favorites, but also are skewed by big and sometimes inexplicable bets. This year, Easy Goer, King Glorious, Houston and Is It True are every book's first four Derby favorites, a fair reflection of how most fans would rank them. But how about the fifth choice at 18-to-1, Barkada? He is such a stranger that Caesars Palace has him listed as Barkado.

Barkada, a son of Devil's Bag and half-brother to Manila, won a Churchill Downs maiden race by 10 lengths but has yet to run in a stakes race and is fighting stomach problems. His trainer, David Whitely, said neither he nor the colt's owner bet and they cannot imagine why anyone would. Someone, however, bet enough to turn a 100-to-1 shot into 18-to-1, but the book operators are not saying who it was.

The linemakers also sometimes seem badly out of date on racing information. The Frontier is still taking bets at 6-to-1 on Fast Play, who has been declared a highly unlikely Derby starter. Caesars last month was soliciting bets on a colt named Chromite, who broke down in August. Caesars has stopped taking bets on Fast Play and Chromite, but the Frontier still has Chromite, who was officially retired to stud last month, listed at 50-to-1 for the Derby. The shortcomings of the winter books reflect those of betting on horses at Las Vegas casinos in general. Track owners do not care who wins a race, since they extract the same fixed percentage from the betting pools regardless of the outcome. A casino, however, can lose money if too many people bet on a winner because it pays off at the track odds regardless of what is actually bet in the casino.

Several thousand horseplayers spend their days in Las Vegas horse books, and it is in some respects an appealing way to play the horses. Bettors have their choice of races from at least five major tracks a day and can watch live telecasts on huge television screens. These books are clean and comfortable, offering free drinks and *Racing Forms* and large work desks.

But a winner can never score the way he can at the track. At Caesars, full track odds are paid only on the first $100 of a win bet, with a 20-to-1 limit thereafter. At the Union Plaza, only the first $5 of an exacta is paid at the track price. Anywhere you go, the maximum return on a trifecta is $1,500, even if it pays $15,000 at the track.

This is the crucial difference between parimutuel and casino betting. A casino is a bettor's adversary, while a racetrack is a disinterested stakeholder. While it is far more appealing to take money from the pocket of a faceless casino than from that of a fellow horseplayer, it clearly is not as easy: It is the casinos that are building new swimming pools and penthouses every year, not the horseplayers.

The talk of Las Vegas the morning after the Super Bowl was not of the game but of Bob Stupak, who walked into Little Caesars casino Sunday morning and bet $1,050,000 on the Bengals plus 7 points. The Bengals lost but covered and Stupak won a cool million. Stupak owns a casino called Vegas World. Perhaps he will install a race book.

HORSE RACING'S BIGGEST BETTORS ARE REAPING RICHEST REWARDS

BY JOE DRAPE

APRIL 26, 2004 — In horseplaying parlance, Maury Wolff is a whale, one of the thousand or so professional bettors who collectively wager as much as $1.5 billion a year on thoroughbred races in the United States. He will not attend the Kentucky Derby at Churchill

Downs on Saturday. In fact, he and the other whales rarely set foot in a racetrack.

He will watch the Derby from his home in Alexandria, Va., where a pile of *Daily Racing Forms*, a stack of videotapes of past races and a computer will give him all the insight he needs into the horses competing. When he decides which horse he believes will win the race, Mr. Wolff will call in his selection.

Even before the starting gates open at Churchill Downs, Mr. Wolff will have an advantage over many other horseplayers. He bets through what are called rebate shops, which are off-shore, on Indian reservations or in states with fewer regulations. Rebate shops offer from 4 percent to 10 percent back on every dollar wagered—win or lose.

When someone bets more than $100 million a year, as one man did through a North Dakota rebate shop in 2002, the savings add up quickly and often mean the difference between winning and losing money. The practice is legal. Mr. Wolff likens his rebates to the cash or airline miles that credit-card users often receive.

"Racing is like a lot of businesses in which the best customers get the best deals," said Mr. Wolff, a former racetrack executive and an economist. "Rebates are targeted tax cuts to the consumer who is most responsive to your product. When you turn people into winners from losers, you're going to get astronomical growth."

National figures compiled by the Jockey Club, considered the official statistician of the industry, show that rebate operations may have had an impact. In 1997, before they became prevalent, $12.5 billion was bet on horse racing held in the United States; in 2003, more than $15 billion was wagered, a 20 percent increase.

But the proliferation of rebate shops has stirred intense debate and raised thorny questions within the horse racing industry.

- Do rebate shops siphon revenue from the racetracks and from the trainers, jockeys and horse owners who put on the show?

- Do well-financed gamblers have an unfair advantage over the $2 bettor or even $500-a-day players?

- Is gambling on a horse race a game, or is it a financial market that a skilled player can manipulate for profit?

Unlike casinos, where bookmakers set odds or determine point spreads, horse racing is based on the parimutuel system, which means bettors are wagering against one another and not against the house. All the betting money, including wagers made at the racetrack and at rebate shops, is commingled, or linked into one pool.

In the Kentucky Derby on Saturday, for example, Churchill Downs will return to bettors at the track about 82 cents of every dollar wagered in the form of winnings. The remaining 18 cents, known as the takeout, will be used to pay for expenses like racing purses, state taxes and track maintenance.

This business model worked fine 25 years ago. But the advent of telephone and computer wagering has drastically changed the flow of money in the industry.

Despite the increase in the amount of money wagered on races held in the United States, the purse money given away at racetracks declined in 2003, for the first time in nine years, by nearly 2 percent, to $1 billion, according to the National Thoroughbred Racing Association. The decline is referred to as "handle up, purses down," and the N.T.R.A. formed a task force last month to examine the problem.

"We have witnessed over the past few years a significant change in betting patterns where the tracks in the U.S. are receiving less net revenue from interstate simulcasting," said Greg Avioli, deputy commissioner for the N.T.R.A. and the task force's chairman. Simulcasting allows racetracks to sell off-site access to their betting pools. "Money is leaking out of the system and not going back to live racing."

Track owners attribute the loss to the rebate shops. The N.T.R.A. says there are currently eight rebate shops, but the number is rising. While rebate shops often pay a higher fee for a track's simulcast signal, they have far less overhead because they need only a small office, a computer system, telephones and a lean staff of operators and technicians.

"What you've done with rebates is you have put people in business with your own product and allowed them to undercut your price and steal your best customers," said Chris Scherf, executive vice president of the Thoroughbred Racing Associations, which represents 45 tracks. "That's not how they teach you to do things at the Wharton School of Business."

Rebate-shop operators, however, say they are attracting new and more money to horse racing and paying a fair share of it to the tracks. Since opening in 1998, Racing & Gaming Services Inc., on St. Kitts, says that its total handle has grown to more than $692 million in wagers in 2003, and that its more than 120 horseplayers increased the amount of their average wagers to more than $21,000 a day last year, from $2,985 in 1998.

In 2003, Racing & Gaming Services says, it paid more than $30 million to racetracks as fees to carry their signals; in six years, it has paid more than $105 million to tracks in the form of fees.

Laura A. D'Angelo, a lawyer in Lexington, Ky., who represents Racing &

Gaming Services, says it has "contributed more to purses than numerous racetrack entities, so it is a mystery why they are repeatedly criticized for 'contributing nothing to racing.'"

Even the most proficient horseplayers are hard-pressed to make a profit at the track because they cannot beat the takeout, which can range from 14 percent to 25 percent, depending on the track and type of wager. Only the rare handicapper will beat the takeout, while the average bettor will collect 80 cents on his dollar bet.

A horseplayer must still figure out the probabilities to maximize his profit, but rebates have transformed skilled horseplayers into high-volume, low-margin investors. One Las Vegas–based horseplayer, for example, says that since he began betting with rebate shops, he has increased the amount he wagers from $3 million to $24 million a year in the hope of making 4 percent on his money, or $960,000 in profit.

"I'm a professional and work long hours to be among the top 1 percent of handicappers," said the man, a 37-year-old Kentucky native who detailed his finances under the condition that he would not be identified. "I don't like the word rebate—I call it a track takeout reduction. When I get an average of 10 percent back, I'm 2 points above break-even and am playing for that extra 3 or 4 points of profit at the end of the year that is usually there after the luck evens out."

The $500-a-day bettor on the racetrack, meanwhile, starts the day down 20 percent, or $100, because of the takeout, and must be precise in his selections if he hopes to reach the break-even point or make money. Industry officials are concerned that this core audience, which makes up roughly 50 percent of its customer base, will eventually become alienated and move off-site as well.

While some racetracks give promotional offers to loyal customers, heavy regulation from state to state prevents them from returning cash to bettors in amounts that match the rebate shops.

"Our view in general is we believe that offering better pricing for your largest-volume customers is consistent with American business practices," said Karl Schmitt, the president of Churchill Downs Simulcast Network, which oversees simulcasting at Churchill's six racetracks. "But we obviously need to find a way to be more competitive and keep the core and the high-end customer happy."

Some within horse racing are also uncomfortable with the idea that sophisticated bettors are treating horse racing like a financial market and profiting handsomely from it.

"It's a game, not a financial market, and if people at the racetrack think they are chum and have been thrown out in the water for five or six players to take down, then the chum is going to move on to another game and the whales will move on to another financial market," said Mr. Scherf of the Thoroughbred Racing Association.

But Mr. Wolff, who is a member of the N.T.R.A. task force, disagrees. For decades, he said, horse racing has marketed itself as a thinking man's game, and skilled players could expect to be successful and make a profit. If the racetracks will not deliver on that expectation, the whales will find an enterprise that will.

"It's a competitive industry targeted at bettors who now want competitive pricing," he said. "The high end is always going to seek the best return. It may be purer to win without a rebate, but when you go to the grocery store, they don't ask you if the money you're buying your milk with is from your winnings or your rebate. Horse racing was built on betting, and if bettors cannot win and they decide to go away, you do not have an industry or a game."

AT THE DERBY, RACING TAKES ON ITS DRUG PROBLEM

BY JOE DRAPE

LOUISVILLE, MAY 1, 2005 — Beneath its twin spires, Churchill Downs has completed a sparkling $121 million makeover in time for the 131st running of the Kentucky Derby, America's most famous horse race. But this year's Derby, which will be Saturday, may be best remembered for the plainclothes investigators roaming the dusty barn areas and for testing the horses for illegal performance-enhancing drugs before and after the Run for the Roses.

After decades of rumors about "juiced" thoroughbreds and ineffective attempts at regulation, the horse racing industry has acknowledged that it has a drug problem.

"It's a very serious problem, and the public perception is that it is a huge problem," said C. Steven Duncker, chairman of the Thoroughbred Owners and Breeders Association's Graded Stakes Committee, which mandated the increased postrace testing for the Derby and the rest of the most important races in the United States.

"I don't know if you can put a dimension on how widespread it is because, like in every other sport, our testing seems to be a step behind the cheaters."

For as long as horses have been racing, some trainers have sought an advantage. Sometimes, it has been as primitive as using a battery-type device to shock a horse during a race; recently it is believed to have become as exotic as using injections of the venom of the cone snail, which is found in the ocean and is prized for its joint-numbing qualities.

The ability of racing authorities to police the industry has been hampered by its patchwork of regulatory agencies. The industry has no national standards, the way professional sports leagues like Major League Baseball or the National Football League do. States set their own policies and Kentucky, home of the thoroughbred breeding industry and the most famous two minutes in sports, is among the most permissive when it comes to drug policy.

"We've been in denial the last 20 years," said John T. Ward Jr., the trainer of the 2001 Derby winner, Monarchos. "Over the years, you've heard a lot of rumors, but there has been no clear-cut evidence. But now we have to think of the future. When you look at the problems in the Olympics and the new-age chemicals out there, it is about time we secure all of our racing—especially our premier events."

Whether or not the horses in past Kentucky Derbys have been competing cleanly is hard to know, many trainers and industry officials say. Only one horse in the history of the Derby has been disqualified for a drug offense: Dancer's Image, who won in 1968.

The increased surveillance and testing at Churchill Downs this year come after positive test results in horses in California—including one trained by Jeff Mullins, who will saddle Buzzards Bay for the Derby—and the federal indictment of a New York trainer on charges of doping one of his horses and telling gamblers associated with the Gambino crime family about it.

In baseball or Olympic sports, the use of performance-enhancing drugs has little direct economic impact on its fans. But in horse racing, the bettors, who wagered $15 billion in the United States last year and $99.4 million on the Derby, have a financial stake in the outcome of a race.

Beginning Thursday, Louisville police officers and Jefferson County sheriff's deputies will take up posts on Churchill Downs' backside along with extra private-security guards hired by the track. And an independent team of investigators from the Thoroughbred Racing Protective Bureau and the Kentucky Horse Racing Authority will also be watching the barns of Derby horses.

"Frustrations are higher than ever among the honest guys," said Jim Gallagher, the executive director of the authority. "Now it's more important than ever we make people know that we are doing everything in our power to protect the integrity of the game."

In 2002, the Racing Medication and Testing Consortium was created in Lexington to come up with a uniform drug policy for the 38 jurisdictions in the United States, and to update testing for a wide range of therapeutic medications, as well as for drugs that are simply performance-enhancing.

So far, 13 of the jurisdictions have agreed to uniform guidelines, and another 13 are expected to sign on by the end of the year. Kentucky is among those that has agreed to the guidelines, although the stricter rules will not be enacted in time for this year's Kentucky Derby.

Among Dr. Scot Waterman's duties as the executive director of the consortium is to sort out "what's real and what's rumor," he said, about the use of performance-enhancing drugs. He has been busy.

With the help of investigators from the Thoroughbred Racing Protective Bureau, the consortium looks into accusations against trainers and veterinarians. Waterman acknowledged that some of those accused have fielded horses in prestigious races, including the Derby.

The consortium also spent more than $300,000 last year and has earmarked $650,000 for this year to come up with tests for chemicals like cone-snail and cobra venom.

"It's a fairly small percentage of people pushing the envelope," Waterman said. "Most vets and most trainers are playing by the rules. But we're shooting to get rid of it all."

For the first time at the Derby, for example, the top finishers will undergo what is being called a super test, which will screen for hundreds of drugs and metabolites.

In another first, each of the Derby starters will have a prerace blood test to detect alkalizing agents, which is evidence of what is known as a milkshake, a concoction of baking soda, sugar and electrolytes that helps a horse ward off fatigue. Twenty horses are expected to start the Derby on Saturday.

It is the method that the New York trainer Gregory Martin is charged with using to fix a race at Aqueduct, according to a federal indictment of 17 people accused of being involved in an illegal gambling ring. [Note: Martin later admitted fixing the race and was sentenced to two years' probation.] It also is what California racing officials suspected Mullins of doing, when a horse he trained tested for an illegal level of sodium bicarbonate in February.

Mullins denied the milkshaking charge and said that the elevated reading could have come from feed, supplements or stomach medications. Still, for 30 days, Mullins's horses were housed in a detention barn and were under 24-hour surveillance. And for another 15 days, Mullins's barn was monitored. In the 60 days before the penalty, Mullins's horses won 28 percent of their races. That dropped to 13 percent while he was under surveillance. He lost additional good will within racing when he was quoted as saying that horseplayers were idiots and addicts, remarks for which he eventually apologized.

Duncker, who is also co-chairman of the New York Racing Association, says uniform regulations, increased testing and greater surveillance are progressive steps. The New York association will take an extraordinary measure when Belmont Park opens Wednesday. All horses will be isolated in a detention barn six hours before their races, with only the state veterinarian having access to them.

"We need a paradigm shift in what our punishment is; it needs to be tougher," Duncker said. "Right now in many places, a trainer can get suspended for seven days, pay a small fine and have his assistant run his horses while he's out. That's meaningless. What the tracks can do, however, is take away their stalls and not allow their horses to run at their tracks."

Ward, the trainer who has seen one of his horses draped with the blanket of roses, says that trainers, owners and track owners should embrace the new vigilance.

"Finally, we have awakened," he said. "This is just the start of it, and hopefully we're only going to get more sophisticated. These are difficult times in all sports to maintain a level playing field, but I think we can do right for these athletes and do right for all of us."

EDITORIAL: MINT JULEPS AND MILKSHAKES

MAY 7, 2005 — William Faulkner pointed out that "the horse is economically obsolete." But he did so in celebrating the Kentucky Derby as a peerless crucible for thoroughbred horses to "endure and survive until man's own nature changes." Strong odds today are that human nature won't change. So the Derby is on again as a classic American oddity—that special moment each year when throngs across the country gather to watch and to pretend to speak knowledgeably about what in truth can be only a deep puzzlement for most of them: the relative strengths of the latest herd of finely bred horses.

But that's the beauty of the Derby. It's a two-minute competition that demonstrates how ignorance can be mass bliss as another winter yields to spring. The cliché-ridden can happily sip mint juleps, the bourbon highball that is soon to be forgotten for another year, along with the names of the horses. And this year, the knowledgeable will talk of "milkshakes"—backstretch jargon for the illegal concoction of baking soda, sugar and electrolytes that can make a champion of an also-ran.

In a candid departure, racing officials at the major tracks are taking the occasion of Derby day to admit that they have a serious drug problem in the barns and must catch up with the cheaters. The details extend to doping horses with the venom of cobras and cone snails. New countermeasures include platoons of security guards, far more stringent blood tests and even the isolation of horses in protected barns hours before they compete.

All this only proves Faulkner's point about human nature. Cheaters have been around the barns ever since the first bets were placed, but the thoroughbreds remain gloriously innocent. Too bad the same can't be said for their self-doping human counterparts. The contrast is yet another reason to savor the horses as they plunge into the Derby's grueling test of champions.

WISE GUYS HAVE THE HORSE RIGHT HERE

BY JOE DRAPE

LOUISVILLE, MAY 4, 2006 — The critical mass occurs as the Kentucky Derby approaches, as railbirds, deep-pocketed horseplayers and pundits with a contrarian streak reach a consensus on the contender best suited to upset the favorites. The result is the "wise-guy" horse, a designation that seems to belong in *Guys and Dolls* and, in reality, falls somewhere between a high honor and a kiss of death.

Remember Noble Causeway, Tapit, Ten Most Wanted and Saarland? There is little reason to remember, except for the fact that over the last four years each horse pulled into Churchill Downs as a contender of sorts, was transformed into a wise-guy selection and then immediately lost steam (and their backers' money) once the starting gate opened. Last year, Noble Causeway finished an inglorious 14th. In 2004 and 2003, Tapit and Ten Most Wanted, respectively, stumbled past the finish line in ninth place. Saarland clunked home in 10th in 2002.

Those results do not say much for recent wise-guy picks, but the tradition lives on, and people pay attention. And so who is the wise-guy pick for the 132nd running of America's most famous race? It is Sweetnorthern-saint, much to the chagrin of his trainer, Mike Trombetta.

As his big bay gelding was on the receiving end of a sudsy sponge bath in front of Barn 42 earlier this week, Trombetta, who is here with his first Derby starter, was clearly conflicted when told the wise guys had landed on his horse as the one to run away with the roses at a good value.

First he blushed, and then he unloosed a rueful smile.

"Yeah, I heard," he said, with a resigned shrug of his shoulders. "I'd rather be one of the people that they're talking about than the one people are not talking about."

There is much to like about Sweetnorthernsaint. He has won three of four starts this year and looked like a world-beater in his last race—a 9¼-length victory in the Illinois Derby. Last Saturday, Sweetnorthernsaint further burnished his credentials with the fastest six-furlong workout of the morning, a "bullet" in racing parlance.

On Wednesday, at the draw for the Derby, the Churchill Downs odds-maker Mike Battaglia made Sweetnorthernsaint the 10–1 fourth choice in a full field of 20 horses, although many people in racing figure he will go to the gate on Saturday at considerably lower odds.

"He's definitely the wise-guy horse," said Trombetta's fellow trainer and barnmate, Kiaran McLaughlin. "He's got the right number on the sheets."

McLaughlin, who has two horses in the Derby, pays close attention to the Ragozin Sheets, technology's contribution to the wise-guy phenomena. They are handicapping tools that cost $35 for a single track's full card, according to its Web site thesheets.com, and are often favored by committed horseplayers. To the uninitiated, they look like a number puzzle.

In theory, they quantify how a horse performed in a given race. As the Web site notes, the sheets take into account any number of factors, such as "speed, weight, allowance for unusual track condition, racing wide or saving ground, headwinds or tailwinds, peculiarities of track construction such as downhill areas." The casual bettor probably does not think about which way the breeze is blowing, but wise guys apparently do.

The sheets "are helpful and fairly accurate on a daily basis," said McLaughlin, whose Closing Argument finished second in the Derby last year. But the Derby, he cautions, is "an altogether different race" because of the 20-horse field and the mile-and-a-quarter distance, and he wonders how useful the sheets are in figuring it out.

In fact, there is a racetrack contingent that believes the whole wise-guy notion no longer applies.

"It's a phrase that might have held some meaning 15–20 years ago before everyone had access to speed figures, trip notes and video replays, when professional and serious players perhaps knew about a big figure or a brutal trip that the rest of the world, including most sportswriters and turf writers, didn't appreciate," said Steven Crist, chairman and publisher of *The Daily Racing Form.*

"Now there are no big secrets like that out there for what has become the most overexposed, overanalyzed handicapping event of the year," Crist added. "I think it's just not a valid premise anymore, especially since now everyone tries to be a smart-aleck and routinely opposes the logical favorites. I think the wise-guy horse has gone the way of the dodo."

Still, the lingo remains part of racetrack lore, and perhaps part of its romance. The tote board is likely to show a lot of "smart money" on Brother Derek, the morning-line favorite, and wise-guy dough on Sweetnorthernsaint.

Horse racing is a game of opinions. Cliff Guilliams charts the races for Churchill Downs and cuts a dashing figure as its resident sage. In his honeysuckled baritone, Guilliams offers an opinion that even casual race fans might want to heed when trying to pick a Derby winner.

"I have a philosophy where I refuse to be pushed into backing a horse by anyone who drives a 10-year-old car and doesn't own a tie," he said, evoking the image of the prototypical wise guy. "Nobody really knows anything when it comes to the Derby, so make your own mind up."

ESSAY: GUY WALKS INTO A BAR

BY BILL BARICH

I had every intention of watching the '86 Kentucky Derby, of course, but the glories of eastern Idaho in springtime were competing for my attention. For nearly a week, I'd been fishing some of the prettiest trout streams on earth, starting with Henry's Fork of the Snake River and moving on to the upper Teton, a lovely spring creek that flows through willow-lined meadows in the shadow of the Teton Range. I hadn't shaved since my arrival, nor had I made any bold moves toward a shower, and the only food I'd eaten was the greasy fare in roadside cafes. In other words, I felt splendid.

On Saturday I planned to take a leisurely drive to Jackson, Wyoming, check into a decent hotel, scrub off the accumulated grit, and plant myself in front of the biggest TV I could find, so I could revel as Snow Chief rallied to what I assumed, with my usual nonchalance, would be an easy victory. I'd first seen the colt at Bay Meadows when he won the El Camino Real Derby stylishly, and after he added the Florida and Santa Anita Derbies to his already impressive portfolio, I cast my lot with those who thought he couldn't lose at Churchill Downs despite being a lowly Cal-bred. Betting isn't exactly encouraged in Idaho, so I called a New York friend with an OTB account and put a hundred on the nose.

That Saturday dawned with a splash of warm sunshine ideal for bringing on a hatch of insects. Soon the bugs were thick in the air, and hungry trout began to feed with an astounding lack of caution. I couldn't cast without hooking one. There's a witchery to rivers, and the Teton had me in its spell. Try as I might, I couldn't pull myself away. Only around noon, when the heat and light finally put down the fish, did I realize I'd never get to Jackson in time for the Derby. Worse, the towns in farm country were few and far between, and often consisted of just a general store and a John Deere outlet. I figured my chance of locating a TV of any kind had to be a longshot.

Yet longshots do come in, and so it was for me. No more than ten miles down the highway I passed a lively looking tavern, its parking lot full of pick-ups. Though I hadn't always been welcomed with open arms at such places, not to say threatened with bodily harm, I was a desperate man, so I walked through the door and into a small, smoky room, where a gang of burly farmers were gathered around an ancient Sony, fiddling with a rabbit-ears antenna to produce the best possible picture on the twelve-inch screen. That they were tuned into the Derby rather than a clash of monster trucks seemed a very miracle. Better yet, they were a friendly crew and invited me to join their pool.

The dude in charge was a wiry little guy in oil-stained coveralls. "Want to pick a horse?" he asked, holding out a baseball cap where scraps of paper lay in wait like portents. "It's a five-dollar buy-in."

I closed my eyes to banish any suggestion I might be a cheater, remembering how Fast Eddie Felson got his fingers broken in "The Hustler," and dipped into the hat. Ferdinand! What an insult! I nearly crumpled up the scrap and tossed it on the floor. I'd scratched Ferdinand from my shortlist of potential winners long ago. His name alone was practically enough to rule him out, a reminder of the fairy tale bull who wanted to smell the flowers instead of tangling with a matador. Moreover, Ferdinand had only two wins from nine runs, plus Snow Chief had already blown him away at Santa Anita. His trainer Charlie Whittingham, though in his seventies, had never won the Derby, and his jockey was the aging Bill Shoemaker, a geriatric double bill. Little wonder, then, that the horse's odds hovered around 17–1.

Well, I'd only be out five bucks. My smart money rested with the state of New York. I settled in with a beer and a growing sense of confidence as the race unfolded, with the speed merchant Groovy grabbing the early lead. Briefly, I wished I'd thrown some cash at Groovy, too, because his name, unlike Ferdinand's, held positive associations. For a split-second, I flashed (as the hippies used to say) on my younger self in the Haight-Ashbury, stoned and carefree, with no mortgage or responsibilites, able to go fishing whenever I pleased—an enviable situation I'd forfeited in overburdened middle-age, and I might have sighed "Ah, youth!" with Joseph Conrad if the ghost of idle days past hadn't loosened its grip on me.

I turned my attention to the race again. Halfway through, Alex Solis had Snow Chief in a perfect position, fourth on the outside and traveling smoothly, while Groovy faded like reefer smoke. At the five-sixteenth pole, Solis kicked it up a notch, and his colt responded by sweeping to the front. The move was so powerful I grew even more confident, and fell victim to a bad habit of counting my profit in advance and parlaying it into absurd fantasies (a bamboo fly-rod, a case of Pouilly-Montrachet), but Snow Chief suddenly stalled. The knock against him—or against Mel Stute, his trainer—was that he'd run too often before the Derby, and though that couldn't be proven without a doubt, the energy was obviously leaking from him as from a dying battery.

Not once had the race caller mentioned Ferdinand, but now, unaccountably, with just over a furlong to go, the big, gawky colt steamed into the picture, driven along the rail by Shoemaker in a brilliant ride to win by 2½ lengths. When I studied the replay, I was even more appreciative of the jockey's artistry, since Ferdinand had some trouble at the start, shuffled back and knocked around. As I collected the pot, enough to cover my loss on Snow Chief, I ignored the fact that dumb luck, not my "skill" as a handicapper, had contributed to the score. Our successes in life may come from out of the blue, unwilled and undeserved, but we seldom fail to take credit for them, anyway. How clever I appeared to myself in that Idaho tavern!

Naturally, I became a Ferdinand aficionado. The colt could do no wrong, I believed, so I backed him in the Preakness, where a reinvigorated Snow Chief beat him, and in the Belmont, where he finished third. I did manage to recoup the following year when he licked Alysheba in the Breeders' Cup Classic and earned an Eclipse Award as Horse of the Year.

That would be poor Ferdinand's last high note, though. His record as a stallion at Claiborne Farm was so unremarkable his owners sold him to the Japanese in 1994, who exiled him to Arrow Stud on Hokkaido Island. He performed no better there and later vanished—this time to a slaughter-house, apparently, a tragic end for a Derby champion.

Bill Barich is the author of A Fine Place to Daydream *and* Laughing in the Hills.

PART VI

"Goodbye, soul brother."
—ANGEL CORDERO, AS SEATTLE SLEW PASSED HIM
IN THE 1977 KENTUCKY DERBY

Belmont Park: Seattle Slew and jockey Jean Cruguet in early morning workout prior to winning the Belmont Stakes and Triple Crown in 1977. BARTON SILVERMAN/ *THE NEW YORK TIMES*

It always is dangerous to argue great horses and golden eras unless you are among horsemen in a kitchen beyond the backstretch early in the morning or on a bar stool alongside horseplayers late at night. It is hard to beat the 1970's, however, as the Golden Era for Great Triple Crown champions: Secretariat, Seattle Slew and Affirmed were each two-year-old champions carrying great expectations. In 1977, just four years after Secretariat, Seattle Slew became the only winner of the Kentucky Derby, Preakness and Belmont Stakes to sweep the Triple Crown as an undefeated colt. In 1978, Affirmed and Alydar gave all of sports one of the great rivalries of all time.

Of the three, however, Seattle Slew's achievements are often over-looked or assessed less than enthusiastically. He had the misfortune of fol-lowing Secretariat, one of the most beloved horses of all time, and he did not have a particularly auspicious start. Mickey Taylor, a lumberman in Washington State, as a present for his wife, Karen, purchased Slew at auc-tion for the bargain basement price of $17,500. Since Taylor's friend Jim Hill, a veterinarian, picked out the colt, the Taylors made him and his wife, Sally, partners.

None of this group had roots in old line breeding. They were young, out-spoken and clearly enjoyed the success of their colt. Seattle Slew's trainer, Billy Turner, and his jockey in the Triple Crown, Jean Cruguet, were also larger than life characters who alternately entertained and aggravated the media.

The "Slew Crew," as they became known, rubbed the racing establishment the wrong way. But the dollar-and-a-dream-crowd loved them.

In the end, Seattle Slew's success brought new owners into the game and helped fuel the auction market. Slew also became a dominating stallion, siring 102 stakes winners—including the 1984 Kentucky Derby winner, Swale, and the 1992 Horse of the Year, A. P. Indy. His offspring won more than $75 million in purses, and at the apex of his breeding popularity, Seattle Slew commanded $750,000 per coupling.

For Cruguet, Slew's greatness was on full display in the Kentucky Derby. The colt smacked into the starting gate and slammed into a horse next to him, but quickly recovered and ended up winning by nearly two lengths.

"All you would have to do is keep quiet and be smooth," said Cruguet. "The only time I ever moved on him was when he came out of the gate. I wouldn't even have to make a move after that. He would just take off.

"He wanted people to know how good he was."

BARN 42, WHERE THE ACTION IS

BY RED SMITH

LOUISVILLE, MAY 3, 1977—There may be days this summer when management of the New York Mets will wish the club could draw a crowd like the one around Barn 42 this gray and spattery morning. Before the late Col. Matt Winn had sipped his first bourbon julep, Barn 42 was the place where Kentucky Derby horses lived through the first week in May. It still is, only this week it's where the Derby horse lives—Seattle Slew. Others share the barn, like the Blue Grass Stakes winner, For the Moment, and Sanhedrin, who chased Slew home in the Wood Memorial, but it was the unbeaten favorite for Saturday's big heat that packed them in. Counting visiting press, sightseers and his own entourage, this horse plays to more people than the Atlanta Braves. Drawn up opposite his stall was the camper that houses the family of Mickey Taylor, who, with his wife, Karen, owns the colt. The space between the camper and barn was roped off, and inside the ropes Mickey's sister, Star Lee, petted her Doberman pinscher, Lance. In addition to security guards at each entrance, Mickey's father, Chester, was on duty as self-elected chief of Seattle Slew's household troops. Hour after hour, Mickey and Karen stood chatting with visitors while another cluster held Billy Turner, the trainer, as though in aspic. Dr. Jim Hill, the veterinarian who is Slew's attending physician, ambled from one group to the other and back again. Traffic slowed, questions never ended, patience never wore thin.

This was only the beginning. On Saturday, when relatives and guests of

the Taylors, Hills and Turners are here along with key employees of the
Taylors' lumber business in the state of Washington, Seattle Slew will have
a private rooting section numbering 89. "The people here have been good
to us," Mickey said. "They came up with good boxes. Of course, having
the favorite helps. If I had a 10-to-1 shot, I'd ask for four seats."

Just a few months ago, the sort of attention he gets now would have
had Slew kicking the barn down. The colt has matured, though, and
learned to relax. He took no notice of the commotion around him today.
Mike Kennedy, his exercise rider, had taken him out for his constitutional
gallop of a mile and a quarter and now he was cooling out under the shed,
plodding serenely with a blanket slung rakishly over his loins.

Except for George Steinbrenner's Hollywood Derby winner, Steve's
Friend, Slew is the oldest of the Derby eligibles. He was foaled on Feb.
24—about six weeks after Steve's Friend—and he was fairly well advanced
physically when he won the Champagne Stakes last October. Since then he
has grown more than two inches but added only 25 pounds. Now he
weighs 1,145 and measures 16 hands 2 inches at the withers.

Mickey Taylor was saying how delighted he was with the way the colt
won the Wood, rating kindly when Fratello Ed ran with him down the
backstretch, expending only enough effort to make the victory sure. "It's
unbelievable how much he has relaxed since the Flamingo Stakes," he
said. Laz Barrera came by, and the Taylors excused themselves to go to
greet him. The trainer of last year's winner, Bold Forbes, is here with a
speedball named Affiliate and he says he didn't come merely to round out
the field.

As for Steve's Friend, there was only one question of major importance
today. John Fulton, the young trainer, was asked whether the Yankees'
owner enforced a dress code for his racing stable. "Yes," the trainer said, "I
got a haircut yesterday."

On the far side of Barn 42, Lou Rondinello was in high spirits. He
trains Sanhedrin for John Galbreath's Darby Dan Farm, and after seeing
his colt close ground on Seattle Slew in the Wood, he rated the winner's
performance as "impressive but not awesome." Of Slew's record, he said,
the favorite was "in a class by himself," but Slew and all the others have yet
to prove that they can stay a mile and a quarter.

"That's why we're all here," he said, "to take a shot at him. I can talk
this way because I don't have Seattle Slew and can relax. My horse is
strictly an 'if.'"

"When did you decide to try the Derby?" he was asked.

"About 10 seconds after the Wood. I telephoned Mr. Galbreath and
asked, 'Do you think—?' and he said, 'Of course we're going.'"

Somebody recalled that when Jean Cruguet, now Seattle Slew's jockey, rode a colt named Media for John Campo in the Wood two years ago, Campo was noisily dissatisfied with Cruguet's work. Saying, "If the owner didn't insist, I wouldn't let him ride my pony." Campo put the pair in the Derby, where they finished fifth to Foolish Pleasure.

Rondinello laughed. He said somebody had asked Campo how he thought Cruguet would do with Seattle Slew. "Two minutes is a long time for the Frenchman not to make a mistake," John said.

SEATTLE SLEW CAPTURES KENTUCKY DERBY BY 1¾ LENGTHS

BY STEVE CADY

LOUISVILLE, MAY 7, 1977—America loves a story with a happy ending, and it got one today at Churchill Downs in the 103d running of the Kentucky Derby.

Undefeated Seattle Slew won the blanket of roses, just as his trainer, his jockey and most racetrack realists expected he would. But Karen Taylor's dark brown Kentucky-bred colt, the people's choice, had to work for his victory. And work hard, unquestionably harder than in any of his previous six victories.

But Slew had the answer to the eight-column headline on the front page of today's *Louisville Courier-Journal*: "Can He or Can't He? Slew Will Say Today." With sentimentalists in the crowd of 124,038 clutching their mint juleps in trepidation, the 1-to-2 favorite overcame an atrocious start, blasted his way into contrition to duel for the lead and then held off late challengers in the severest test of his career.

With much-criticized Jean Cruguet riding him brilliantly, Seattle Slew had a 1¾-length margin over Run Dusty Run at the finish of the mile-and-a-quarter race for 3-year-olds. Late-closing Sanhedrin finished third, only a neck farther back. Despite the relatively slow time of 2:02 ⅕, it appeared that Seattle Slew had something left to give had it been needed.

In becoming the first unbeaten horse to win the Derby since Majestic Prince in 1969, the favorite returned $3 for $2 to his backers in the fourth largest Derby crowd. He also earned $214,700 from a purse of $267,200, the second largest ever, but that's not what really mattered most to the people in his camp today.

What mattered to them, to Karen Taylor and her husband, Mickey, and to Cruguet and Billy Turner, the colt's trainer, all of them in their 30's, was that the critics had been answered. All week long, nonbelievers had been saying that Slew was overrated and undertrained, that he didn't have the foundation to go the Derby distance. And Cruguet's detractors had called attention to a nationally published comment by a prominent New York trainer: "Two minutes is a long time for the Frenchman to go without making a mistake."

But 37-year-old Cruguet went more than two minutes today, and all Turner could say about his performance was: "I thought he rode a very, very cool race, and that's what wins Derbies."

Turner, 37 himself, also had good things to say about the lightly raced colt he has brought along so patiently. Said Turner, proudly but without recrimination against the skeptics: "He was challenged, and he met the challenge. That's the most thrilling thing to me. And he overcame adversity."

For the Taylors, 32-year-old Karen and her soon-to-be 32 husband, the success in America's most glamorous horse race represented the fulfillment of a dream that began with the purchase of a yearling son of Bold Reasoning out of My Charmer at the Fasig-Tipton Kentucky Sales in July of 1975. The colt, not a strikingly handsome individual, went to them on a bargain-basement bid of $17,500. And he turned out to be Seattle Slew.

Other owners have turned arrogant over horses that couldn't carry Slew's feed bucket. But not the Taylors, Turner or Cruguet. Too poor to get married until seven years after they started going together, Mickey and Karen like the lifestyle of White Swan, Wash., a logging community 140 miles east of Seattle where Mickey struck it rich with pulp wood in 1972.

"I'm a logger," says Taylor, "and Karen's an ex-stewardess for an airline. What else is there to say?"

Lots and lots, the media has decided, and today's victory by the Taylor colt will only increase the volume of talk.

From the moment the linked starting gates opened, one with 14 colts in it, the other with only Nostalgia, Seattle Slew battled adversity. The black and yellow silks worn by Cruguet couldn't be seen in the initial wave of half-ton horses as they began the long run to the first turn.

With Slew in early trouble, Angel Cordero immediately sent For the Moment, the 7-7 third choice, to the front. Would this be a front-running repeat of last year's Derby, in which Cordero kept Bold Forbes ahead of favored Honest Pleasure, a full brother to For the Moment, every step of the way?

It wasn't. Seattle Slew, under attack constantly, was guided quickly through traffic along the rail in the run to the first turn. By the time the leader swept past the gold-topped finish line the first time around, Slew was right alongside, just half a length back. Those two stayed well ahead of third-place Bob's Dusty, a stablemate of Run Dusty Run sent out as a pace-setting rabbit. But Bob's Dusty never made the lead, and was rabbit stew after three-quarters of a mile.

Approaching the far turn, Cruguet hit Seattle Slew with the whip for the first time since the colt won last fall's Champagne Stakes at Belmont Park by nearly 10 lengths. The black and yellow silks now surged forward, drawing away from For the Moment as that Blue Grass Stakes winner began a late fade to eighth place.

With about an eighth of a mile to go, Run Dusty Run had ranged up into second place and Sanhedrin and Get the Axe were coming on with strong late bids. But Seattle Slew, three lengths in front at that point, didn't come back to them quickly enough to make it a nerve-racking finish. Through the final sixteenth of a mile, just flicking the whip alongside his mount's neck, it appeared almost as if Cruguet was trying to save a little for the Preakness, the next step on thoroughbred racing's annual Triple Crown.

THE FAVORITE'S DAY

BY RED SMITH

LOUISVILLE, MAY 7, 1977 — Like most of the other tourists at the 103d Kentucky Derby, Seattle Slew had precious little sleep last night, and perhaps that is why he was dozing in the gate when J. T. Wagoner pressed the starter's button today. Jean Cruguet woke his mount up hastily and the unbeaten colt ran the race of his young life to whip 14 of the best 3-year-olds in America. He had raced six times before without ever finding a horse that could test him but this time they asked him the question. He had the answer, putting the pace-making For the Moment away as he turned into the stretch and holding off Run Dusty Run in the last punishing quarter. He did it on three hours' sleep, for it was 1 A.M. and the Churchill Downs stable area was silent before he lay down on his bed of straw last night. Within minutes he was snoring.

"He snored like a pig," said Chester Taylor, self-appointed head of security for the horse his son and daughter-in-law own. Three hours later the colt was awake and ready for breakfast. Chester, who had stood watch over him until then, retired to the motor home his family occupies a few steps away, and John Polston, the groom, gave the horse two quarts of oats laced with powdered vitamins. He cut up three or four carrots for dessert. Seattle Slew eats a lot of rich hay but John said he wouldn't get that today unless he got fidgety.

Billy Turner, the trainer, arrived about 5 o'clock. A friend gave him a packet of antacid tablets, the prescribed Derby Day breakfast for trainers of favorites. "Thanks," Billy said. "I had Rolaids, but when I looked this morning there was only one tablet and some dust." Billy said he had slept well, though briefly. He said that when he and his wife, Paula, got back to the Executive Inn, he saw himself being interviewed on television. "I asked her to switch to the basketball game so I could go to sleep," he said, revealing a taste in entertainment that does him credit. "Who won the game?" he was asked. "I don't know. I slept till 4:30, when I always get up."

Dr. Jim Hill, the veterinarian who is Seattle Slew's attending physician, made a house call, but Mickey and Karen Taylor, the owners, stayed away until midafternoon, preferring to do their stall-walking in the privacy of their motel. It was just beginning to grow light when Polston led Slew out to be ponied around the track instead of taking his usual gallop. When the colt got back, Polston washed him down and Donald the hot-walker—nobody seemed to know his last name—led him around and around the barn to cool out. Returned to his stall, Slew assumed his customary position facing the rear. He may have napped.

Lance, the Doberman pinscher owned by Mickey Taylor's sister, Star Lee, was tethered between camper and barn in a roped-off space where the signs warned: "Beware of the dog." Chester Taylor said the dog tolerated nobody but him, his wife and Star Lee. "He don't like to be looked at or spoken to," he said. Last year, he said, Lance was on sentry duty one night at Taylor & Taylor, the family lumber company in White Swan, Wash., when somebody climbed the cyclone fence that protects the logging equipment. "Next morning," he said, "we found the seat of a pair of pants."

Antisocial among people, Lance is Seattle Slew's great friend, Chester said. "Sometimes we tie him to the stall and they touch noses."

With Chester, Polston, Donald and a Pinkerton named Bob Doar all keeping an eye on the horse, Turner left the barn to deliver admission badges to some friends. Hours crept by quietly. Now and then visitors wearing press badges stopped by. A few small TV crews ambled about. Seattle Slew turned and thrust his head out the stall door. Polston spoke to him softly, snapped off the single electric light bulb in the stall and adjusted the tuning of a radio playing popular music.

"When he faces the door," Chester said of Slew, "he'll start playing. He's a good feeler. He has lots of life but he's growing into a man, getting over his coltsie ways."

Chester watched until the horse withdrew his head. "He's gonna explode," he said. "When he gets in the race, he's gonna fly."

A little after 11 o'clock Star Lee stepped out of the camper wearing a yellow jumper over a black blouse, the stable colors. She was joined by Karen Taylor's brother, Delman Pearson, in a three-piece suit, and they were off to the races. Lieut. Comdr. Mac Johnston of Bethpage, L.I., a Navy pilot who is a friend of Jim and Sally Hill, had joined the group at the barn. Also joining the group were Ron Bracco, a commercial artist who sometimes helps with the chores, and David Pierce, the blacksmith who shoes Seattle Slew.

A faint sprinkle of rain had started about 10:30 and it kept up intermittently. Rain didn't daunt a small friend of Seattle Slew named Brandon Hill. Brandon is the daughter of Jim and Sally Hill and she wanted to visit her friend, so Susan Small brought her through a tiny shower. Susan is from Uniondale, Pa., where Billy Turner grew up riding steeplechasers for her father. She waited while Brandon walked down the shedrow to Slew's and stood for a while gazing in.

Two young men arrived from the stable kitchen with lunches for Polston and Donald on paper plates—fried chicken, baked beans, potato salad, scallions and carrots. The groom and the hot-walker sat in the tack room eating and watching television. Slew had his radio, still playing dance music.

On the last day of a frantic week, peace reigned. Gone were the hordes of visitors, the guys with ballpoints and note paper, with tape recorders and cameras, who had swarmed through the stable area each morning. Even the animal cries of horseplayers rooting for losers in the pre-Derby races were so muted as to be barely audible. Not one thrice-asked question harassed Turner when the trainer returned at 2:30 P.M.

He found his horse as tranquil as the scene. The long, long wait had dwindled to less than two hours. Then a pony girl named Cindy Hostettler would lead Slew to the post for the biggest race of his life, but the horse didn't know that. As Eddie Sweat, Secretariat's groom, said of that smasher, "He don't know nothin' but eatin' and runnin'."

RIGHT ANSWER AGAIN

BY RED SMITH

BALTIMORE, MAY 21, 1977 — Tommy Ennis, best of a splendid lot of sign painters from Charleston, W.Va., scurried up a bright red ladder on top of the doll house that stands in the winner's circle at Pimlico, slapped black and yellow paint on a weather vane fashioned like a mounted race-horse and scurried down in 1 minute 56¾ seconds this afternoon, a Preak-ness record. Skeptics tended to scoff at the clocking. They said no wonder Tommy could get the job done that fast, he was so sure Seattle Slew would win that he didn't cumber himself with any paint except in the colors Jean Cruguet was wearing aboard the unbeaten favorite. While Ennis swung his brush, 77,346 witnesses—the greatest crowd ever funneled into this 107-year-old cavalry post—were rending their haberdashery and bawling approval of the winner's eighth victory in eight races. Once again, the best 3-year-old colts in America had asked him the question, once again Slew had come up with the answer, and now he was two-thirds of the way along toward possession of the American Triple Crown. "I think he will run the mile and a half of the Belmont the same way he's been running these races," said Billy Turner, the trainer, making the best forecast he could about the final contest in the classic trilogy.

The Belmont comes on June 11, striking mutual clerks permitting. The strike in New York has complicated Turner's immediate plans. In ordinary circumstances he would van the horse to the home barn at Belmont Park tomorrow, but he said he didn't want to risk taking him through a picket line and might decide to stay in Baltimore a little longer.

After Seattle Slew had swept under the wire with his nearest pursuer a length and a half away, a great many people said a great many things and the most memorable statement came from Robert Pineda. Robert had been aboard Sir Sir, who was beaten 18 lengths by Slew in the Flamingo Stakes, 11 lengths by Slew in the Kentucky Derby and 13½ lengths by Slew today.

"He could run better in the Belmont," Pineda said of his mount.

They will all have to do much better in the Belmont if they are to whip the big horse. Slew got off better today than in the Derby, where he was left at the post. He broke alertly but had to bear left as Run Dusty Run came over on him from the outside post position. Cruguet aimed him toward the rail but Cormorant, who had the inside post position, got there first and kept Slew outside of him all the way round the clubhouse turn and down the back stretch.

Cormorant, however, wasn't showing the speed Seattle Slew's people were expecting from him.

"I thought we'd be a length and a half off Cormorant on the back side," Turner said.

"When did you know you could take him?" Cruguet was asked.

"Take Cormorant?" he said. "Oh, he was dead all the way."

"It was a fast race," Billy Turner said, "and one of Slew's best performances.

"For one day he got out of the gate in good shape. I can't say this had anything to do with my training. Maybe Eddie Blind and his crew of assistant starters were responsible. They handled the horses well and they broke well."

Slew's people won't say so, but the fact is an assistant starter had hold of the colt when he dawdled in the gate in Kentucky.

Seattle Slew isn't a shy dude like Secretariat and maybe he'll never win such an emotional following as the red horse had, but he is winning converts. Eddie Arcaro has found that out from the flap he caused by saying after the Derby that Slew was only the best of an ordinary lot.

Evidence refuting Eddie has been piling up. In the Derby, Slew beat Run Dusty Run, who had been first or second in 13 of his 14 earlier starts. That record didn't mark Run Dusty Run as mediocre.

Today Slew beat Run Dusty Run again. He also beat J. O. Tobin, who was England's 2-year-old champion last season and can't be brushed off as ordinary. Slew also beat Cormorant, a winner of seven straight before losing the Withers Mile by the scantiest possible nose a week ago. Nosed out in the Withers by Iron Constitution, Cormorant came back to take the lead one jump beyond the finish, and there is nothing ordinary about that.

From the first day he went to the races, Seattle Slew has done every-thing asked of him, and the gut feeling here is that he has reserves that have not yet been called upon.

It says here that he has the ability to become the 10th winner of the Triple Crown. At the same time, it says in the record book that 10 others got this close to the bauble, and no closer.

UNBEATEN SEATTLE SLEW TAKES BELMONT FOR TRIPLE CROWN

BY STEVE CADY

ELMONT, N.Y., JUNE 12, 1977—Once upon a time, an ordinary-looking horse was sold at public auction in Kentucky for the very ordinary price of $17,500.

His owners named him Seattle Slew, dreamed of Triple Crown glory—and crossed their fingers. And yesterday the impossible dream came true when their horse became thoroughbred racing's first undefeated Triple Crown champion. He did it at Belmont Park by winning the 109th run-ning of the $181,800 Belmont Stakes before a near-record crowd of 70,229, and he did it easily as a 2-5 favorite who returned $2.80 for $2.

At the finish of the one and one-half mile "test of the champion," Seat-tle Slew was coasting along four lengths ahead of second-place Run Dusty Run, the honest rival who finished second to him in the Kentucky Derby five weeks ago and third back of him in the Preakness three weeks ago.

And while Slew was coasting home on a muddy track, his French jockey, Jean Cruguet, was standing up in the stirrups 20 yards before the wire. With his right hand holding the whip he never had to use to any serious extent, Cruguet was waving a salute to the second largest crowd in Belmont's history.

Even in Seattle Slew's proudest moments, though, the dark brown

Kentucky-bred colt hadn't convinced all his detractors. Some of them were pointing out that the time of 2:29⅗, even considering the off track, was a full 5⅗ seconds slower than the track-record clocking made by Secretariat in that colt's 31-length Belmont triumph in 1973 that earned him the ninth Triple Crown. Seattle Slew's Belmont was the slowest since Pass Catcher's in 1971.

But Cruguet said before yesterday's race, "If a jockey in Europe wins by more than three or four lengths, he's considered a bad rider. You have to think of the handicap races, where lengths mean extra pounds."

There were questions raised, too, about Seattle Slew's late arrival in the paddock. His regular route had apparently been blocked by cars, and he arrived 10 minutes late, forcing a delay of five minutes in the post time. But he wasn't late at the finish line.

Sanhedrin, the stretch-running challenger who had been expected to give Seattle Slew some trouble at the longer Belmont Stakes distance, never threatened seriously. He wound up third in the field of eight 3-year-old colts, two lengths back of Run Dusty Run and two and one-quarter lengths ahead of Mr. Red Wing. Then came Iron Constitution, Spirit Level, Sir Sir and Make Amends.

Seattle Slew's ninth and most significant triumph vindicated the campaign strategy of his trainer, Billy Turner, and his owners, a syndicate consisting of Mrs. Taylor and her husband, Mickey, of White Swan, Wash., and Jim and Sally Hill of Garden City, L.I. They were patient, waiting until last Sept. 20 before sending their bargain-basement colt into his first race, and the patience paid off as Seattle Slew became not only the 10th Triple Crown winner but the first with an unblemished record.

There was vindication, too, for Cruguet, criticized earlier this year for letting Slew run too fast in the Flamingo Stakes and for previous alleged inadequacies. But Cruguet had the last laugh yesterday, taking both the Belmont and the $85,800 Mother Goose Stakes during a four-winner afternoon.

Cruguet's vindication may have been the sweetest of all, because he got a kiss on the cheek from rotund Johnny Campo, the trainer who was quoted in a national magazine earlier this year as saying, "Two minutes is a long time for the Frenchman to go without making a mistake."

Campo saddled Elmendorf's Road Princess, the 42-to-1 long shot ridden to victory by Cruguet in the Mother Goose Stakes, second part of the New York Racing Association's triple crown series for 3-year-old fillies, at a payoff of $86.40. That was two races before the Belmont, and Campo leaned across the presentation table to show his gratitude to the jockey.

Cruguet also won the first and last races on the card on a big day of seven trips to the post. The purses earned by his winners totaled $178,760, which translates into $17,376 for Cruguet as his 10 percent cut of the loot.

As for the Belmont, Cruguet explained it perfectly when he said, "Relaxation was the whole story. I knew if I could make him relax, I'd have no trouble."

Seattle Slew is a great-grandson of the late Bold Ruler, and descendants of that fabled sire have often had trouble if they weren't on a clear lead. Their headstrong desire to run, and run fast, sometimes has drawn them into suicidal early speed duels. And that kind of duel is not designed to produce Belmont winners at a mile and a half.

But front-running Seattle Slew, though he was in front every step of the way, relaxed better than in any of his previous races. The clue to this Belmont came early, as first Spirit Level and then Run Dusty Run went up almost head to head with the leader. They were both still there after a mile. But the fractional times by then had told most knowledgeable viewers that the race was over. Seattle Slew, under a hard hold, had gone the first quarter in 24 ⅗, the half in 48 ⅖, the six furlongs in 1:14 and the mile in 1:38 ⅘. That is about as slow as racing's newest equine celebrity can be conned into going. Predictably, he ran away from everything in the last half-mile.

"There was no pace in the race," groaned Jacinto Vasquez, rider of Mr. Red Wing. "Those jocks didn't go after him. But I'm glad he won."

Cruguet had said that the "first horse that tries to go by me early gonna die." And John Russell, trainer for the Phipps family, had predicted that none would try.

"Are there any heroes left?" he had asked. "For the Moment tried it in the Derby, and Cormorant tried it in the Preakness. I think these horses today are going to concentrate on getting second money."

For Cruguet, the blanket of white carnations draped over Seattle Slew joined the blanket of roses from the Kentucky Derby and black-eyed Susans from the Preakness. The jockey had been expecting them. When he arrived at the track shortly after 11 A. M. with his wife and daughter, both were wearing white carnations.

And after Cruguet came through along the rail to win the ninth race, an admirer said, "With a jockey like that, why does France need the Concorde?"

By winning, Seattle Slew joined a select Triple Crown honor roll that began with Sir Barton in 1919 and continued with Gallant Fox (1930), Omaha (1935), War Admiral (1937), Whirlaway (1941), Count Fleet (1943), Assault (1946), Citation (1948) and Secretariat. But the son of Bold Reasoning and My Charmer, purchased as a yearling at the Fasig-Tipton auction in July 1974, became the only Triple Crown winner who still hasn't needed an excuse to explain why he lost a race.

When they bought him, the Taylors and the Hills owned no breeding farms or brood mares or even any shares in an outstanding sire. They had been in racing only two years, but they struck pure gold on the night they went to $17,500 to get their dream horse.

First-place money in the Belmont lifted the colt's bankroll to $717,720. But when the "official" sign on the tote board went up and $2.80 appeared for Seattle Slew's payoff, none of the figures of payoffs or earnings could begin to reflect his real value. And if he keeps winning and stays undefeated, even the skeptics may start comparing him to Secretariat.

THE FRENCHMAN'S RARE DAY
IN JUNE

BY RED SMITH

ELMONT, N.Y., JUNE 12, 1977—Three or four strides before he reached the finish line, Jean Cruguet stood up in his stirrups and flung his right fist aloft in triumph. It was a typically Gallic gesture, an emotional flourish such as had not been witnessed in 108 earlier Belmont Stakes, but this was the 109th and Cruguet was astride Seattle Slew, the only undefeated horse that ever won a Triple Crown. Cruguet had a right to his moment of melodrama, but that didn't silence the dramatic critics in the jockeys' quarters.

"You do that again," said Jacinto Vasquez, who had finished fourth aboard Mr. Red Wing, "and you'll fall on your butt."

Not yesterday. Jean Cruguet has been riding races for 18 of his 37 years, but he never knew a day like this. Fall off this colt, which he has ridden every step that Slew ever took in a race? Mess it up now when he and his horse had their ninth straight victory in hand with the Kentucky Derby and Preakness behind them and the Triple Crown only yards away?

This was a day when nothing was beyond him. Not only did he and Slew complete the most sensational winning streak ever compiled by an

American horse at this stage of life, but the little Frenchman also polished off three other races, including the $85,800 Mother Goose Stakes. Jean took that one, the second event in the fillies' triple crown series, aboard Road Princess, who was trained for Elmendorf Farm by Cruguet's severest critic, John Campo. It is a rare day in June when Jean can look good in John's eyes.

Indeed, he looked so good that when he got off Road Princess, the trainer kissed him. However, Cruguet reported later that Campo had not been all sweet surrender. Even as he smooched the rider he growled in his ear: "You're still a bum."

Why had the jockey saluted the crowd as he coasted down toward the wire? It was the second-largest crowd that ever saw the Belmont Stakes, by the way, 70,229 immortal souls who tore their pants shoving $6,498,117 through the mutual wickets.

"Happiness," Cruguet said, "just happiness."

This is the rider whose chances in the Derby were assayed by Campo thus: "Two minutes is a long time for the Frenchman not to make a mistake." He has been on and off Seattle Slew since the colt got to the races last Sept 20. That is almost nine months, and the Frenchman has yet to make his first mistake with him.

"What can I say," Billy Turner said when the trainer was asked about Seattle Slew's Belmont. "He runs the same race every time."

He meant the colt wins every time, and that is all the trainer asks. Actually, every one of his races differs from the last. Where he has shown devastating speed in the past, he took his time with this job, obediently cooperating with the rider trying to conserve him for a mile and a half.

The result was a comparatively slow trip over a bridle path drenched by 36 hours of rain.

"We knew up front," Billy Turner said, "that this wasn't a track for record-breaking, and this isn't a record-breaking horse. He does what he has to do. If something presses him, it's like his first race this year when he destroyed the track records, but it's hard to find a horse to press him."

One of his old rivals and one who had never hooked him before tried pressing him in the Belmont. A newcomer named Spirit Level went after the favorite right after the start, ran with him to the far turn and chucked it, finishing sixth in the eight-horse field. Run Dusty Run ranged up alongside Spirit Level and Seattle Slew turning into the backstretch, but the winner went along on his untroubled way. Run Dusty Run is always close. He can't run with Slew, but he ran second.

As a rule, no horse that comes to the Belmont has ever tried the Belmont distance of a mile and a half and there are always doubts about a steed's ability to stay that far until he does it. Before this race, as a voice in the jock's room was saying, "It's another quarter-mile. He has to go a quarter-mile farther."

"Yes," said Joe Imperato, who had no Belmont mounts, "another quarter-mile to look at his rear end."

TRIPLE CROWN LEGEND IS GONE: SEATTLE SLEW DIES IN SLEEP AT 28

BY JOE DRAPE

MAY 8, 2002 — It was Sept. 16, 1978, and Angel Cordero finally landed the ride of his life: he was aboard Seattle Slew for the Marlboro Cup Handicap. The colt swept the Triple Crown the previous year and had won 11 of 13 races overall with the jockey Jean Cruguet, but now it was Cordero's turn atop a horse he had long admired.

Seattle Slew emerged from the breezeway at Belmont Park and immediately began his prerace dance, high-stepping like a Radio City Rockette, eyeballing the other horses and even glancing up at rival jockeys. Cordero had been on the receiving end of Slew's withering gaze many times and was hardly surprised.

But Cordero was startled when the horse got in the starting gate, stilled his feet and began breathing deeply. Never before had Cordero felt a horse get lost in concentration.

Seattle Slew's chest expanded, his neck got taut and he stared through the gate, just raring to go.

And he did go, leading every step of the mile-and-an-eighth race, and dusting by three lengths a pretty good horse named Affirmed, who happened to be that year's Triple Crown winner.

"If Seattle Slew was human, he'd be Muhammad Ali," Cordero said of the champion horse, who died early yesterday at age 28, 25 years to the day that he won the Kentucky Derby. "Jumping, strutting and cocky, but good—the best horse I've ever been on."

A son of Bold Reasoning, Slew was the last living Triple Crown champion, as well as the only winner of the Kentucky Derby, Preakness and Belmont Stakes to sweep the prestigious series as an undefeated colt. He had won all six of his races before the spring classics.

His death leaves the thoroughbred racing world without a living Triple Crown winner for the first time since Sir Barton first accomplished the feat in 1919.

"He was the most complete thoroughbred the industry has seen," his owner, Mickey Taylor, said of Seattle Slew. "He just kept raising the bar with every record he broke."

He was equally dominating as a stallion, siring 102 stakes winners— including 1984 Kentucky Derby winner, Swale, and the 1992 Horse of the Year, A. P. Indy. His offspring won more than $75 million in purses, and at the apex of his breeding popularity, Seattle Slew commanded $750,000 per coupling.

The horse had been suffering from arthritis the past two years and underwent two delicate spinal fusion operations, the most recent of which was last month. The Taylors moved to Kentucky from the state of Washington two years ago to be closer to Seattle Slew.

Just last week, Billy Turner, who trained Slew through his Triple Crown campaign, celebrated the 25th anniversary of that feat by remembering a "big, gangly colt," blessed with intelligence but sometimes difficult to handle because of his burning desire to run.

The sadness was palpable throughout Kentucky's Bluegrass yesterday, especially at Three Chimneys Farm in Midway, where Seattle Slew spent the bulk of his retirement. "He saw himself as king of the world," said Dan Rosenberg, the president of Three Chimneys. "He held himself royally here."

Unfortunately, Seattle Slew may have been eclipsed in the public's consciousness at the height of his racing prowess. He followed Secretariat, whose 1973 Triple Crown was punctuated by a 31-length victory in the Belmont, and he preceded by one year Affirmed, who had the advantage of memorable, and triumphant, Triple Crown duels with Alydar.

Neither was better than Seattle Slew, in Cordero's estimation. One of racing's greatest jockeys, Cordero rode the horse in his final four starts, three of them victories, the other a loss by a nose to Exceller in the Jockey Club Gold Cup.

But it is Cordero's memory of being vanquished by Seattle Slew in the

1977 Kentucky Derby that most embodies the horse's character and drive. Cordero's mount, For the Moment, led the field when Seattle Slew motored past, but not before taking a look at Cordero and his horse.

"Goodbye, soul brother," Cordero remembers calling out.

Goodbye, indeed.

Belmont Park: Affirmed after nosing out his rival, Alydar, to win the 1978 Belmont Stakes and Triple Crown.

IN 1955, Nashua, a Kentucky-bred, was the nearly even-money favorite over Swaps, an equally accomplished colt from California. When Swaps galloped to a length and a half victory to win the roses, a rivalry was born of geography. Later that year, the two met again in a nationally televised match race in Chicago. Nashua won and later was named Horse of the Year.

Rivalries amp up the tension and increase the drama of the Triple Crown. In 1990, Unbridled and Summer Squall went at it twice, splitting decisions in the Kentucky Derby and the Preakness. In 2001 and 2005, Point Given and Afleet Alex rebounded from disappointing Derby losses to thump the Derby champs, Monarchos and Giacomo in the Preakness and Belmont Stakes. There have been a number of these split decisions, and perhaps the most memorable of them was in 1989, when Sunday Silence outran Easy Goer in the first two legs of the Triple Crown only to lose to him at Belmont. But it was Affirmed and Alydar's duels in the 1978 Triple Crown that electrified a generation of fans who to this day swear allegiance to one horse or the other. Affirmed won each time, by consecutively smaller margins in the Kentucky Derby and Preakness, culminating in a classic Belmont Stakes that was run head to head for the entire mile and a half.

Little did anyone know that not only were we seeing our last Triple Crown champion, but also perhaps an end of an era?

Affirmed was more than gritty. He was a racehorse that had never been babied by his trainer, Laz Barrera. Affirmed won seven of nine races at age 2, four of them graded stakes, including the Hopeful at Saratoga and the Futurity at Belmont, both Grade I's. Over his glorious career, Affirmed started 29 times in his career and won 22 races. "In our time, horses were tougher," said Patrice Wolfson, who bred and owned Affirmed with her husband, Louis. "Laz thought three weeks was a long layoff."

When Affirmed and Alydar were joined in their epic battle, Steve Cauthen, Affirmed's teenage jockey, was on the cover of magazines ranging from sports to newsweeklies. Alydar and his trainer, John Veitch, became one of the most famous runners-up in all of history. Veitch does not feel bad about that at all.

"You can't say Affirmed without saying Alydar," he said. "It was a wonderful thing just to be a part of something so great. You had a noble horse, and everyone around Affirmed acted nobly. I wouldn't trade it for anything in the world. We live in an era where there is very little greatness and nobility. So people don't experience it and they don't recognize it. I was fortunate."

What Veitch remembers almost as fondly was the spirit of sportsmanship: between the Wolfsons and Alydar's owners at Calumet Farm, between Cauthen and Jorge Velasquez, between the Hall of Fame trainer Barrera and himself.

"There was never a word of animosity spoken; they were the epitome of class, of champions," Veitch said of Affirmed's camp.

HE WAS NAMED FOR ALY, DARLING

BY RED SMITH

HIALEAH, FLA.,MARCH 24, 1978—The tack boxes spaced along the shedrow at Barn AA are painted red and blue, the devil's red and deep blue of Calumet Farm's racing silks. These are the colors Whirlaway and Citation carried when they swept the Triple Crown races of 1941 and 1948. They are the colors flown by Pensive and Ponder and Hill Gail and Iron Liege and Tim Tam when those good ones dashed home first in the Kentucky Derby.

The red and blue silks have never disappeared from the winner's circle, but after a disqualification made by Forward Pass, the farm's eighth Derby winner, they were seen there less and less frequently until last year. In 1977, Calumet's Our Mims was the best 3-year-old filly in the country and her young stablemate, Alydar, just missed out as the champion 2-year-old. Beaten out by Affirmed in that election, the colt came back this year to win Hialeah's Flamingo Stakes like breaking sticks, and—with Affirmed spending the winter in California—consolidated his position as the Eastern favorite for the Derby. He will hold that rank until April 1, at least, that being the date of the Florida Derby at Gulfstream, his next assignment.

In the morning, John Veitch walked back to Barn AA from the grandstand after watching a set of his horses at work. John Veitch is the trainer in charge of the Calumet renaissance, a young man rather short on hair above the intellect but long on breeding and background. His father, Sylvester, is a trainer who was installed last August in the Racing Hall of

Fame at Saratoga. His Uncle Leo was a trainer. And ever since he left off squandering his youth in a cradle, John has lived with the horses.

He grew up working on C. V. Whitney's farm. He worked at Greentree Farm and on George D. Widener's farm and put in three years at the track under Elliot Burch when that astute horseman trained for Paul Mellon's Rokeby Farm. Whitney, Greentree, Widener, Rokeby, Calumet—in American racing that reads like Burke's peerage.

John walked past a pickup truck with a bumper sticker reading: "Seattle Slew Is Back and Hialeah's Got Him." Management hoped that boast would draw multitudes to this year's meeting, but illness kept the glamour horse of 1977 from running at Hialeah. Slew is still on the grounds, but racing always looks ahead to the rising stars.

"Alydar," John Veitch said, and a chestnut head emerged from a stall. "He knows his name," the trainer said, offering a cube of sugar. The names of horses often are suggested by the names of one or both parents, as in the case of Believe It, the son of In Reality that Woody Stephens is preparing for the Derby, but Mrs. Gene Markey, the mistress of Calumet, named Alydar for the late Aly Khan, a great favorite of hers whom she addressed as "Aly, darling."

Alydar was vanned to Gulfstream yesterday and pleased his trainer by working three-quarters in 1:10. A one-mile work is planned for Monday. Then if all goes well in the Florida Derby, the colt will go to Keeneland for the Blue Grass Stakes 10 days before the Kentucky Derby.

"I sort of hope Affirmed stays in California," Veitch said, "and I don't think Mr. Barrera is anxious to hook me before the Derby." At last report, Laz Barrera, the trainer, was undecided whether to try the Blue Grass, take his colt to Kentucky via the Wood Memorial in New York, or ship directly from California to Churchill Downs.

The colts hooked up six times as 2-year-olds, finishing one, two five times, with Affirmed the winner of four. "Any excuses for Alydar?" Veitch was asked. He shook his head.

"No," he said. "Well, in Alydar's first start, the Youthful Stakes, he was knocked down leaving the gate and he ran green all the way and was off the board. After that, it was just the way the races were run. In the Champagne, Affirmed was in the deeper going inside and we ran by him in the stretch. In the Laurel Futurity, where it had rained for three or four days, Alydar was inside and couldn't catch Affirmed.

"In the Futurity at Belmont they ran nose and nose for three-eighths and at the wire Affirmed had his head down for the camera. What are you looking for?"

Alydar had finished the sugar and was licking his lips. His eyes begged the trainer for more, but a sudden commotion made Veitch whirl. Hot walkers had been leading half-a-dozen horses around an oval path when a 2-year-old by Sir Ivor was startled by a goat, kicked, and ran off. Veitch raced after the loose horse, crept up and caught him by the shank.

"Clyde?" said John Veitch's mother, who had stopped by for a visit. The man who had been kicked in the ribs was on the ground. "That's Clyde Sparks. He worked for John's father when John was 2 years old."

"He's Alydar's groom," John said, returning to the shedrow. He watched with concern while a blanket was brought to cover Sparks, who lay propped up on an elbow. "You take Alydar today," John said quietly to a passing groom. When an ambulance had come and taken Sparks away, the morning routine was resumed.

"Were you always going to be a trainer?" John was asked.

"Always, I guess."

"Never wanted to be a cop or a fireman or a ballplayer?"

"No," John Veitch said. "Ballplayers don't make any money."

ROYAL CONFRONTATION: ALYDAR VS. AFFIRMED IN KENTUCKY DERBY

BY STEVE CADY

LOUISVILLE, MAY 1, 1978 — There has been talk about other horses, talk about how racing luck or the right jockey or tactical brilliance could decide the outcome of next Saturday's Kentucky Derby.

But as Jimmy Conway, a trainer who knows what it's like to saddle a Derby winner, observed last week: "Let's face it, it's a race between Affirmed and Alydar."

Conway, the man who won the 1963 Derby with Chateaugay, clapped his hands together, quick and hard. "Those two are like that," he said. "They must adjust to possible speed, like Sensitive Prince. But other than that, they must race each other. They'll have to look each other in the eye somewhere along the line, and that could be your Derby."

"I'm glad they haven't met yet this year," said John Veitch, trainer of Alydar. "It makes the Derby all the more exciting."

"Yes," agreed Laz Barrera, trainer of Affirmed, "it's a confrontation. Affirmed needs a horse like Alydar to make him run."

If racehorses are the nonviolent weapons used by the rich to wage vicarious combat, then Harbor View Farm's Affirmed and Calumet Farm's Alydar are the ultimate weapons, about to be detonated at Churchill Downs in the 104th running of America's favorite horse race. Seldom have two 3-year-old thoroughbreds with such awesome credentials faced each other in the opener of racing's annual Triple Crown series.

And seldom has a Derby scenario offered such glamour and intrigue. If a Hollywood scriptwriter tried to sell the story, he would probably be told to stop drinking.

Consider, for example, the main plot: the inherited wealth of Mrs. Gene Markey, 85-year-old owner of Calumet Farm in Lexington, Ky., against the wealth of 65-year-old Louis Wolfson, the controversial proxy-battling retired self-made financier who didn't come into racing until 1959 when he started buying land in Ocala, Fla., for Harbor View Farm. By that time, seven horses carrying the devil's red and blue silks of Calumet Farm had won the Derby, and two of those, Whirlaway in 1941 and Citation in 1948, had gone on to sweep the Triple Crown.

But the Calumet dynasty, founded by Mrs. Markey's first husband, Warren Wright, the baking-powder magnate, collapsed when the sons of Bull Lea, the famous Calumet foundation sire, failed to carry on the quality line.

From 1941 through 1961, with Ben Jones training most of the horses, Calumet led the national money-winning list 13 times. But in 1976, Calumet horses won only $83,000. The renaissance, though, was already under way.

Sweet Tooth, a Calumet mare descended from Bull Lea, had foaled Our Mims, last year's champion 3-year-old filly, and Alydar, who was only a yearling when young John Veitch took over as Calumet trainer in 1976.

Ironically, it was Affirmed's grandsire, Raise A Native, a horse owned, raced and then syndicated by Wolfson, who sired Alydar for the rival Calumet. Raise A Native, bought by Wolfson for $39,000 at Saratoga, won four straight races as a 3-year-old before a leg injury ended his competitive career. He was syndicated for $2.6 million and became a breeding stallion at Spendthrift Farm at Lexington. Wolfson now owns only two shares in the syndicate, the same number as Calumet.

Then there's Mrs. Louis Wolfson, the former Patrice Jacobs, 41, whose

late father Hirsch Jacobs, was one of racing's best-loved and most successful trainers.

On the other side of the main-plot fence, Mrs. Markey will be getting
support from her husband of 26 years, 83-year-old Admiral Gene Markey,
an engaging sportsman whose previous wives included the actresses Hedy
Lamarr, Joan Bennett and Myrna Loy and whose 11 novels include one
called *Women Women Everywhere*.

If that's not a rich enough plot, add 18-year-old Steve Cauthen as a
jockey for Affirmed—the same Kentucky-bred Steve Cauthen who last
year became racing's first Six Million Dollar Boy by riding mounts whose
purse earnings exceeded $6 million. Along the way to acclaim as athlete of
the year, Cauthen broke Jorge Velasquez's New York record for number of
winners. And who will be riding Alydar in the mile-and-a-quarter Derby?
Jorge Velasquez.

Though he was conceived in Kentucky, Affirmed was foaled in Florida.
Thus, as a Florida-based horse, he is something of a resented "alien" in the
bluegrass country. But his jockey, young Cauthen, comes from Walton,
Ky., not Lexington. That poses a conflict for Kentuckians who cherish
Alydar as a hometown boy from Calumet Farm but who are also proud of
homegrown Cauthen.

As 2-year-olds last season, they met six times. Affirmed, a son of Exclusive Native (and grandson of Raise A Native, Alydar's sire), won four of
those encounters. But almost every race was a head-to-head battle decided
in several cases by the photo-finish camera. If it weren't for Alydar, Affirmed would be going into the Derby with a perfect 13-for-13 record. If it
weren't for Affirmed, Alydar would now have a record of 12 firsts in 14
starts.

Each colt has won all four of his starts so far this year, always as an
odds-on favorite returning a profit of less than even money. Alydar followed the Florida route used by so many previous Derby winners, taking
three races there and then winning the Blue Grass Stakes last Thursday at
Keeneland, in Lexington, by 13 ¼ lengths. Affirmed comes to the Derby
off four California victories at Santa Anita and Hollywood Park. He has
earned $700,127, a record for a horse going into the "Run for the Roses."

"I know my horse," says Barrera, 52, who won the 1976 Derby with
Bold Forbes and has been voted an Eclipse Award as America's leading
trainer the last two years. "He's better than last year. People make rumors.
They say he ran slow in the last part of his California races, but that's because he needs a horse like Alydar to make him run. Nobody has made him
run except Alydar."

Says Veitch, Alydar's 32-year-old trainer: "My horse is stronger than last year, and more mature. He knows how to relax, and he's been finishing very strong. He couldn't be better."

So the scene is set for the next chapter in the Derby script. Among the romanticists, sentiment seems to be building for the Markeys.

"It's a sport with her," says Admiral Markey, a cigar in his hand and a glass of brandy on the table beside him. "Nothing commercial. She's always been like that about horse racing."

"That's very kind, dear," says Mrs. Markey. "I hate pushers with a poison-ivy passion."

"Have you ever had a poison-ivy salad with Roquefort, dear?" the Admiral asks his wife. "It's delightful."

They are sitting in red-leather easy chairs in the sunny living room of their white-column house at Calumet Farm, where they will watch the Derby on television.

The Markeys, their mobility sharply curtailed by arthritis, can stand up to greet their guests; they get around mostly in wheelchairs. However, they remain mentally alert and cheerful.

It costs $10,000 a year to keep Calumet's 25 miles of white plank fences looking picture-postcard neat, but Mrs. Markey wouldn't have it any other way. Other horse farms, looking to economize, have switched to cheaper creosote-stained dark fences that require much less maintenance. But not Calumet, an 890-acre showcase of sloping bluegrass pastures and white red-spired barns where eight Derby winners have been raised.

"I guarantee there'll always be white fences here," Mrs. Markey said.

In a way, the white fences are symbolic of Mrs. Markey's popularity in the racing world. She has paid her dues. Even when the Calumet dynasty suffered a decline, she kept buying horses and breeding them and hoping for another Derby winner.

Will it be Alydar?

"I've seen the best horse lose," she said. "It can happen, can't it, darling?"

"Yes," the Admiral agreed. "All Ben Jones would ever say is, 'I think he'll run good.' And they usually did. If the Lord smiles, we'll win the Derby."

"I don't see it that way, dear," said Mrs. Markey. "If the horse is good enough and doesn't get into trouble, he'll win."

Then, like any battle-tested horse owner, she added, "I think."

9-5 AFFIRMED, CAUTHEN UP, WINS KENTUCKY DERBY

BY STEVE CADY

LOUISVILLE, MAY 6, 1978—A Kentucky Derby can have only one winning script, and the dramatic scenario in today's 104th running of America's favorite horse race belonged to a golden colt named Affirmed and an 18-year-old jockey named Steve Cauthen.

In a tumultuous three-horse battle royal at Churchill Downs, Kentucky-bred Cauthen brought his 3-year-old Florida-bred colt home a length and a half ahead of Calumet Farm's favored Alydar, who led third-place Believe It by a length and a quarter.

They said it would be Affirmed or Alydar, just as it was last season in their six close encounters as 2-year-olds, and that's how it went again. Through the final eighth of a mile in their mile-and-a-quarter test, it was the flamingo pink and black silks of Harbor View Farm ahead, and the famed devil's red and blue silks of Calumet gaining.

"Here comes Alydar," thousands of fans in the crowd of 131,004 hollered.

"Keep going, Stevie," came the cry from thousands of others. "You got it."

Alydar went past Believe It, made up ground on Affirmed, but never was able to get close enough to hook him in the kind of hand-to-hand combat they waged last year.

One of the reasons Jorge Velasquez couldn't get the favorite up in time was that Cauthen had taken Affirmed back off a brutal early pace as the field of 11 settled into the backstretch.

The prophets of doom had suggested that Affirmed might burn himself out by running too fast too early against speed horses like Raymond Earl, and particularly the undefeated Sensitive Prince. But as Raymond Earl went the first quarter in 23 ⅗ and Sensitive Prince west past him for a half in 45 ⅗ and three-quarters in 1:10 ⅘, Cauthen had restrained Affirmed and dropped him four or five lengths off the pace.

But midway through the final turn, the youngster turned his mount loose and Affirmed, along with Believe It, ridden by Eddie Maple, stuck his head in front with about a quarter of a mile to go. But Affirmed rapidly drew away from him and kept going.

First place from a gross purse of $239,400 was worth $185,908. But it was the glory more than the gold that mattered most, as it always does, on this cool but sunny day. On a fast track that had been rolled out to make it faster, Affirmed ran the distance in 2:01 ⅕, equaling the fifth-fastest time for a Derby.

Despite the fact that Affirmed had beaten Alydar four times last year and had never finished behind any other horse except that rival, he was sent off as the second choice at 9-5. He paid $5.60, $2.80 and $2.60.

Alydar, the sentimental favorite because of the popularity of 85-year-old Mrs. Gene Markey, the Calumet owner, was also the betting choice at 6-5. Alydar returned $2.60 and $2.40. Believe It paid $2.80.

It was the pro-Cauthen sentimentalists who got to spill a tear into their mint juleps as the youngster won the Derby on his first try. Two years ago around this time, Cauthen finished far back on King of Swat in the first ride of what would become a meteoric jockey career. Last season, the kid from Walton, Ky., became the first rider whose mounts earned $6 million in a single year. And today, he and Affirmed and the trainer Laz Barrera got the roses and silenced the skeptics who had said the chestnut colt had not been finishing his races as strongly as Alydar.

It was also vindication for 65-year-old Wolfson, the controversial one-time financier who bred Affirmed, and for Wolfson's wife, the former Patrice Jacobs, whose father, the late Hirsch Jacobs, failed in nine Derby tries as a trainer.

Barrera, who had been saying all week his horse should be favored, had shown his confidence before the race when somebody told him, "May the best horse win."

"Yes," replied the 52-year-old trainer. "May the best horse win—again."

Afterward, Barrera lauded the coolness of Cauthen, who only turned 18 last Monday.

"He rode his horse perfect," said the Cuban-born trainer, who won the 1976 Derby with Bold Forbes about two weeks before Cauthen made his debut as a jockey. "I think he rode a long time ago and came back with 80 years experience. What do you call it? Reincarnation?"

Typically, when somebody told Cauthen he did a great job, racing's first Six Million Dollar Man replied, "I did my best. Winning is never easy."

So after months of debate and growing anticipation, the race they call the "most exciting two minutes in sports" had burned away speculation and opinion and replaced it with cold, hard fact. Or had it? Did Alydar, lagging in ninth place for half a mile and in eighth after three-quarters, launch his bid too late? Did the fast, bouncy racing surface favor Affirmed, who raced last winter and earlier this spring in California?

"The track was too hard," said Velasquez, who had swept to earlier victories this year aboard Alydar in the Flamingo, the Florida Derby and the Blue Grass Stakes. "He couldn't handle it. He only started running the last eighth of a mile."

But before the race, Alydar's 32-year-old trainer had said he didn't mind the hard track.

Whatever the case, it appears virtually certain that Alydar and Believe It, at least, will challenge Affirmed again two weeks from today in the Preakness, the second part of racing's annual Triple Crown series.

AFFIRMED OUTDUELS ALYDAR AGAIN IN THE PREAKNESS

BY STEVE CADY

BALTIMORE, MAY 20, 1978 — Affirmed beat Alydar again today, but their stretch duel in the 103d Preakness kept a track painter, a record crowd of 81,261 at Pimlico, and a national television audience in suspense right to the end. The margin this time for Affirmed, a 1-2 favorite, was only a neck.

While the two outstanding 3-year-old colts stormed through the stretch together, the painter stood on a ladder waiting to put the winning colors on the blouse of a metal jockey atop a metal horse that stands on an infield weathervane.

Would it be the flamingo pink and black of Harbor View Farm, carried to victory in the Kentucky Derby two weeks ago by Affirmed? Or would it be the devil's red and blue of Calumet Farm flown by Alydar?

Nobody could tell for sure, because this was the kind of head-to-head battle the two adversaries had waged last season.

It was a renewal of the equine war, with different battle strategies from the ones employed in the 1¼-mile Derby when 18-year-old Steve Cauthen rode Affirmed to a 1½-length victory over late-running Alydar, ridden by Jorge Velasquez.

Once again, though, the result had a familiar ring: Affirmed first, Alydar second. The Florida-bred colt, a chestnut son of Exclusive Native, now has defeated Kentucky-bred Alydar six times in eight closely contested meetings.

By winning the $188,700 Preakness, at 1 3/16 miles, Affirmed put himself in line to become thoroughbred racing's 11th triple crown champion. The only barrier left is the 1½-mile Belmont Stakes on June 10, when he undoubtedly will have to contend with Alydar again.

But the pattern appears to have been set. Affirmed, now with 13 firsts and two seconds in 15 starts, became the youngest equine millionaire in the history of racing today by adding the first-place purse of $136,200 to his bankroll. His earnings now stand at $1,033,227. Twenty other horses have earned $1 million or more, but none ever did it this early in a racing career.

Cauthen, himself a budding millionaire, remains just as cool as his golden chestnut colt. While Alydar was being led back to the barn by a groom, Cauthen was steering Affirmed into the infield for the blanket of black-eyed Susans as nonchalantly as a farmboy riding bareback atop a docile old plow horse.

Young Cauthen, as brilliant today as he was in the Derby, told the whole story in a few words during a press box conference after the race.

"My horse and I were waiting for Alydar," he said. "I set my horse down at the head of the lane and Jorge set his horse down. And my horse beat him."

On a fast track that had dried out well from recent rainy weather, the time of 1 minute 54⅖ seconds came close to the stakes and track record of 1:54 set by Canonero II in 1971. Affirmed's clocking tied the mark for the second fastest Preakness, a time shared by Secretariat and Seattle Slew. Both those colts went on to sweep the triple crown, and both Cauthen and

Laz Barrera, Affirmed's trainer, are confident their horse can duplicate that feat.

Affirmed, only a head in front of Alydar at the top of the stretch, ran the final three-sixteenths of a mile faster than any other horse in Preakness history except Little Current in 1974. It took only 18 ⅕ seconds, the same time required by stretch-running Little Current.

The fast finish by both Affirmed and Alydar left the others in a field of seven 3-year-olds far back. Believe It, third in the Derby, finished third again today. But he was 7½-lengths back of Alydar this time, and his jockey, Eddie Maple, voiced a familiar refrain: "You just can't get past that first guy, Affirmed. My horse went to him at the three-eighths pole, but the other horse was just pricking his ears."

Second choice to Alydar when he won the Derby, Affirmed paid a meager $3 for $2 today as the solid odds-on favorite.

Alydar was the 9-5 second choice this time. The exacta on those two paid only $4, a striking reflection of their superiority.

Affirmed and Alydar have now finished first or second in 30 of their combined total of 31 races. Against each other, they have now raced just over 7½ miles—and the overall net margin in favor of Affirmed is still under three lengths.

But Affirmed, the pride of Lou Wolfson and his wife, the former Patrice Jacobs, showed again today that when the head-to-head combat comes, he usually has the ammunition to turn back Alydar.

In the Derby, when he dropped 17 lengths off the early pace, the Calumet colt had excuses. He had none today except the obvious one—Affirmed. Sharpened by recent fast workouts, Alydar was never more than about five lengths back of the leader today. After three-quarters of a mile, Velasquez had him within two lengths of pace-setting Affirmed and they were head to head at the top of the stretch.

This was the confrontation the fans had turned out on a sweltering 88-degree day to see, and they weren't disappointed.

All the way down through the stretch, it appeared that Alydar, on the outside, might blast past his nemesis at any moment.

But Affirmed is a fighter. And Cauthen, a manchild who seldom makes a mistake, was riding another perfect race.

Cauthen's key decision came fairly early in the race when Maple, on Believe It, decided not to send that colt to the lead. Instead, the early pace-setter was Track Reward, a long shot trained by Barrera's 24-year-old son, Albert.

But Track Reward, after leading through a quarter in 23 ⅗, began bearing out.

So Cauthen gunned Affirmed past the front-runner, and the favorite led the way by a length after a leisurely half mile in 47 3⁄5. The time after three-quarters was still on the slow side for these horses, 1:11 4⁄5, and Affirmed reached the mile in 1:35 1⁄5.

At that point, though, Cauthen still had not asked his favorite horse to get ready to fight. The real race, between Affirmed and Alydar, was only beginning.

In contrast, Seattle Slew ran the first mile of the Preakness last year in a record 1:34 4⁄5. Bold Forbes, the Barrera-trained colt who won the 1976 Derby and Belmont but lost the Preakness, reached the mile here in 1:35 1⁄5 after setting records of 45 seconds for the first half and 1:09 for three-quarters.

But Affirmed is a more versatile horse than the game but headstrong Bold Forbes. Like the fancy-footwork boxer who can also counter-punch with devastating efficiency, Affirmed can do anything.

But Barrera, apart from his jubilation of saddling his first Preakness winner, reportedly wasn't as happy about everything as might have been expected. The trainer was annoyed that security guards had whisked Cauthen into an elevator bound for the press box but had left Barrera cooling his heels downstairs. He never did come to the press box for an interview.

That minor flap, though, isn't expected to have any effect on the winner's camp as preparations are made for the Belmont Stakes. By winning today, Affirmed became the 10th horse in the last 20 years to take both the Derby and the Preakness.

Except for Secretariat and Seattle Slew, seven of those recent double winners have failed in the Belmont. But Barrera already has said he thinks the Belmont will be the easiest of the triple crown races for Affirmed to win. And John Veitch, Alydar's trainer, already has disagreed.

The Preakness, in past years, had proved to be a major roadblock to triple crown fame. Nine horses who won both the Derby and Belmont failed in the Preakness. Eight others won the Derby and the Preakness but lost in the Belmont, and six won the Preakness and Belmont after losing the Derby.

Thus, there were 26 near-misses involving the horses who ran in all three events, but met defeat in one of them. In addition, seven horses, including Man o' War, won the Preakness and Belmont but didn't start in the Derby, a race that didn't gain full national popularity until after World War I. Two other horses, Burgoo King and Bold Venture, won the Derby and Preakness but didn't race in the Belmont.

MAN HERE LOVES HIS HORSE

BY RED SMITH

ELMONT, N.Y., JUNE 10, 1978 — As all readers of bad fiction know, horsemen are callous schemers steeped in guile, to whom a thoroughbred of royal lineage and generous courage is merely a tool to be used while it can produce money and then discarded or destroyed. In movies they wear a snap-brim hat over eyes that regard the world with a larcenous stare. They talk out of the corner of the mouth, almost always in conspiratorial tones because they are almost always conspiring to fix a race, break a jockey's arms, swindle a sucker or nobble another man's horse. When they aren't talking, a cigarette droops from the corner of the thin-lipped mouth. Lazaro Sosa Barrera could be a hell of a horseman, except that he is hatless, amiable, patient, humorous, warm, cooperative and accommodating, looks like Cupid with a suntan and doesn't smoke. Probably his trouble is that he is a Latin, for Latins are notoriously emotional. This Latin is openly and unashamedly emotional about a horse named Affirmed, who may or may not add victory in the Belmont Stakes this afternoon to his scores in the Kentucky Derby and Preakness and thus become history's 11th winner of the triple crown, the third in five years and the second in 12 months.

Laz has been training racehorses for 38 of his 53 years, in his native Cuba, in Mexico, California and New York. He has worked with a one-horse string and with a stable worth $30 million or more. He has had good horses and rogues, sound horses and cripples, fast horses and horses that could run just enough to keep a man broke. Last year and the year before he saddled winners of $5,248,546 and twice hand-running he walked away with the Eclipse Award as trainer of the year. He has not had a winner of the triple crown, but two years ago he passed a triple miracle by getting a sprinter named Bold Forbes up to a mile and a quarter to win the Derby, patching him together after the colt was cut up running third in the Preakness and sending him out to run in front every step of the Belmont's searching mile and a half.

He knows better than to let himself grow so attached to a horse that it might warp his judgment. Yet when he speaks of Affirmed, his soul strands in his dark eyes.

"Did you ever have a smarter horse, Laz?" a visitor at Belmont asked. They were standing under the shed of Barn 47, in front of Affirmed's stall.

"Not like this one," the trainer said.

He spoke of the two races Affirmed has lost in 15 starts, the two occasions in their eight meetings when he finished second to Alydar. The first time, he said, was in the Great American Stakes at Belmont last July. Affirmed gave Alydar five pounds that day and hit the starting gate, cutting his lip and knocking out a tooth. Alydar won by 3 ½ lengths.

In the Champagne in October, Laz said, Affirmed was fighting for the lead with Darby Creek Road and Sauce Boat and didn't see Alydar when that one blew past them on the outside to win by a length and a quarter.

"He knows better now," the trainer said. "Watch his ears in the stretch." He said that when a horse charged at Affirmed now, the colt called the attention of Steve Cauthen, his rider, to the threat by pointing with an ear. Laz made horns of his forefingers and waggled them alternately back and forth. "A horse comes upon the outside"—the right finger pointed back. " 'Hey Stevie!' a horse on the inside—back went the left horn. 'Stevie, look.' "

Laz talked about his horse's agility, his quick, athletic way of going. "He hits the ground and gets out of there so quick," he said. "Very light. He don't kick too much dirt." He recalled a half-mile work by Affirmed at Pimlico on the Thursday before the Preakness. Fog was so dense that work couldn't be clocked.

"We couldn't see anything," Laz said, "but I said, 'here come my horse.' 'You crazy,' they told me, but I could hear him. The other horses all were 'thumpety-ump, thumpety-ump.' My horse you could only hear, 'thrrip, thrrip, thripp.' "

The trainer walked his visitors to the barn door. The stable area was a hog-wallow of mud but there was no need to ask Barrera what an off track would mean to Affirmed. Laz had answered that question before the Preakness: "My horse never said no to any track."

In the 1976 Preakness, Bold Forbes burned himself out running three-quarters in 1:09 and the mile in 1:35⅕. During the next three weeks, Barrera knocked the speed out of him with easy gallops and the colt won the Belmont in moderate time, staggering home with Angel Cordero holding him together.

During the first week after this year's Preakness, Laz took it easy with Affirmed. In the second week he sent him out for a full open gallop of slightly more than a mile and a half. "He went the last quarter in 25 and change," the trainer said, "and wasn't breathing hard. Next time we worked him three-quarters he went in even 12's." He meant Affirmed ran 12-second furlongs, which is winning time at the classic distances.

Laz respects Affirmed as an athlete who will place himself wherever the trainer and rider want him in a race. He believes his horse can set the pace and win, be rated off the lead and come on, or win from far back. "If they go the first quarter in 24," he said, "I'll be on the lead. If it's faster, I won't be."

At that point John Russell, trainer of Judge Advocate, was asked whether his colt might set the pace.

"With Laz Barrera having a horse in the race," Russell said, "the lead may be already spoken for."

AFFIRMED WINS BELMONT STAKES FOR TRIPLE CROWN

BY STEVE CADY

ELMONT, N.Y., JUNE 11, 1978 — Affirmed fought off Alydar one more time yesterday, and his courage under the fiercest of pressure in the 110th Belmont Stakes brought him a sweep of the triple crown.

No horse ever worked harder for it, or deserved it more. For the last half-mile of the mile-and-a-half "test of the champion," Affirmed and Alydar ran head to head. At the finish, with a crowd of 65,147 at Belmont

Park and a television audience of millions on the brink of a nervous break-down, Affirmed's head was still in front.

At the parimutuel windows, that meant $3.20 for $2. To Affirmed's people, it meant the fulfillment of a lifetime dream.

Even Steve Cauthen, the Harbor View Farm colt's unflappable 18-year-old jockey, didn't know quite how to explain what his golden 3-year-old had done in those last desperate yards.

"I can't believe it," he said, reflecting the unanimous reaction of racing fans to what had to be one of the most dramatic Belmonts in history.

Not since 1962, when Jaipur beat Admiral's Voyage by a nose, had there been a closer finish. And never has a triple crown sweep been sealed by such a narrow margin. It took a photo-finish camera to determine that Affirmed had won by a head.

But young Cauthen, who brought home three other winners yesterday, knew he had it. He stood up in the saddle a few yards past the finish, and waved his left hand high in the air.

Jorge Velasquez, Alydar's rider, was among the first to salute Cauthen and Affirmed, but the Panamanian didn't forget his Calumet Farm colt.

"They proved they are the greatest," said Velasquez. "You see how far they be ahead of the rest every time they run."

Only three other colts challenged the Big Two in yesterday's $184,300 race, and the one that was closest to them at the finish, Darby Creek Road, was 13 ½ lengths back. Judge Advocate finished fourth and Noon Time Spender was last in the five-horse field, the smallest since Secretariat trounced four rivals en route to his triple crown in 1973.

Florida-bred Affirmed, now with 14 firsts and two seconds in 18 starts, became the third triple crown winner in six years and the second in two years, the first time there were consecutive sweeps. Seattle Slew accomplished the feat last year. But that was a runaway. Yesterday's Belmont, making Affirmed the 11th triple crown winner, was the kind of close-combat struggle that demonstrated why humans have been so fascinated by thoroughbred race-horses for centuries.

After months of hope and anticipation and anxiety, it all came down to one final wait on the part of Affirmed: a wait for Alydar. This time the at-tack by the Calumet colt came much earlier than in either the Derby or the Preakness. Halfway down to the backstretch Velasquez let his horse range up alongside the pace-setting Affirmed.

From then to the wire, there was never any daylight between the flamingo pink and black silks of the Harbor View Farm and the devil's red and blue of Calumet. And Velasquez, free to whip right-handed as he drove Alydar along just outside his rival, rode as brilliantly as Cauthen.

In the upper stretch, it appeared that Alydar pushed his head in front.

Now Cauthen, who had hit his mount nine times right-handed, was forced to switch the stick to his left hand. It was the first time he had ever hit Affirmed left-handed, and he rapped him nine more times from that side.

From a slow early pace that helped front-running Affirmed, the last half-mile was furious. The final time of 2:26⅘ was the third fastest in Belmont Stakes history, bettered only by Secretariat's 2:24 and Gallant Man's 2:26⅗. No final half-mile in the Belmont was ever run any faster than Affirmed and Alydar ran it.

And racing history itself has seldom seen two 3-year-olds as good as Affirmed and Alydar in the same season.

Never in that long history have two horses fought each other so frequently in a rivalry that has produced such close margins. In nine meetings, Affirmed and Kentucky bred Alydar have raced a total of nine miles. Affirmed has won seven of those battles, but his net margin is still just under three lengths.

His total margin in the triple crown series was fewer than two lengths, by far the slimmest of any triple crown winner. He beat Alydar in the Kentucky Derby five weeks ago by a length and a half, and beat him in the Preakness by a neck.

It's a good thing Affirmed is a racehorse, not a sentimentalist. He was just about the only one in his camp with completely dry eyes after today's excruciatingly tense duel in the sun.

From owners and trainer to jockey and stablehands, the winners have paid their dues. That's why the romantics had to be pulling for Louis and Patrice Wolfson, Affirmed's owners, and for Laz Barrera, the colt's 53-year-old trainer, and for Cauthen.

As Governor Carey presented the trophy to the Wolfsons, Mrs. Wolfson hugged Cauthen and threw kisses to friends in the crowd. But she may also have been thinking of her father, the late Hirsch Jacobs, a famous trainer who saddled more winners than anybody else but never managed to win a Kentucky Derby, much less a triple crown.

But the fans also had to feel a debt to Alydar, his 32-year-old trainer John Veitch, and Adm. and Mrs. Gene Markey, now in their 80's, dedicated horsepeople who bred the colt and hoped he could turn their once-dominant Calumet empire into a winner again.

So there were mixed feelings as Cauthen, resplendent in the Harbor View Farm silks, rode Affirmed into the winner's circle while Alydar, unsaddled and without his rider, was led back to the barn once more by his groom.

In 33 combined starts, the two colts show 23 firsts and nine seconds. No horse except Alydar has ever beaten Affirmed, and almost no other horse except Affirmed has beaten Alydar. He now has nine victories and seven seconds in 17 starts, and six of those seconds came in competition with Affirmed.

"My horse don't let nobody go in front of him," said Barrera, "but Alydar is a great horse, too. He fights like a tiger."

Alydar was never more of a threatening tiger than he was yesterday as he matched Affirmed stride for stride on the fast track in their frantic drive to the wire. The triple crown seemed to be slipping away, but once again it was Affirmed who kept his head in front of the 11-10 second choice. The winner's purse of $110,500 pushed Affirmed's bankroll to $1,133,807.

"What can I say?" said Veitch after the 3-5 favorite had beaten his colt again. "It was a helluva horse race and we got beat. He'll be back to try Affirmed again, and maybe we'll get him sometime, somewhere."

Beyond the drama of the moment, substantial long-term gains appeared to be in store for Spendthrift Farm, in whose breeding shed at Lexington, Ky., both Affirmed and Alydar were sired. Affirmed, bred by his owner, is a chestnut son of Exclusive Native and a grandson of Raise a Native, a horse raced by Wolfson. Alydar is a son of Raise a Native. And all spring, Brownell Combs, the manager of Spendthrift Farm, has been smiling like a poker player who has been dealt back-to-back aces.

Yesterday's result did nothing to change that attitude.

If there was a single disappointment for management, it was that no more than 65,417 spectators turned out on a perfect day of pleasantly dry 73-degree temperatures. In 1971, before the impact of offtrack betting, a record crowd of 82,694 saw Canonero II fail in his bid for a triple crown. Seattle Slew's sweep last year drew 71,026, and 67,605 saw Secretariat win in 1973.

THE SCRIPT MAY BE ALL EASY GOER

BY STEVEN CRIST

LOUISVILLE, MAY 5, 1989 — It was shortly after 3:30 P.M. last Aug. 19, in front of the ancient and rickety wooden stands of Saratoga Racetrack in upstate New York, that it began to look as if the 115th Kentucky Derby here at Churchill Downs might be different from most. A reddish colt with a splash of white on his forehead had just won a race for 2-year-old maidens, the kind of dash that often yields a promising young racehorse and sometimes much more.

The Teletimer said that this colt had just run seven-eighths of a mile in 1 minute 22⅗ seconds, the kind of clocking that accomplished older horses hang up when they win important stakes races.

But you didn't have to know the time to know this colt was something special. He hadn't so much run as he had glided, carried by the wave of his own quiet power. Racetrackers knew at that moment that he not only had the ability to win a Derby, as someone must every year, but also had the flame that might put him among the few truly great horses who have won the race.

The colt's name is Easy Goer, and on Saturday he will be the heaviest favorite to win the Kentucky Derby in 10 years.

His career since that maiden victory last August has seemed almost scripted in both its neatness and its similarities to those of Secretariat and Seattle Slew in the 1970's. He won Belmont Park's big fall races and was

189

named the champion 2-year-old. He wintered in Florida, where he fleshed out and matured. He prepped in New York, where he set a track record and then proved he could go longer distances. Finally, he trained perfectly at Churchill Downs.

While this Derby has attracted an unsually large field of 16 that inexplicably includes at least half a dozen thoroughly overmatched colts, Easy Goer is no favorite by default. Sunday Silence, the blackish colt from California who won the Santa Anita Derby by 11 lengths, is good enough to be a Derby favorite, and possibly a winner, in many other years.

Houston remains a puzzle after only five career starts, but there is no denying his tremendous talent on his best days. Awe Inspiring is getting better by the day, and Triple Buck is better now than when Easy Goer beat him by three lengths in the Wood Memorial on April 22.

Easy Goer will race a furlong farther than ever before on Saturday, and against a much bigger field than he has yet to work his way through. He must break from post 14 and could be forced wide on the first turn or bothered by two wild long shots with rookie jockeys just outside of him.

The weather has also turned nasty here, and there are forecasts for a windy, cold Derby Day with a few showers and possibly sleet.

The last time Easy Goer lost a race was Nov. 5, when he ran second in the Breeders' Cup Juvenile. It was over a wet and sticky surface on this same Churchill Downs track, after a rocky trip in a large field. These variables sometimes do keep the best horse from winning: Native Dancer's only defeat in 21 career starts was after a traffic jam in the 1953 Derby.

But horses as special as Easy Goer more often do find a way to win. Secretariat was dead last heading into the first turn of the 1973 Derby, then looped the field and set a track record. Seattle Slew was behind a wall of rivals four years later and bulled his way through to take the lead. Spectacular Bid was all over the track and jostled a few times before almost disdainfully burying his rivals in 1979.

Easy Goer's handlers are looking for their first Derby victory, but each has what it takes. Ogden Phipps has been mating and racing high-class thoroughbreds for 58 years, and Easy Goer is the product of generations of refined Phipps bloodlines. Shug McGaughey is the sport's outstanding young trainer. Pat Day's chilly patience in the saddle sometimes gives horseplayers heart failure, but he is the king of Churchill Downs and his style seems to fit this colt.

People who watch just one race a year usually choose the Derby, and hope to see a winner good enough to take the Preakness two weeks later and then bid for a Triple Crown in the Belmont Stakes in June. This year, there is a feeling afoot that the crown may be worn for the first time since Affirmed reigned in 1978. The answer will come shortly after the gates spring open at 5:33 Saturday afternoon.

SUNDAY SILENCE TAKES DERBY IN UPSET

BY STEVEN CRIST

LOUISVILLE, MAY 6, 1989 — Sunday Silence scored a two-and-a-half-length upset victory over Easy Goer in the 115th Kentucky Derby today at Churchill Downs, but the only thing that seemed right about the race was that the two best colts beat the others.

This had shaped up as an extraordinarily good Derby, a virtual match race between two special colts, and those with a piece of Sunday Silence or a bet on him were delighted by the outcome. But many in the crowd of 122,653 seemed dazed and unsatisfied with the way the showdown unfolded.

Both colts had traffic problems. Sunday Silence weaved strangely through the stretch as he shied from his rider's whip. Easy Goer's jockey said his colt had failed to handle the track or fire his best shot. The time of the race was the slowest in 31 years, and fewer than 10 lengths separated the first dozen finishers, who had figured to finish much farther apart.

Sunday Silence, who paid $8.20 for $2 to win as the second favorite and ran the mile and a quarter under Pat Valenzuela in 2:05 on a track labeled "muddy," took the lead turning for home and ran a crooked course to the wire while well clear of the field. Easy Goer passed four rivals in the final furlong to be second, a head in front of Awe Inspiring, with whom he was coupled as the Shug McGaughey–trained entry that was favored at 4-to-5.

Dansil, who forced Easy Goer to alter course through the stretch, was fourth, a nose ahead of Hawkster. Northern Wolf, Irish Actor, Houston, Triple Buck, Shy Tom, Wind Splitter, Flying Continental, Clever Trevor, Faultless Ensign and Western Playboy completed the finish in that order.

Sunday Silence may well turn out to be the better of the two favorites who clashed today, but this was a Derby that seemed to demand a rematch. If he and Easy Goer come out of the race uninjured, they might meet again in the Preakness Stakes at Pimlico on May 20. If Sunday Silence wins that race and the Belmont Stakes at Belmont Park on June 10, he will earn $5 million and become the first winner of racing's Triple Crown since Affirmed in 1978.

Sunday Silence, a son of Halo and the Understanding mare Wishing Well, has now won five of seven career starts. He lost photo finishes in his two other races and is 4 for 4 as a 3-year-old. He came into the Derby off an 11-length romp in the Santa Anita Derby on April 8, and is the fourth straight Kentucky Derby winner to have prepped in that race. Twice spurned by buyers at auctions, Sunday Silence races in the colors of Arthur B. Hancock 3d, who raised him at his Stone Farm in Paris, Ky. Hancock owns 50 percent of the colt and Charlie Whittingham, the trainer, and Dr. Ernest Gaillard, a Louisville surgeon, each own a 25 percent interest.

"If ever a horse could win the Triple Crown, this one could," said Whittingham, 76, who also sent out Ferdinand to win the 1986 Derby. "He was green today and he still won. He's learning all the time."

Easy Goer, who had been widely regarded as a likely Triple Crown winner and was sent off as the first odds-on Derby favorite in 10 years, simply did not run as well as he had in winning all three of his preps this spring.

"He never grabbed hold of the bit like he has in his other races this year," said Pat Day, his jockey, who had ridden five straight winners on the card going into the Derby. "I really don't know why."

"It seemed like he had a little trouble handling the racetrack down the backstretch," said McGaughey. "But I'm not making excuses. You have to congratulate Charlie and Sunday Silence."

The outcome was particularly disappointing to Ogden Phipps, 80, who bred and owns Easy Goer. His family has failed to win the Derby in 10 attempts dating back to 1927.

Both colts had decent position coming out of the first turn, though, and down the backstretch Houston, the third choice in the race at 5 to 1, continued to set the pace through fractions of 23, 46⅗, 1:11⅖ and 1:37⅖.

Entering the stretch turn, Sunday Silence swooped to the lead, but Easy Goer began dropping back and Awe Inspiring got past him.

When they straightened away, Sunday Silence opened a clear lead but then ducked sharply every time Valenzuela hit him. He changed lanes at least four times down the stretch. Easy Goer, meanwhile, had to change course when Dansil drifted in front of him, then split horses and just outlasted his entrymate for second.

"When Sunday Silence began to move away from us, I nudged Easy Goer and got no response," Day said. "At the three-eighths pole I started getting into him some more and again I got no response. When I really got into him at the end, he came on enough to be second. But it wasn't his performance. It wasn't his race."

SUNDAY SILENCE WINS PREAKNESS BY NOSE

BY STEVEN CRIST

BALTIMORE, MAY 20, 1989 — Sunday Silence, who raised more questions than he answered when he beat Easy Goer by two and a half lengths in the Kentucky Derby two weeks ago, proved himself a worthy Triple Crown contender today by winning the 114th and closest Preakness Stakes ever at Pimlico Race Course. The blackish colt from California raced head and head with Easy Goer for the length of the stretch before regaining the lead in the final yards to win by a nose.

The last time a Preakness was decided in a photo finish was when Affirmed held off Alydar by a neck in 1978. Now Sunday Silence is one victory away from becoming racing's first Triple Crown winner since Affirmed, and his rivalry with Easy Goer, a son of Alydar, is the tightest Triple Crown battle since then. The two colts will hook up again in the Belmont Stakes at Belmont Park on June 10, where victory would bring Sunday Silence's owners a total of $5 million in purses and bonuses for the series.

The winner had to survive a claim of foul from Pat Day, Easy Goer's rider, who alleged interference by Pat Valenzuela and Sunday Silence through their stretch duel. After reviewing the films for seven minutes, the stewards let the order of finish stand. Another unrelated foul claim, by the rider of Dansil, who was fourth, against Rock Point, who was third, was also disallowed.

The bettors in a record Pimlico crowd of 90,145, unconvinced by Sunday Silence's weaving Derby finish and the slow final time of that race, made Easy Goer the 3-to-5 favorite today and let Sunday Silence off as the second choice at 2 to 1. Sunday Silence paid $6.20 for $2 to win after running the mile and three-sixteenths in 1:53 ⅘, the third fastest Preakness ever, behind Tank's Prospect's 1:53 ⅖ in 1985 and Gate Dancer's 1:53 ⅗ in 1984.

Rock Point, who skipped the Derby after running second to Easy Goer in the Wood Memorial last month, was up for third, five lengths behind Easy Goer and two lengths in front of Dansil. Hawkster was fifth with Houston tiring to finish sixth, and it was 26 more lengths back to the outclassed locals, Pulverizing and Northern Wolf. Awe Inspiring, as expected, was an early scratch.

Sunday Silence has won six of eight career starts and is undefeated in five races this year. Sunday Silence survived a serious illness and a vanning accident early in his career, was twice rejected by buyers at yearling sales, and came back this week from a bruised right front foot that forced him to miss two days of training.

The tight finish capped a race in which the two principals both looked as if they would win easily at some point. Each appeared to fire his best shot, and while there will be plenty of interest in a rematch, and some excuses made for the loser, the race seemed more genuine than the Derby.

"I think this puts to rest the talk that Easy Goer is the better horse," Valenzuela said. "I think his horse was overrated and mine was underrated. I knew Pat was going to claim foul. He was grasping at straws. He didn't want to let the public down and he didn't want to let the Eastern writers down."

Shug McGaughey, Easy Goer's trainer, said within moments of the finish that he was eager to try Sunday Silence one more time in the Belmont. But McGaughey seemed even more dispirited today than he was after the Derby, which he had hoped was a fluke.

"We'll just try again," McGaughey said. "I guess I'm going to start hearing a whole lot about Affirmed and Alydar now, but I hope we can put that to rest in the Belmont."

The race unfolded as expected and looked much like the Derby at first. Easy Goer got the only poor start, jumping in the air and spotting the field a length. Northern Wolf and Houston were head and head for the lead through a moderate first quarter-mile in 23 ⅖ before Houston pulled away to lead by 2½ lengths after a half-mile in 46 ⅖.

Then Easy Goer, running better than he did in the Derby, made a bold move that seemed tactically brilliant at first. Day sent him up to the lead on the outside of Houston and managed to shut off Sunday Silence, who checked for a moment as he had nowhere to go between them. Easy Goer led by a head after six furlongs in 1:09 ⅗, and seemed just about to blow the race wide open.

Then Sunday Silence gathered himself together and swooped up to join Easy Goer. For a moment, he looked ready to take a commanding lead. But as the two colts straightened out at the top of the stretch, Easy Goer came back on the inside, and the battle was on.

It was Sunday Silence by a head at the furlong pole, but then Easy Goer got a nose in front again with a sixteenth of a mile to go. At the wire, Sunday Silence was surging again, and clearly won the photo.

Day said after the race that the slow start and the tight quarters in the stretch could have added up to more than the narrow margin of defeat. McGaughey wondered whether Day had sent Easy Goer to the lead too soon. The Sunday Silence camp, however, thought this race merely confirmed the Derby outcome.

Hancock, who owns a 50 percent interest in Sunday Silence and raised the colt at his Stone Farm in Paris, Ky., spoke somewhat bitterly after the race about the lack of respect his colt had been afforded after winning the Derby. He began a news conference by mockingly wondering what excuses Easy Goer's backers would make this time. Whittingham predicted his colt would have no trouble with the Belmont distance of a mile and a half.

LAST BOUQUET FOR EASY GOER

BY STEVEN CRIST

MAY 15, 1994—When I heard that Easy Goer had died Thursday at Claiborne Farm in Paris, Ky., felled by a heart attack in just his fourth year as a stallion at the Bluegrass nursery where he was born and raised, my impulse was to send sympathy flowers. Roses would have been tactless, black-eyed Susans downright cruel. The only flowers appropriate to honor this wonderful horse are white carnations.

They covered the only one of the Triple Crown victory blankets that Easy Goer got to wear, and no horse ever redeemed so many hopes and dreams in triumph. For many New York racing fans who came of age too late for Secretariat in 1973, Easy Goer's victory in the 1989 Belmont Stakes was the sweetest moment ever spent at a racetrack. It was five years ago this month that Easy Goer went to the Triple Crown as the heaviest favorite since Spectacular Bid a decade earlier. He had rolled through New York's landmark prep races—the Cowdin and Champagne as a 2-year-old, the Gotham and Wood as a 3-year-old—by a combined 23 lengths.

A fast and powerful 2-year-old, he had gotten even bigger and better at 3, running the Gotham in an otherworldly 1:32.40, still the fastest mile ever by a 3-year-old. There were some other quick horses in California that spring, but it seemed a long shot that fate had dropped more than one colt of such rare talent in the very same crop of foals. This particular long shot came in. Easy Goer failed to take home either the roses in the Kentucky Derby or the black-eyed Susans in the Preakness, instead finish-

196

ing second to Sunday Silence both times. You could make reasonable excuses for both defeats, excuses I will defend to my grave: the muddy track at Churchill Downs, jockey Pat Day's premature move at Pimlico.

Still, there was no denying that Sunday Silence was something special himself, and a nimbler, more aggressive racehorse who would always have a strategic edge over Easy Goer's massive, raw talent. It seemed Easy Goer might make only ironic history, becoming what his sire, Alydar, had been to Affirmed 11 years earlier: the runner-up in every leg of someone else's Triple Crown.

Only those who had taken an oath of loyalty to Easy Goer were still with him on Belmont Day. The majority of the customers were reluctant to be betrayed a third time and made Sunday Silence the 9-10 favorite this time. They looked smart for a mile, as Sunday Silence established perfect position, stalking the suspect pace setter Le Voyageur from second place, while Easy Goer lagged farther back in third. Once again, it seemed Sunday Silence would pounce first, gain the edge, and leave Easy Goer with too much to do too late.

Then suddenly, turning for home, came the move that the faithful had been waiting for since pledging their hearts to this colt months earlier.

Easy Goer's enormous stride and Belmont Park's majestically sweeping turns were made for each other, and as he reached the end of the backstretch he accelerated into the turn as if his entire career had pointed for this moment. Sunday Silence thrust his head in front of the tiring Le Voyageur with three-eighths of a mile between him and a Triple Crown, but the lead lasted only a moment as Easy Goer furiously swooped past them from the outside.

A length in front with a quarter of a mile to run, Easy Goer was just starting to soar, gliding to a 4½-length lead with a furlong to go and reaching the finish line eight lengths in front of his nemesis. His time of 2:26.01 remains the second fastest ever, surpassed only by the incomparable Secretariat's 2:24.

Those who had kept the faith were hugging strangers and deciding that sometimes life is fair after all. Even those who had bet on or fallen in love with Sunday Silence seemed willing to acknowledge that they had seen something historic and humbling that afternoon, and to concede that this was a rare year of two brilliant colts.

No one left the track that day grousing about how a favorite had lost again or that the game was maddeningly unpredictable or that it was another disappointing season because no one had won the Triple Crown for the 11th straight year. That particular lament is heard almost every year from the people who blindly root for every Derby winner to go on to victory in the Preakness and the Belmont. They seem to think that everything that ails thoroughbred racing can be cured by a marketable four-legged hero with a certificate of achievement.

In fact, when the next colt good and lucky enough to win the Crown does come along, all he will do is generate a few more stories from the people who pay attention to racing three or four times a year. The sport's genuine problems—the punitive economics of owning or betting on horses, decades of customer neglect by track management, the industry's loss of its virtual monopoly on legal gambling—will not be addressed, much less lightened, by another Triple Crown winner.

So there is never a reason for anyone who treasures racing and quality to root for anything less than an Easy Goer or a Sunday Silence to win the Triple Crown. Call me a sourpuss, but I will be rooting against Go for Gin in the Preakness on Saturday and, if he wins it despite me, in the Belmont three weeks later. He is a perfectly nice racehorse and better than most of our recent Kentucky Derby winners, but he has done nothing to suggest he deserves to keep company with Sir Barton, Gallant Fox, Omaha, War Admiral, Whirlaway, Count Fleet, Assault, Citation, Secretariat, Seattle Slew and Affirmed.

Instead, I will be watching the 2-year-olds this summer and fall, including Easy Goer's first offspring, hoping for that one brilliant colt who just might be the next Secretariat—or at least let me think that he is for a while. He doesn't have to win the Triple Crown and it's 3-5 he will break my heart along the way. If he gives me just one day at the races like the 1989 Belmont, though, I will be forever in his debt, as I am to the late, great Easy Goer.

PART VIII

◆◆◆

"What can you say? It's a horse race!"
—RACETRACK LAMENT

Pimlico Race Course: 1986 Kentucky Derby winner Ferdinand with jockey Willie Shoemaker and trainer Charlie Whittingham. AP IMAGES

Sometimes the Racing Gods have cursed the Triple Crown, and other times they have blessed it. How else do you explain the great Native Dancer suffering his only defeat in 22 starts by a diminishing head to Dark Star in the 1953 Kentucky Derby? Native Dancer had twice beaten Dark Star, a horse that would never win again.

"Losing the Kentucky Derby is almost always a quick trip to the bottom of a trivia deck," writes Alfred G. Vanderbilt in a story collected here and shows why Native Dancer is the exception to that rule.

The series also inevitably gives us moments that cannot be conjured by a fiction writer—like when old-timers Charlie Whittingham and Bill Shoemaker teamed up for an improbable Derby victory with Ferdinand in 1986.

Just because they constitute the Triple Crown doesn't mean these races aren't prey to the same bedevilments that afflict all other races. Horses have stumbled, jockeys have erred and impossible long shots have simply outrun the favorites. Fillies have beaten the boys. Hall of Fame trainers like D. Wayne Lukas and Nick Zito have set milestones, and relative unknowns have left their names in the record books.

Leave it to Zito, a loquacious New Yorker with a horseplayer's emotional demeanor, to sum up the appeal of horse racing. In 2005, he became the first trainer ever to saddle five horses for five different owners in the

Kentucky Derby. Among them was the post time favorite, Bellamy Road, who was owned by New York Yankees owner George Steinbrenner. But May 7, 2005 turned out not to be Zito's day. Bellamy Road finished seventh, and Zito's other horses—Andromeda's Hero, High Fly, Noble Causeway and Sun King—staggered home in eighth, 10th, 14th and 15th place. A 50-1 longshot named Giacomo wore the blanket of roses.

"There's no locks in this game," Zito said, standing on the track moments after the race.

Zito was obviously disappointed—he had hoped that one of his brigade was going to bring him his third Derby victory. Suddenly, however, a smile crept across his face as he saw the prices flash on the tote board. The trifecta of Giacomo, Closing Argument and Afleet Alex paid $133,134.80 for a $2 bet; the superfecta with Don't Get Mad as the fourth-place horse picked paid $1.7 million for a $2 bet.

"Look at that board," he said, pointing at the payoffs for the four horses that were not his. "You just have to salute the winners. It just shows you what a great game this is, what a tough game."

A SHATTERED ROMANCE

BY ARTHUR DALEY

LOUISVILLE, MAY 3, 1953 — It's a dreadful and blighting experience to fall madly and blindly in love with a racehorse. But that's what happened to this tourist to the blue grass belt. The unashamed admission must be made that he fell in love with Native Dancer. But he was not alone in becoming enamored of the big gray. Almost half of the press box tenants at Churchill Downs yesterday also were ga-ga over him.

The Dancer is a distinctive horse, big and handsome. He glows with a peculiar sort of personality, an equine magnetism. By way of adding to his appeal, he is trained by Bill Winfrey, as nice a guy as anyone ever met, and owned by Alfred Gwynne Vanderbilt, a very charming young man. In eleven races the Dancer had been overpowering in performance. It was love at first sight.

Because love thrives on dreams and lives in dream castles, it was natural to envision the gray as the winner of yesterday's Kentucky Derby, as the winner of the Triple Crown and as one of the truly great horses. Here was another Citation, another Man o' War.

But Native Dancer didn't win the Derby. He missed his date with destiny. This reporter was never as emotionally affected by a horse race as he was yesterday at the Downs. At the end he felt heartbroken. Since he didn't have a pfenning bet on the outcome, it had to be pure sentiment which moved him, a bitter and brooding feeling that the best horse hadn't won the race.

Even the jockeys confirmed that impression in the jockey room afterward. Doug Dodson had one of the best vantage points in the joint. He rode Ram o' War, who finished ninth.

"The gray horse was the best," he said, "but not today."

Eric Guerin, the rider of the Dancer, walked past on his way home for a good cry. His face still bore a stunned and disbelieving look.

"He just wouldn't run," he said.

There had been some talk earlier that Guerin had given the Dancer a slightly less than perfect ride. But when that thought was offered out loud, little Johnny Adams disagreed.

"When a horse ain't goin' good," he said, "it looks like you're ridin' him bad. The funny thing about that race is that Correspondent didn't run good enough to challenge Dark Star. If he had, he'da killed off Star and the gray would win easy."

Later on, one knowing horseman offered his impression. "I've been wondering," he said, "if Guerin wasn't too confident. The Dancer broke well from the gate, but Guerin took back with him, never letting him go. He could have been an effortless third around the first turn but let himself get jammed in the middle of the pack. And he had a tight rein of him all down the backstretch. Then when he wanted him to go at the head of the stretch, the Dancer wouldn't respond. Horses will do that, you know."

Maybe the gray did get discouraged and disinterested as a result of Guerin's restraint. No excuses could be offered for him over the last quarter-mile from the head of the homestretch to the wire. Both Correspondent and Invigorator swung wide into the straightaway and that left the inside rail wide open and inviting. Guerin took it and only Dark Star, the winner, was ahead of him.

If Native Dancer deserved his accolade of greatness, the opportunity was there. One explosive lift would have hurled him past Dark Star. But he didn't have it. "He wouldn't run until the last sixteenth," said Guerin sadly. It was too late. The first three-sixteenths of that final quarter-mile were wasted.

Thus does Native Dancer fall into the same category as Bimelech, who was "the greatest horse I ever owned," according to the late Col. E. R. Bradley, who had owned many great ones. But Bimelech fluffed out on the Derby of 1940 and never achieved the recognition he deserved, even though he later took both the Preakness and the Belmont with ridiculous ease.

Bimelech was deemed such a Derby shoo-in that some writers actually wrote the story of his victory in advance, merely leaving blanks to fill in the time, margin and name of the second horse. It was a foolproof system for beating uncomfortably tight deadlines. The catch to it, though, was that Gallahadion, a 35-to-1 shot, took the Derby.

No one tried to beat the gun on Native Dancer. But there still were more broken hearts in the press box at his defeat than any race in recent memory. His embittered swains couldn't help but recall that Money Broker, who finished eighth yesterday, had beaten the triumphant Dark Star by sixteen lengths in the Florida Derby only five weeks ago, Dark Star finishing thirteenth. And this, gentle readers, was the winner of the Kentucky Derby.

The course of true love never runs smooth.

GRAY GHOST IS HAUNTING TRIPLE CROWN

BY ALFRED G. VANDERBILT

JUNE 1, 2003 — Native Dancer's descendants have won six Kentucky Derbies in a row and eight of the last nine. Funny Cide, a great-great grandson, has a chance to win the Triple Crown in Saturday's Belmont Stakes.

The Dancer, which was what everyone called him, was my father's best horse. He won his first two starts a week apart in 1952 at the old racetrack at Jamaica, Queens. Then, the team of Alfred Gwynne Vanderbilt, his owner and my father, and Bill Winfrey, his trainer, shipped him to Saratoga. There he won four major stakes in 26 days, an average of more than a race a week. No horse had ever done that before and none have done it since. Today, resting three weeks between races is considered the bare minimum for a thoroughbred.

As John Eisenberg observed in his book *Native Dancer: Hero of a Golden Age*, "Racing was the nation's No. 1 spectator sport." Major tracks regularly drew 30,000 people on weekdays and 50,000 on the weekends. As Eisenberg noted, the prospect of seeing horses compete from thousands of miles away was also proving to be an irresistible lure to television buyers. Native

Dancer, the Gray Ghost, whose body seemed to shimmer on black-and-white screens, brought more people into showrooms than Milton Berle.

The Dancer and I turned 3 years old the same year, and my memories of him and his races have been clarified and enhanced over time by conversations with my father and, more recently, with Eisenberg and Eva Jolene Boyd, the author of *Native Dancer*. The Dancer went into the 1953 Kentucky Derby undefeated. He had run two weeks before, in the Gotham Stakes, and just a week later in the Wood Memorial, ridden as always by the great Eric Guerin. As the field came into the first turn in the Derby, the Dancer was in sixth place. Guerin asked him to move up, but a horse called Money Broker cut them off, going from the far outside to the rail in three short strides. It looked as if it had been done on purpose.

Guerin had to stand in his stirrups and pull his horse up to prevent a full-speed collision. The horses still made contact, and Native Dancer dropped back to eighth, almost last in the field.

To make sure he was clear of trouble, Guerin moved his horse to the outside. The race was now more than a third over and Native Dancer had lost a tremendous amount of ground. He ran the middle quarter-mile of the race in 23 seconds. *The Morning Telegraph* of May 3, 1953, wrote: "That is as fast as horses travel." By the time they reached the stretch, Dark Star—whom the Dancer had beaten twice and who would never win again—was gamely hanging onto a three-length lead with Henry Moreno aboard.

Native Dancer thundered behind them. The crowd roared and Guerin called for his horse. For several strides they gained no ground at all, then the big colt actually seemed to fade. Moreno used the milliseconds to move Dark Star from the center of the track to the rail, cutting off the Dancer's best route. It was a smart move.

As he sped toward the wire, Native Dancer found some unfathomable reserve of strength and he began to gain ground again. He had been asked for speed twice already in the race, he had been bumped hard and pulled up, moved to the outside, then forced to circle most of the field. He had covered more ground than any horse in the race. One enormous stride brought him to within a length of Dark Star. Another, and his nostrils flared at Moreno's fast-moving hands. With one more jump, the Derby and immortality—a perfect record—would have been his.

It was not to be. He lost by a head. As he walked past the winner's circle, Dark Star was being photographed and wreathed with roses. Native Dancer kept looking back at him, over his shoulder.

If all we gauged of the greatness of horses was a performance in one race—or even in the three great races of the Triple Crown—we would miss the most valuable lesson. They are what we would like to be: beautiful and fast and free.

A few years ago, visiting friends near my father's old breeding farm in Maryland, a distinguished-looking gentleman asked if I was Alfred Gwynne Vanderbilt's son. He told me how he used to drive past Sagamore Farm every day and see Native Dancer standing out in his field. "It was like seeing Winston Churchill out there," he said.

Native Dancer won the Withers, then a week later, the Preakness. Next was the Belmont Stakes, the longest race of the Triple Crown series and properly called the Test of the Champion. In one of the most thrilling finishes in Belmont history, the Gray Ghost caught Jamie K. and the master, Eddie Arcaro, right at the wire. It was one of the fastest Belmonts and, incredibly, the Dancer ran the second half of the race faster than the first. Losing the Kentucky Derby is almost always a quick trip to the bottom of a trivia deck. But for the Gray Ghost it was different. He defined the modern era of thoroughbred racing, winning with frequency and ease while dominating the news media's attention as no horse had done before him.

The public paid him a rare tribute when the horses were being saddled for the 1953 Travers Stakes. The paddock at Saratoga was unrestricted back then and nearly 30,000 people strolled in to get a better look. They clustered around Native Dancer, my father and Winfrey. Some reached out to touch the big horse. Some even tried to pull hairs from his tail. The situation could have ended badly, but the Dancer stood quietly as he had when he allowed me, as a 3-year-old, to playfully pull on his tail in his stall.

The stands and betting windows had all but emptied. Somehow, Guerin got through the crush and mounted, and the two went onto the racetrack to win by five and a half lengths. Native Dancer never lost again. He won the 1954 Metropolitan Handicap in what Joe Hirsch, the dean of American turf writers, called, "one of the finest races of the century." In his last start, at Saratoga, he romped to a nine-length victory carrying a staggering 137 pounds. If he had continued to run, the handicappers would have continued to raise the weights until either they beat him or he broke. It was reason enough for my father to retire him.

The nobility of great horses has always moved us. Asked to run at speeds no other animal can sustain, they risk their lives for a sugar cube, a carrot, or a pat on the neck—just so long as it comes from one of us.

There should be no question where Native Dancer ranks among the great horses. In the opinion of many, the Kentucky Derby he lost was the best race he ever ran. And, as it happens, he was avenged in this year's Kentucky Derby not only by Funny Cide, but by every horse in the race.

All 16 were his descendants.

Alfred G. Vanderbilt is a public relations consultant, a writer and a musician.

'HAD TO BE SOME HORSEMANSHIP'

BY DAVE ANDERSON

LOUISVILLE, MAY 9, 1988 — When his alarm clock buzzed at 3:30 yesterday morning, D. Wayne Lukas's first thought upon waking was not that one of his horses, the filly Winning Colors, had finally won the Kentucky Derby.

"No," he was saying now with a smile, "my first thought was, 'Boy, am I tired.'"

Tired from not having had enough sleep. But also tired of hearing the talk that he's silenced now, the talk that he would never train a Derby winner.

"I could take some shots at people," he said, "but that's not my way."

Outside Barn 39 on the Churchill Downs backstretch, the 52-year-old trainer was wearing a blue windbreaker, blue jeans and brown lizard boots as he held a folded brown leather shank. On Saturday, as he walked Winning Colors over to the paddock in his blue blazer and paisley tie, he was dressed like the corporate executive that some hardboots seem to resent.

"Going over, the railbirds were yelling, 'You're 0 for 13.' They'd already conceded that I wouldn't win this time," he said. "But on the way back, when I walked past the grandstand, the people stood up and applauded. Some of the same guys who had been yelling at me before."

This, too, is racing. Over the last five years Lukas's horses have won more races and more money than those of any other trainer in the nation. But his twelve previous Derby horses had been unable to do better than one third, Partez in 1981, his first year here. And his mod methods contrasted with those of three of racing's most popular trainers who had won recent Derbies—Jack Van Berg with Alysheba last year, Charlie Whittingham with Ferdinand in 1986, Woody Stephens with Swale in 1984.

"I hope this puts to rest all those theories that we were businessmen instead of horsemen, but with $17 million," Lukas said, referring to the record earnings of his horses last year, "there had to be some horsemanship there. The president of AT&T can't do it. Lee Iacocca can't do it. But neither can I save Chrysler."

Now, coincidentally, Chrysler sponsors the Triple Crown Challenge that assures $5 million to the owner of a Triple Crown winner.

"I think she's got a shot at it, I don't think it's impossible," Lukas said. "I think the Preakness fits her style more. I don't think we had her peaked here. We took a little bit of a shot here. We used the Derby as a springboard for a super Preakness, then we've got three weeks to the Belmont which favors a front-running horse. The Belmont is conducive to speed if they can stay on the pace."

"Sea Trek and Proper Reality were on each side of her and when they spread, she broke clear. In the backstretch, she was in perfect rhythm. You know how they run. She was relaxed and in her stride. Right about then I thought, 'Switch leads now, baby, switch,' and she switched."

But a filly has never won the Triple Crown, and a filly hasn't won the Preakness since Nellie Morse in 1924. Genuine Risk, the only filly to run in the Preakness after having won the Derby, in 1980, finished second to Codex, a colt trained by Lukas that had not run in that year's Derby.

"I'll be going back to the scene of the crime," Lukas said. "But that year we thought Codex was the best horse. I was grooming him. He was big, the picture of health. I knew that if the battle went to the strong and the swift, Codex would win."

Codex beat Genuine Risk by 4¾ lengths, surviving a foul claim against Angel Cordero Jr. by Jacinto Vasquez, the filly's jockey. And now Gary Stevens, a 25-year-old Californian who had been a high school wrestler, will be riding a filly with a chance for the Triple Crown.

"There are so many great riders around now," Lukas said, "but sometimes the mesh is more important. Maybe one rider will fit that horse better. I use a lot of different riders. I tell 'em, 'We're not going to get married, we're just going to do business for two minutes.'"

Three years ago Lukas used Stevens on Tank's Prospect in the Derby, but switched to Pat Day for the Preakness, which Tank's Prospect won.

"Gary is the 'now' rider," Lukas said, "but when he goes into a slump, I don't want him to take me down with him. The confidence level with riders is as important as it is with baseball hitters. I've had to sell riders on a horse, but I've never had to sell Gary on this filly. From day one he was a believer."

Lukas will also be training another Preakness horse, Tejano.

"Tejano's owner, Bob French, deserves the same shot at the Preakness with his colt that Gene Klein does with his filly," Lukas said. "But Tejano doesn't have the filly's speed. I think if we ran the filly at Tejano 10 times, that the filly would win all 10."

Lukas sounded more concerned about Woody Stephens's colt, Forty Niner, which finished second to Winning Colors, which the 75-year-old Stephens has derided.

"But after the race," Lukas said, "Woody told me, 'The filly's a good one, she's for real.' But he told me I'll never win five Belmonts, and I agree."

But who's to say that Wayne Lukas won't win five Kentucky Derbies? Or maybe even six? That would tie the record set by Ben Jones when Calumet Farm was in its glory with Lawrin in 1938, Whirlaway in 1941, Pensive in 1944, Citation in 1948, Ponder in 1949 and Hill Gail in 1952.

"Next year," Lukas said, "I might have three Derby horses. Tijuana, a Slew o' Gold colt out of Terlingua; Houston, a Seattle Slew colt out of Smart Angle, and Upstart, a Saratoga Six colt out of Kitchen Winner. I really feel like we're going to win a lot of Derbies."

Especially now that he's finally won his first.

SILENT SHOE'S LAST RIDE

BY STEVEN CRIST

JUNE 4, 1989 — It is a rainy Saturday at Santa Anita Park, and a tightly bunched pack of horses is turning for home in the afternoon's third race. The jockeys are jostling for position, waiting for a hole to charge through in a final burst toward the wire.

As the horseplayers in the stands start cheering their choices, the most famous and successful jockey in racing history makes his move. Sitting in a lounge chair in the Santa Anita jockeys' room, he disgustedly gathers up the playing cards in front of him and concedes another game of solitaire.

Shoemaker's hands have been shuffling cards more often than usual this year while his younger colleagues ride the races. This is his 41st season in the saddle and it will be his last. As he nears his 58th birthday, he admits that the big mounts have finally stopped coming. On this particular afternoon, he has just one ride on the nine-race card, a long shot he is riding as a favor for an old friend. The horse will finish far back.

His longevity and successes in recent years have defied everyone's expectations. Only three years ago, at the age of 54, Shoemaker won his fourth Kentucky Derby, becoming by far the oldest jockey to win the roses. In 1987, he enjoyed his richest season ever, riding the winners of more than $7.1 million. But last fall, after his best mount was retired to stud and his most loyal patron stopped having him ride regularly, Shoemaker decided it was time to stop.

"I can still ride," he says. "I think I'm getting buried before my time a little bit. But I don't want to be a hanger-on."

Last month, when Sunday Silence, a colt trained by Charlie Whittingham, won the Kentucky Derby and the Preakness, Shoemaker was a sad footnote to the races. He and Whittingham had been the most successful trainer-jockey team in racing history, winning more than 100 stakes races together, including the 1986 Derby with Ferdinand. This year, though, Shoemaker was never asked to ride Sunday Silence, who won at Churchill Downs and Pimlico with a 26-year-old rider named Pat Valenzuela on his back. On Derby Day, Shoemaker's only stakes mount was in the National Jockey Club Handicap at Sportsman's Park, a minor-league track near Chicago.

When Sunday Silence races for the Triple Crown, racing's premier event, in the Belmont Stakes this Saturday at Belmont Park on Long Island, Shoemaker will be making the first of more than two dozen farewell appearances at foreign tracks from Malaysia to Paris. He hopes to start a career as a trainer next year, saying he already has some owners lined up. He might even double as an exercise rider.

"I want to stay around racing," he says. "I enjoy doing this. The whole fun of it is to get a horse with some real ability."

He owns most of the sport's riding records, though none is secure. His 8,800 winners as of May 18 is the most imposing mark, but Chris McCarron is well ahead of Shoemaker's pace after 14 years and Jose Santos is ahead of McCarron's pace after four. Shoemaker's mounts have earned more than $120 million (of which he has received about 8 percent), but Laffit Pincay Jr. and Angel Cordero Jr. have both passed that mark in the last three years. When Shoemaker first led the nation's jockeys in earnings in 1951, it took $1.4 million to win that title. Last year, Santos nosed out McCarron with a total of $14.8 million.

It is unlikely, though, that American racing will ever see so widely recognized a jockey as Shoemaker, as much an international symbol of horse racing as Pelé was of soccer. Shoemaker's career spans four decades of American racing history. He has ridden champions and their great-grandsons at tracks that were torn down years ago. He is the last of his breed from an era when jockeys were as celebrated as their horses and welcomed into the pantheon of American sports heroes. In the 40 years since Shoemaker rode his first winner, the role and reputation of jockeys in thoroughbred racing has changed as much as the role and reputation of racing itself in the hierarchy of American sports.

Jockeys generally fall into two categories of riding technique. There are slashers, who furiously pump and whip their mounts and muscle them home. Then there are sitters, who coax and nurse a horse home.

"When I started out," Shoemaker says, "I was about the only sit-still jockey around. I might have been the first guy that did that. Today a lot more people ride that way, and it's better for the sport. Some horses respond to a strong ride, but you'll do better in the long run getting them to relax for you."

Shoemaker's quiet style in the saddle initially drew the scrutiny of California racing officials, who were concerned the fans would think he was not trying hard enough. But trainers liked the young rider's style, and he was deftly promoted by the agent Harry Silbert, who booked his mounts from 1949 until his death in 1987. Shoemaker was second in the nation with 219 winners in 1949, tied for the lead with 388 in 1950, and set a record that stood for 20 years when he won 485 races in 1953.

He was known then as Wee Willie Shoemaker or, more often, as Silent Shoe, because of his monosyllabic replies to interviewers. A decade later, after extensive oral surgery, Shoemaker admitted that his reticence was due largely to embarrassment over crooked teeth and a deformed jaw. He later became more responsive, but remains a tough nut with strangers and a quiet man even among friends.

His light touch with the reins has always been accompanied by an unusually even temperament. Jockeys often stomp off the track mad after a race, and many respond to a rival's bump on the track with a right hook in the locker room.

"Shoe never blew his temper," says Johnny Longden, who held the record for career winners with 6,032 until Shoemaker passed him in 1970. "He never lost a race that way and that's why you won't find anyone on the track who's his enemy."

The first horse to bring Shoemaker nationwide accolades was Swaps, who in 1955 became one of the first California-based colts in the modern era to win the Kentucky Derby. Swaps and Shoemaker set three world time records, and the colt was the first of Shoemaker's four Derby winners. Tommy Lee in 1959, Lucky Debonair in 1965 and Ferdinand in 1986 were the others. Shoemaker also won the Preakness Stakes with Candy Spots in 1963 and Damascus in 1967, and the Belmont Stakes on Gallant Man (1957), Sword Dancer (1959), Jaipur (1962), Damascus (1967) and Avatar (1975).

The ride for which Shoemaker will be most remembered was his losing performance in the 1957 Derby, when he stood up prematurely after mistaking a pole a sixteenth of a mile from home for the finish line. He realized his mistake after two strides but the error probably cost Gallant Man the race. The track stewards suspended him for 15 days but the colt's owner, Ralph Lowe, gave Shoemaker a new Chrysler and kept him on the colt. Shoemaker later funded a sportsmanship award in Lowe's name.

In the course of Shoemaker's career, the public's attitude toward jockeys and toward thoroughbred racing has undergone significant changes. A series of race-fixing scandals at northeastern tracks in the 1970's blackened the sport's image; these cases resulted in more than 40 convictions and suspensions. While many of the most prominent jockeys who were implicated were never formally charged, they spent their subsequent careers riding amid widespread suspicion.

The increasing role of television in sports may have hurt racing the most. The racing industry initially was reluctant to be televised, due to a shortsighted fear that on-track attendance and betting revenues would decline. A generation of fans and news executives grew up without much exposure to racing, and its fan base began to age.

Meanwhile, bettors throughout the game were undergoing a change of methodology that diminished the role of the jockey. Sophisticated analysis of horses' running times, once the province of a few sharpies, became popularized and adopted by a new generation of ambitious bettors. With such an approach, the raw abililty of the horse became the dominant factor, and the choice of a jockey seemed less relevant.

Shoemaker, however, seemed to transcend the change. While horseplayers were no longer paying as much attention to riders, Shoemaker remained the sport's most recognizable figure.

Shoemaker says he tries not to be bitter about the owners and trainers who no longer ride him, but sees in their attitude a change in the sport.

"Loyalty used to mean a lot more around the track," he said. "There was a smaller group of people in the game. Now you have new faces all the time and people just want to go with whoever's hot right now."

But Shoemaker holds no grief for the good old days of racing. He says that the game has improved significantly during his career, especially when

it comes to riding. "I don't know that the jockeys today are themselves better, but the techniques have improved," he said between hands of racetrack
rummy in the Santa Anita jockeys' room recently. "Riders ride with their
stirrups a lot shorter nowadays so there's less leg movement. They help
their horses a lot more instead of bouncing around on them. When you
have more control, you can have more strategy. When I first came around
people didn't think I was doing enough on a horse, but now I think most
riders are more like that."

Shoemaker is widely respected by his colleagues for taking a leadership
role in their welfare. He served for more than a decade as national president
of the Jockeys' Guild and fought for greater safety measures at tracks. Un-
officially, he has mediated disputes among California jockeys for the last 20
years. New arrivals ask him to appraise their riding and he gladly does so.
When he sits down to play cards for much of the afternoon, younger riders
like to sit by the table, hanging around for any scrap of insight.

When Shoemaker won the 1986 Kentucky Derby on Ferdinand, his
colleagues greeted him in the locker room with respectful applause. Almost to a man, they said that if they could not win the race, they were
pulling for Shoemaker to win it one last time. They certainly did not make
it easy for him on the track. Ferdinand, breaking from the inside post in a
field of 16, was pinched back at the start and then knocked into the rail
twice during the run to the first turn. Shoemaker gathered his colt up and
waited. He began picking up horses one by one down the backstretch, saving his colt for the moment it would matter.

At the top of the stretch, a hole opened and Shoemaker went for it a
split-second before the other jockeys did.

"Maybe that's where the experience comes in," he said later. "When the
hole opened, I didn't think about it, I just went through it."

He gave Ferdinand a little slack and the colt opened a clear lead and
drew away by more than two lengths at the finish.

It was Shoemaker's first Derby victory in 21 years and the first ever for
Charlie Whittingham, then 73 years old, and Shoemaker's leading patron
for the second half of his career. Whittingham has saddled more stakes
winners than any trainer in racing history, and until this year Shoemaker
has been on most of them.

Having had one of the most illustrious careers enjoyed by any jockey in
history, Shoemaker was not asked to ride a single one of the 76 horses who
ran in the seven Breeders' Cup Day races last Nov. 5. Only a week before,
he had casually announced that 1989 would be his last season of riding.

"I knew I was going to have to do it someday," Shoemaker said recently.
"It was later than I thought it would be. There was no one specific thing. I
just feel like it was time to do it."

Ferdinand's retirement and the lack of Breeders' Cup offers may not have meant as much as the fact that Whittingham was no longer using him regularly. Whittingham won 11 of the nation's 122 Grade I stakes races last year, but only two of them in partnership with Shoemaker.

"It wasn't my doing," Whittingham said. "On his best day, Shoe can ride as good as anyone and better than most. It's the owners. They don't want to ride a guy who's 57 years old. They pay the bills."

"I'm not as good as I was when I was 25," Shoemaker says, "but I'm better than a lot of 25-year-olds."

A POPULAR VICTORY BY OLD GUARD

BY GEORGE VECSEY

LOUISVILLE, MAY 2, 1993 — You see it at the Oscars sometimes, when a Hollywood insider finally wins the Academy Award. You can see the hometown crowd sigh and smile while bursting into applause.

You see it at the Super Bowl when Wellington Mara of the New York Giants or Art Rooney of the Pittsburgh Steelers finally wins it. They have paid their dues.

And you could feel it all over Churchill Downs yesterday, when Sea Hero commandeered the rail and won the 119th Kentucky Derby. Paul Mellon, 85 years old, is the owner, and Mack Miller, 71 years old, is the trainer, and neither had ever won the grandest American horse race.

"The Kentucky Derby is a collage," said Tom Meeker, the president of Churchill Downs, who works for the establishment, and speaks for it, too. "Sometimes the new people win it, and sometimes the old people win it. There is something for everybody. Mr. Mellon and Mack Miller have been so great for this business."

There have been a number of one-time wonders who came out of nowhere with a hot horse and won the Derby and strutted on Saturday night and moved on, which is fine. All sports are lightning in a bottle. Win it now. But the Super Bowl means something because people like the Maras and the Rooneys stuck it out, and racing exists because the Mellons and the Millers kept at this game, decade after decade.

Mellon has been in racing for 60 years, and is now the only owner to ever win the English Derby (pronounced "Darby"), the French Arc de Triomphe and the Kentucky Derby. He showed no sign of a gaping hole at the center of his psyche from never winning on the first Saturday in May.

"Sure, it's a disappointment," he said, "but we did win the Belmont two times." And besides, the Mellon family had other diversions to keep him busy. His private art collection is one of the finest in the world. His Rokeby Farm in Upperville, Va., is one of the most beautiful estates in the world.

His private jet was waiting at the airport, so when a British interviewer asked him what business he was in, Mellon did not have time to give a crash course on the history of the Pittsburgh Mellons, a bit of steel and banking. "Investments. I guess you would say investments," he replied.

Mellon had been to the Derby three times before, with Quadrangle in 1964, Arts and Letters in 1969 and Head of the River in 1972. He did not feel the need to send inferior horses to the Derby for the sake of the owners' box, and then Sea Hero came along. "I hate to say it, but this horse is not Mill Reef," Mellon said, referring to his horse who won the "Darby" in 1971. "You're lucky to get one like that in your lifetime. On the other hand, he can still do a lot more, so maybe he will be."

Mellon has recently been disposing of his breeding stock, and concentrating on racing. Asked yesterday if he regretted his decision, he said, "You mean, do I want to buy all the mares back?"

That sounded like a no. It also sounded like a no when he was asked how much he had bet on Sea Hero. "I don't ever tell anybody how much money I bet," he said pleasantly, accent on the "ever." Mainly what he wanted was a vodka martini. That wasn't bourbon, but somebody rushed to get him the drink. With two olives.

Mellon was also praised by Gov. Brereton Jones for his "good judgment" in maintaining a 16-year association with MacKenzie Miller of Versailles, which is pronounced "Ver-SALES" in Kentucky.

In 1936, Miller was taken by his father to the opening day of Keeneland, that gloriously rural and ritzy track in Lexington.

"I never even rode ponies," Miller said, but after a day at Keeneland, he was hooked. He started in racing "wielding a pitchfork at Calumet Farms" and he became a trainer in 1949. He lives in Aiken, S.C., and Garden City, L.I., but he keeps a home in Versailles. And in all those years as a major trainer, he had entered exactly one horse in the Derby. Jig Time finished fifth in 1968.

"It's not that I have anything against the Derby—I don't," Miller said yesterday. "But I only entered it if I thought I had a chance to win."

He rushed off to call his wife, Martha, who had stayed home in Versailles. "She said, 'I'm so proud it happened,'" he said in a very soft voice. "It caps off a wonderful life." Somebody asked Miller if he would like something to sip. "A bourbon would put me to sleep. Maybe a gin and tonic." On this day, the man from the Bluegrass could drink whatever he wanted.

ESSAY: FORGET THE ROSE BLANKET, I WANT A DERBY JACKET

BY WILLIAM GRIMES

It's always a thrill to watch the Kentucky Derby. It's an even bigger thrill to cash a ticket on the race. The biggest thrill of all, however, is to run a horse on the first Saturday in May and watch it thunder down the stretch, head-to-head with the best three-year-olds in the land.

I speak from experience. Remember Monarchos, winner of the 2001 Derby? He was one of mine. So was Barbaro, the 2006 winner, and Lion Heart, a runner-up in 2004. In fact, I've run horses in every Derby for the last six years, hoping against hope, screaming my lungs out, and, some years, almost tasting the prize that has eluded me, and so many thousands of others. I am speaking of the limited-edition Kentucky Derby jacket offered as a consolation to 25 of the top finishers in the annual Road to the Roses Fantasy Challenge.

The Road to the Roses has transformed my relationship to the Triple Crown. Created in 1998, it's horse racing's answer to Rotisserie League baseball. As the first Derby prep races get underway, contestants put together a fantasy stable of 10 horses (and another five later on in supplemental drafts), plus two trainers and two jockeys, who accumulate points as the season progresses through about 30 prep races. It starts with February races like the Southwest Stakes at Oaklawn Park and the San Vincente Stakes at Santa Anita and rolls right along through major tests like the Florida Derby at Gulfstream Park, the Bluegrass Stakes at Keeneland and the Louisiana Derby at Fair Grounds. Players can run a maximum of five horses per race, with points awarded for a win, place, or show finish. A win by your trainer or jockey also scores points. A Grade I race scores more points than a Grade II, and so on down through the Grade III and ungraded stakes races. The really heavy points are awarded in the Derby itself.

Six years ago, my wife, Nancy, and I founded Losing Ticket Stable. Having settled on the name, we began poring over the special *Daily Racing Form* supplement that lists every last triple-crown nominated horse (something like 450 of them last year), with past performances if the horse has already run. We searched out previously obscure Web sites, like bloodhorse.com and thedowneyreport.com, to ferret out obscure leads on possible dark horses. We studied the *Sporting Life*, Britain's equivalent of the *Form*, to get the dope on the Euros.

We started seeing the racing game through the eyes of owners and trainers. Outside, the ground was frozen solid, and the jockeys at Aqueduct were wearing gloves. Inside our house, we were sweating with Derby fever. We—which is to say, Nancy—studied until our (her) eyes glazed over, trying to separate pretenders from contenders. That million-dollar purchase and potential wonder horse in the Godolphin Stables? Would it really come over to the U.S., or would it spend the rest of its days staring at the Arabian sands? Which pedigrees suggested potential for a mile and a quarter?

This in itself was a loaded question. A horse that never makes it to the Derby can rack up big contest points in the shorter prep races A Derby loser can be a winner, in other words. Conversely, horses that underperform in the shorter races can come on strong in the contest's stretch drive, overhauling their short-winded competitors. The goal is to put together a stable of horses that can compete at varying distances, avoid injury, and stay on the Derby trail, but not the same horses that everybody else has. This is not easy to do. How many people spotted Funny Cide in February?

On the other hand, it does not help to throw out a "now" horse that piles up victory after victory in the preps. Nancy and I refused to jump off the cliff with Lawyer Ron, a horse with obvious distance limitations, who only went on to win four races in a row leading up to the Derby, including the Arkansas Derby. We stood firm against Smarty Jones, refusing to fall for the hype. When all about us lost their heads, we stayed cool. Eventually the horse would hit a brick wall, as the distances increased. This was obvious. Really.

The Road to the Roses is a marathon run over broken glass. There are the highly annoying Smarty Jones situations, of course. Trainers and owners can get together and take a promising horse off the trail. The mysterious Makhtoums of Dubai can refuse to ship their most likely three-year-old. Likely prospects, for whatever reason, never make it to the races. And injuries can decimate your stable.

In 2005, Corinthian, dismissed by many contestants, looked like he might be the gift that keeps on giving as he upset the field in the Fountain of Youth. (Yes, he was disqualified from first and placed third, but the future looked bright.) Then he suffered a minor leg fracture and dropped off the Derby Trail (only to come back last year and demolish the field in the Breeder's Cup Dirt Mile). Losing Ticket horses too numerous to mention developed nagging coughs, chipped nails, or unspecified attitude problems. Like elderly readers who turn immediately to the obituary pages of their newspaper, Nancy and I began obsessively clicking onto the injury report section of the Churchill Downs Web site. That is, when we were not tracking our performance in the overall standings week by week.

We seek glory, not riches. Well, glory *and* riches actually, but we'll get to that in a minute. The grand prize, considering that it costs nothing to play the game, is substantial: an expenses-paid trip for two to Louisville for the next Derby, a betting voucher of $5,000 plus assorted sweeteners, such as, last year, the "Rare Bobblehead Collection of Champion Thoroughbreds including Pat Day, R. A. (Cowboy) Jones, Julie Krone, Mike Pegram, Spectacular Bid & Nick Zito ($120 Value)."

Early on, Nancy and I decided that outright victory was an unrealistic goal. Because we are poor losers, we assume that the top finishers in the contest either work on the backstretch or are married to racetrack personnel. How else is it possible to field the top three finishers in one race and two in another on the same weekend? Only a pact with the devil can explain it. And who outside of Barclay Tagg and those guys at Sackatoga Stables would have picked Funny Cide?

But the jacket—$75 value!—awarded to finishers four through twenty-five is a possible goal. One year, when our stable was heavy with early-burners, Losing Ticket Stable rocketed into the top of the standings, somewhere in the first 50. That lasted for a week, and then the racing gods began picking off our entries one by one. Overhyped imposters like Lawyer Ron refused to lose, and our carefully selected sleepers failed to deliver. We discovered that it's possible to develop deep, lasting hatreds.

Andromeda's Hero, a stellar nonperformer in our stable, still inflames me when I see it stepping onto the track for a race today. Slam-dunk selections like the trainer Todd Pletcher enter into an inexplicable slump. One year, convinced that Bob Baffert, as always, would be using Victor Espinoza to ride his mounts, we selected Espinoza as one of our two jockeys. Needless to say, Baffert suddenly switched to another rider.

Here's the plus side. Getting in the game early, and studying hard, can earn dividends. Invisible Ink, one of our horses, snuck into the exacta at 55-1 underneath Monarchos (ours too) in 2001, igniting a $1,229 exacta. That will buy you a Derby jacket. Bluegrass Cat, whipped in the Bluegrass Stakes, stayed in our betting plans on Derby Day last year, and rewarded loyalty by finishing second at 30 to 1.

But it was the 2005 Derby that confirmed the value of the Run for the Roses contest, and the handicapping discipline it imposes. The night before the race, Nancy and I had to select five horses from our stable to run on Derby Day. One horse was on the bubble: Giacomo. Should we run him or not? Nancy, after agonizing, decided to go with Bandini instead. But on the day of the race, as we put together a few exacta and trifecta tickets, she found a little space for Giacomo after all. Not that he had a snowball's chance in hell of winning, but still—"If I don't bet on him, and he wins after I left him out of the contest, I'll kill myself," Nancy said.

And that is how the owners of Losing Ticket Stable cashed in on Giacomo at 50 to1.

William Grimes is a book critic for The New York Times.

PART IX

"Wherever the wire is, he'll get me there."
—Ron Franklin, Spectacular Bid's jockey,
after winning the 1979 Preakness

Funny Cide fans watch on television as he loses the Belmont Stakes—and Triple Crown—in 2003. AP IMAGES/JIM MCKNIGHT

Heading into the Belmont Stakes, Ron Franklin had every reason to believe that Spectacular Bid would join Secretariat, Seattle Slew and Affirmed as the fourth Triple Crown champion of the 1970s. Like them, "The Bid," was a 2-year-old champion the previous year, and winner of twelve straight stakes races. His trainer, Grover (Buddy) Delp, shared Franklin's confidence.

"The greatest horse to ever look through a bridle," as Delp was fond of calling him, Spectacular Bid was one of 20 horses that arrived at the grand old racetrack on Long Island needing only to run a mile and a half faster than his rivals to enter the record books. But it was not to be. Two horses, Coastal and Golden Act, ran faster, relegating the third-place Bid to the near-miss ranks. Since then, nine others have fallen one race short of immortality.

They've often done so in tantalizing fashion. In 1998, Mike Pegram, the owner of Real Quiet, suffered what was one of the toughest beats in all of sports. His colt had a four-length lead with a quarter of a mile left to run in the Belmont Stakes. Suddenly, his legs started wobbling while the appropriately named Victory Gallop made his move, catching Real Quiet at the wire. Pegram had to sweat out a photo finish, which showed his colt losing the Triple Crown by a nostril.

Pegram, who owns several McDonald's franchises, is one of the most affable owners in all of racing. When he visited the Kentucky Derby Museum the following May, it finally dawned on him what had been lost. The centerpiece of the museum is a video of the Derby in all its glory on a 360-degree screen. Pegram had watched it often, but this time, tears streamed down his cheeks.

"It dawned on me how close Real Quiet came to be never forgotten," he said. "It also reminded me how for those five weeks we were on the greatest chase in sports. It was a once in a lifetime experience."

Thwarting a bid for history can be at once thrilling and heartbreaking. In 2003, Empire Maker left Funny Cide's Triple Crown bid stuck in the Belmont mud. A year later, Smarty Jones hit the stretch of Belmont Park with a four-length lead and a record crowd of 120,139 urging him on. Behind him, however, Edgar Prado had a 36-1 shot named Birdstone in high gear. In 2002, Prado had been aboard Sarava, an impossible 70-1 longshot, that ended the bid of War Emblem to sweep the Triple Crown.

Almost as soon as he crossed the finish line a one-length winner, Prado reached out to Stewart Elliott, the jockey aboard Smarty Jones. "I'm very sorry that happened, but I had to do my job," Prado told him. "I'm happy and sad—sad because I was looking forward to a Triple Crown. This sport needs heroes."

Twenty-nine years after Affirmed swept the series, the racing world is still looking for a Triple Crown hero. The wait has never been so long.

THE DIFFERENCE A YEAR MAKES

BY RED SMITH

LOUISVILLE, MAY 6, 1979—One year ago tomorrow, an 18-year old apprentice jockey named Ronald Joseph Franklin sat in the home of Grover Delp in Laurel, Md., and watched on television while Alydar strove in vain to catch Affirmed in the Kentucky Derby. Three months earlier, Franklin had ridden the first race of his life on a mare named Pioneer Patty and she had won easily at Bowie. Things had gone well for the kid since then, but Churchill Downs on the first Saturday in May is light years removed from the thickets of Maryland. On May 6, 1978, Ron couldn't have imagined where he would be on May 5, 1979.

He knew that Bud Delp, the trainer who employs him and is virtually his second father, had a gray colt in the barn, a well-made 2-year-old named Spectacular Bid, but the horse had not yet run his first race.

Ron couldn't have guessed that about 5:40 P. M. today he and the colt would be thundering down the Churchill Downs home stretch with a winner's purse of $228,650 waiting at the wire and nine beaten thoroughbreds behind them.

Yet that's how it was in the 105th Derby where Franklin, publicly excoriated after the Florida Derby and threatened with loss of his mount, redeemed himself with a splendid ride.

"It would take an act of God to get this horse beat," Bud Delp said after Spectacular Bid ran into one blind switch after another and still won the Florida Derby for his eighth victory in a row. The streak has now reached 11 in a row, and the colt is the only horse in the world with a chance to win the American Triple Crown, and God hasn't interfered yet.

What he said about the colt and God wasn't all the trainer said in Florida. He called the kid an idiot for riding into those blind switches and threatened to take him off the horse as he had done for two races last summer after Franklin messed up a ride at Delaware Park.

Franklin had to wait almost a week before Spectacular Bid's owners decided to string along with him. That was two months ago, and ever since then trainers have been shaking their heads over what they considered a foolish decision. Ever since then, Ron has read the comments of those trainers in the press, has seen himself described as a blundering novice who would be at everybody's mercy in a race like today's.

Veteran jockeys accustomed to danger and abuse have compared the Kentucky Derby to a vast pressure cooker. They have confessed that the tension can be almost unbearable when the field appears on the track, the band strikes up "My Old Kentucky Home" and the crowd—it numbered 128,488 today—begins to roar.

Yet, "I was very confident going into the race," the kid said after the Derby, "because I knew I had the horse to do it with. I just let my horse do his thing and that's all you've got to do."

Many thought Delp might tell the rider to gun his mount away from the gate and try to stay in front, away from trouble. Franklin did better. Breaking from the third stall out from the rail, he tucked his horse back and steered him to the outside as Shamgo, General Assembly, Flying Paster and Lot o' Gold raced four abreast on the front end. He kept him out in the clear going down the backstretch, moved outside Flying Paster and General Assembly on the second turn, took the lead straightening for home and rapped the colt five times left-handed just to keep his attention as they drew away by almost three lengths.

What instructions had the trainer given the rider? "Don't misjudge the finish line," Delp said, quoting himself, "or you'll get a Size 10½ in the rear." Back in Florida when a change of riders was being considered, the first jockey Delp mentioned as a possible replacement was the gifted Bill Shoemaker, who did misjudge the finish line here 22 years ago.

There was a little bumping on the last turn when General Assembly bore out slightly and forced Flying Paster over on Spectacular Bid, but no foul claims were entered and no inquiries ordered by the stewards.

In 105 years there has never been a foul in this cleanest of all races, no matter who got knocked down.

Somebody at Churchill Downs must live right. After two wretched days of rain, the sun shone today from a cloudless sky, the track dried and the crowds came and bet till the windows closed. They even bet $74,393 on Great Redeemer, the maiden who finished last again.

From here the road leads to Baltimore for the Preakness and New York for the Belmont Stakes, second and third events in the Triple Crown series. If some newcomers show up to challenge him there, Spectacular Bid won't mind.

"He was laughing," Bud Delp said of his horse in the homestretch, "and looking for company."

TEMPER, TEMPER

BY RED SMITH

BALTIMORE, MAY 19, 1979 — The East-West confrontation that racing people have awaited eagerly since mid-winter still hasn't come off, but diplomatic relations between San Juan, Puerto Rico, and Dundalk, Md., are getting a trifle strained. Flying Paster, the California champion whose smashing victories in the Santa Anita and Hollywood Derbies established him as the nation's leading challenger of Spectacular Bid, could do no better in the Preakness stakes than he did in the Kentucky Derby, beating only one horse as Spectacular Bid ran off with the second part of the Triple Crown series.

However, Ron Franklin of Dundalk and Angel Cordero of San Juan had things to say about each other when the race was over. It wasn't the first time.

When Spectacular Bid won the Florida Derby in spite of an imperfect ride by Franklin, the jockey accused Cordero of trying to bushwack his mount. The riders hooked up again at Churchill Downs in the race immediately before the Derby, and Franklin won with a 9-to-2 shot while Cordero finished last on the favorite.

In the Derby itself, Cordero and Screen King were seldom within sight of Franklin and his winner, but when Cordero won today's seventh race with Franklin's mount second, Franklin made an unsuccessful claim of foul.

An hour later they were in the main event. Again aboard Screen King, Cordero carried Spectacular Bid wide on the clubhouse turn and wide down the backstretch.

Responding like a race rider, the 19-year-old Franklin dropped his horse over on Screen King, fetched him a whack, and went on to win as his horse pleased.

"I think the kid is getting about as good as this horse," said Buddy Delp, Spectacular Bid's trainer and surrogate father of the jock.

When a colt runs a mile and three-sixteenths and wins $165,300 eased up, his jockey tends to be tolerant, if not downright forgiving.

"When he started race ridin,'" Franklin said of Cordero, "well, that's all in the game. I jis' moved in and jammed him. He was jis' doin' his job and I was jis' doin' mine. Kin I have that drink of water now?"

"We was in good stride and everything," Franklin said of his jaunt around Pimlico's bridle path.

"We was just where we wanted to be." He said he had eased up on his mount in the homestretch or the colt might have broken the track and stakes record. On a track that was probably a second slower than the one Canonero II negotiated in 1:54 in 1971, Spectacular Bid was only one-fifth back of that mark.

"He woulda taken two or three ticks off the record if anybody'd made him do it," Buddy Delp said.

Tradition dictates that Pimlico management must send a case of champagne to the Preakness winner's barn. "I'd rather have a bloody mary," young Franklin said. Still he was fatalistic about the champagne bit. "Bud's gonna pour it down my throat when I get to the barn," he said.

Someone asked about Ron's plans for the evening. "I had eight hours' sleep last night," he said. "I'm just going partying."

There were only five horses in the Preakness and Spectacular Bid had already whipped the other four, yet this was a significant race all the same. The winner's time in the Derby had not been brilliant, and the people connected with horses that lost were disposed to blame the "cuppy" track rather than concede Spectacular Bid's superiority. By negotiating an off track in near-record time with nothing pressing him, the colt made a lot of converts, not only among the 72,607 customers but also among the losers' trainers and riders.

Nevertheless, some of them will be at Belmont June 9 to try to keep Spectacular Bid from becoming the third Triple Crown winner in three years. Ben Ridder, owner of Flying Paster, said before today's race that his colt would be at Belmont if he came back in one piece tonight.

"I'd like to win them all," he said, "but the Belmont is the horsemen's race."

"He can run all day," Sandy Hawley said of his Preakness mount, Golden Act, who finished second. "I think he's got a good shot at catching him at Belmont. It's been a long campaign for them all but mine is a powerful horse and he could do it."

How would Spectacular Bid like the Belmont distance of a mile and a half?

"He'll get me to the finish line," Franklin said. "There's nothing left to beat him. Wherever the wire is, he'll get me there. By now he knows where it is." Considering that this was the colt's 12th consecutive stakes victory, his rider could be right about that.

Spectacular Bid loves Pimlico. "He ran like this was his home," his jockey said. "He'd run over a rocky road if you asked."

"I'M ALWAYS READY TO LOSE"

BY RED SMITH

ELMONT, N.Y., JUNE 10, 1979 — Hung on the rail around the Belmont Park walking ring was a hand-lettered salute to Spectacular Bid's jockey. "Ron Franklin," the sign read, "is spectacular." Horse players were jammed eight or 10 rows deep around the paddock as the field for the Belmont Stakes paraded, but there must have been at least one fight fan among them. "Franklin will whip your tail," he cried as Angel Cordero, the jockey who moonlights as Franklin's sparring partner, was hoisted aboard General Assembly.

Nobody said anything just then to Ruben Hernandez on Coastal, but earlier in the week when the prospect arose that this colt might be made a supplementary entry, Buddy Delp, Spectacular Bid's trainer, said: "I beat this horse by 17 lengths in Jersey. Why is he coming in here?"

Delp got the answer yesterday, and he accepted it like a champion. Along with 59,073 paying guests, he saw Coastal ramble home on top in the 111th and richest running of the gaudy old cavalry charge, he saw his tired gray colt beaten back to third by Golden Act, breaking a winning streak of 12 straight stakes, and he saw his dream of a Triple Crown shattered. Then he went back to Barn 14, opened a can of Heineken and said:

"He may not be a mile-and-a-half horse. The best horse won. I got beat, that's all. Tomorrow's another day.'

He took a long swallow of beer. "I couldn't see any excuse for my horse at all. He was strong until he ran out of gas. I'm not shocked, I'm disappointed. I understand horse racing better than a lot of people do. I'm always ready to lose. I've lost a lot more than anybody."

Over on the front side of the track, the experts were already dissecting Ron Franklin's ride with the sure touch of sophomores in the biology lab dissecting a frog. "A turf expert," one definition goes, "is a baseball writer with borrowed binoculars."

"Around the racetrack," another says, "an expert is somebody who's been right once."

Now they were saying that Franklin pulled his mount's cork by sending him to the front early and going the first mile in 1:36. On the back side, Buddy Delp sipped his beer.

"The kid rode a fine race," he said again and again.

In a little while Franklin joined him. Trainer and jockey climbed into a car to ride back home to Laurel, Md. A woman handed Franklin a scrap of paper for an autograph. "Make it quick, Ronnie," Delp said. In the front seat, he reached across and scribbled his own signature below the jockey's. "There, lady," he said. "You've got the losers."

At just about that time, William Haggin Perry, who owns Coastal, and David Whiteley, who trains him, visited the press box. They had waited till the last moment to make their colt a starter, putting up $5,000 to enter him last Thursday but deciding only about 2 P. M. yesterday to pay the remaining $15,000 of the supplementary fee. That money was due because Coastal had not been nominated by Feb. 15, as the others were.

Coastal's training for the Belmont had been retarded. He had won two of five starts last year but finished fifth in the World Playground at Atlantic City in September, 17 lengths behind the victorious Spectacular Bid. He suffered an eye injury in the fall when he was hit by a clod, and didn't start as a 3-year-old until April 28. Running in blinkers, he won three times in a row, and the third was a smasher in the Peter Pan, which he polished off by 13 lengths.

It was that race that got Coastal's people thinking about the Belmont. If they didn't remember, there were others who reminded them how Counterpoint, Gallant Man, High Gun and Cavan had all used the Peter Pan as a prep for Belmont, had knocked off that race and gone on to take the big one. So they invested the $20,000—the other starters paid only $3,100 to get the post—and they got back $161,400.

Spectators were astonished when Spectacular Bid took out after Gallant Best soon after the start and went to the front early in the backstretch, though in most of his successful races he had run fairly close to the pace. When David Whiteley was asked about this, a trace of a smile touched his lips. He recalled that at the press breakfast last Thursday, Harry Meyerhoff, the colt's owner, had teased Delp by asking whether he thought Spectacular Bid could spring a mile and a half.

"Maybe they were trying to prove something," Whiteley said, "because the boy was riding him on the back side." He looked around at the assembled press. "You all been comparing him to Secretariat," he said. "Maybe they were worried about 31 lengths." That was Secretariat's stunning margin in the Belmont of 1973.

Beaten in the third and last leg of the Triple Crown series, Spectacular Bid joins a distinguished company that tired and fell back in the past. Starting 35 years ago, eight horses before him won the Kentucky Derby and Preakness but failed in the Belmont. They were Pensive in 1944, Tim Tam in 1958, Carry Back in 1961, Northern Dancer in 1964, Kauai King in 1966, Forward Pass in 1986 (though he finished second in the Derby and was moved up later when Dancer's Image was disqualified), Majestic Prince in 1969 and Canonero II in 1971.

"So your horse won't be remembered with Secretariat," a man said to Buddy Delp.

"No," the trainer said. "He sure won't be, but I'll remember him pretty good."

TOUCH GOLD SNEAKS IN TO STEAL SILVER CHARM'S CROWN

BY JOSEPH DURSO

ELMONT, N.Y., JUNE 8, 1997—After winning the Kentucky Derby and the Preakness in photo finishes, Silver Charm failed to complete his march into history yesterday when he was overtaken in the final 100 yards and lost the Belmont Stakes to Touch Gold by three-quarters of a length before a throng of 70,682 spectators at Belmont Park.

Silver Charm, the gray colt from California, seemed to have won the race in the homestretch when he caught and passed his old rival, Free House. But he simply did not see Touch Gold rushing past both of them on the outside. And, in a flash, the dream of a lifetime was gone: Silver Charm did not become the 12th horse to win the Triple Crown, nor the first since Affirmed did it 19 years ago, and he missed the chance to win the $5 million bonus that went with sweeping America's three classic races for 3-year-olds.

"I saw a shadow out of the corner of my eye," said the jockey Gary Stevens, describing the final seconds of the race aboard Silver Charm. "It was Touch Gold, and Silver Charm never saw him."

Touch Gold, who ran fourth in the Preakness after stumbling badly out of the starting gate, came back three weeks later to run a shrewd and strategic race in the Belmont. And he did it with a fiberglass patch wrapped around his left front foot, which he cut when he kicked himself during his disastrous start in the Preakness.

This time, he stalked the leaders during a slow pace and made the final

turn for home still trailing Silver Charm and Free House. But after a rousing duel down the homestretch, he executed his coup, running down Silver
Charm in the final strides. Free House finished another length behind in
third place.

"It's sad not to have a Triple Crown," said Frank Stronach, the Canadian horseman who owns Touch Gold. "But this is a competition. That's
what racing is all about."

The Silver Charm camp accepted the melodramatic defeat with grace.
Bob Lewis, the beer distributor from Southern California who owns the
colt with his wife, Beverly, said: "The horse is in a class that few reach. It
was a wonderful ride from start to finish. We'll go on from here.

"How can you feel downhearted when you win the Derby and the
Preakness and finish second in the Belmont?"

Bob Baffert, the white-haired wit from California who charmed the
public while training his superstar horse, tossed Silver Charm buttons to
the crowd before the race. Afterward, he said, "These people came for a
show, and they got it.

"Free House made sure he ran with us," Baffert said, reliving a rivalry
that has grown more intense through six straight races. And when Silver
Charm got a head in front in the stretch, he thought they were done.

"But he forgot that Touch Gold was out there too."

The chance for a sweep of the Triple Crown stirred the public's fancy as
no other horse race in recent New York history. The crowd, 20,000 more
than anticipated, was the third largest in the track's history and the largest
since the Belmont Stakes of 20 years ago, when 71,026 watched Seattle Slew
win to complete the Triple Crown. The record crowd was the 82,694 in 1971
who saw Canonero II try, but fail, to win the Belmont and the Triple Crown.

This time, the throng gathered despite unusually chilly winds and temperatures in the 60's and even though racing in recent years has been
marked by declining crowds and competition from off-track betting.
What they saw was a corking good horse race. All seven horses sprang
from the starting gate in good order but by the time they reached the first
turn a quarter of a mile away, Touch Gold had seized the lead by a length
over Wild Rush, his entrymate and the winner of the Illinois Derby, with
Silver Charm right at their heels. They stayed close for another quarter of
a mile but, after they had run one mile on the mile-and-a-half oval, Wild
Rush was in front followed by Silver Charm, with Free House third and
Touch Gold fourth. All were crowded together within a length and a half.

Chris McCarron, who rode a flawed race 10 years ago when Alysheba
ran fourth in the Belmont and missed winning the Triple Crown, had no
trouble this time remembering the words of Touch Gold's trainer, David
Hofmans.

"David told me not to be surprised if I found myself in front early," the jockey said. "He told me the horse was going to be aggressive and would want to run. I moved out and found a comfortable path—the rail was a little dead.

"The pace started to quicken. We all knew we were going slow. The race really began at that point, at the half-mile pole. And I had enough horse to be where I wanted to be. I swung out turning for home, and he had more energy than the others. But I knew Silver Charm was a fighter, and he just doesn't let horses go by him."

But before Touch Gold made his move, it was Silver Charm who forged to the front as the horses swung into the homestretch. He now had the lead, but Free House was staying with him, only half a length behind.

Third on the outside, and looming: Touch Gold.

"Chris used his head by staying away from Silver Charm," said Hofmans, a 54-year-old Californian. "That would have just pumped up Silver Charm.

"Silver Charm is the most dangerous horse to run against. He will eyeball you, and then run on."

This time, 100 yards from home, Silver Charm never got the chance to eyeball anybody. He was still putting away his old nemesis Free House as they roared toward the finish line, and he did not see Touch Gold racing from behind.

"I think that was part of the plan, not letting him know we were coming at him," Hofmans said. "Not giving him an advantage—that surge."

"My horse," Baffert said, "never saw that other horse."

VICTORY GALLOP'S CHARGE KEEPS REAL QUIET SHORT OF POSTERITY

BY JOSEPH DURSO

ELMONT, N.Y., JUNE 7, 1998 — The Triple Crown of horse racing slipped away from Real Quiet in the final strides of the Belmont Stakes yesterday, when he was run down and beaten by a nose by Victory Gallop, the horse who chased him home in both the Kentucky Derby and the Preakness. They staged a roaring duel down the homestretch on a brilliantly sunny and cool afternoon before 80,162 fans at Belmont Park, the second-largest crowd to see the race in its 130 runnings. And they saw a Belmont Stakes of show-stopping drama, the closest in the 20 years since Affirmed nipped Alydar by a head to become the 11th horse to win the Triple Crown.

No horse has completed a sweep since then. Real Quiet became the 14th to lose it in the final race in the series, and lost by the narrowest margin among those 14. Afterward, the stewards suggested that he might have been disqualified if he had won the race because he brushed Victory Gallop twice in the homestretch.

For the second year in a row, the trainer Bob Baffert was foiled on the threshold of completing a Triple Crown. He was thwarted last year when Silver Charm lost the Belmont to Touch Gold by three-quarters of a length. He was foiled again this year when Real Quiet was nipped by Victory Gallop. And in one of those twists of fortune, Silver Charm's losing jockey, Gary Stevens, became the winning jockey this year on Victory Gallop.

"Being beat at the finish line, it hurts a lot," said Kent Desormeaux, who rode Real Quiet in the Derby, the Preakness and the Belmont. "Nearing the finish line, I could taste it, and I even felt it for a moment."

Baffert, the only trainer who has won the Derby and the Preakness two years in a row, took his second straight loss of the Triple Crown with sad stoicism after weeks of a sometimes rollicking buildup.

"He just ran out of gas," he said of Real Quiet. "He ran a great race, but got tired at the end. I'm getting closer. Silver Charm lost by three-quarters of a length, Real Quiet by a nose."

Real Quiet ran a good pattern, but was undone by the rigors of trying to win three classics in five weeks' time, and by the distance of the third. He bided his time in sixth place at the start, while the speed horses Chilito and Grand Slam shot into the lead and kept it for one mile.

Then, as they rounded the turn for home, Real Quiet made his customary move. The big bay colt shot from sixth place to third, then drove past his rivals with majesty and headed home. He opened a lead of four lengths with only a quarter of a mile to go. "We felt we had to let Real Quiet make his move, and weather the storm," Walden said. "Don't try to go with him. He has such a tremendous burst, but let him go ahead and exert that energy and then see if we can come pick up the pieces late. That's exactly how it worked out."

It worked out because, with the Triple Crown within reach, Real Quiet squandered his huge lead. With a resounding finishing kick, Victory Gallop came looming up on the outside and made his late challenge.

They raced together for the final 200 yards, heads bobbing, rushing at the finish line. And as they crossed, Victory Gallop's head bobbed forward, and he won by a whisker.

The three stewards, who serve as race officials, delayed the result until they examined films, looking for contact between the horses as they neared the finish. They found that the wearying Real Quiet had indeed lugged out and brushed Victory Gallop twice.

They said that if Real Quiet had finished first, he probably would have been disqualified. It would not have been an easy step to take; no winning horse has been disqualified from a Triple Crown race for an infraction during the race.

John Joyce, steward for the state Racing and Wagering Board, said: "There was some significant lugging out there. We probably would have D.Q.'d Real Quiet if he had won." But he did not, and Real Quiet thereby lost the biggest payday in racing: $600,000 as the winner's share of the $1 million purse plus the $5 million bonus from Visa for a horse who wins the Triple Crown.

Baffert remembered how Real Quiet had been born with crooked legs and sold as a yearling for only $17,000, and later was dubbed the Fish because he looked so thin. "He flattened out at the end," Baffert said. "The Fish floundered."

CHARISMATIC'S BID ENDS IN INJURY AND DEFEAT

BY JOSEPH DURSO

ELMONT, N.Y., JUNE 6, 1999 — Charismatic, standing on the threshold of sweeping the Triple Crown, missed his date with history yesterday when he ran third in the Belmont Stakes behind the 29-1 long shot Lemon Drop Kid. And, worse, in a stunning finish to the saga of the colt who won the Kentucky Derby and Preakness at long odds, Charismatic fractured two bones in his left front leg as he crossed the finish line.

The injury did not appear to be life-threatening but it ended his racing career.

It also brought a sorrowful close to what had been a rousing day at Belmont Park, with a record crowd of 85,818 on hand in perfect weather to see if Charismatic could become the first horse in 21 years to win the Triple Crown. Instead, he became the 15th horse, and the third in three years, to win the Derby and Preakness but fail to cross the finish line first in the mile-and-a-half race. For Bob and Beverly Lewis, Charismatic's owners, it was the second time in three years that one of their horses came within one race of winning the Triple Crown. In 1997, Touch Gold passed the Lewis's Silver Charm with less than 100 yards to go to win the Belmont.

Charismatic, who ran in a claiming race in February before surging to the top of the 3-year-old racing world in the past two months, will undergo surgery late this morning. Dr. Larry Bramlage, a veterinarian from Lexington, Ky., reported that the colt had cracked the cannon bone just above the ankle and had fractured the sesamoid behind it.

"It is not life-threatening," Bramlage said, "but it definitely means his racing career is over. However, he should be fine as a stallion."

Chris Antley, the jockey who overcame problems of weight and substance abuse and made a roaring comeback aboard Charismatic in the Derby and the Preakness, quickly jumped off the horse at the end of the race and lifted the colt's injured leg off the ground. Antley was clearly shaken by what had happened and was tearful as he spoke. "He broke down right after we crossed the wire," he said. "He gave us a lot. He gave America a lot.

"He was running comfortably turning for home. At about the eighth pole, he let up a little bit. Then the horse from the outside, Lemon Drop Kid, came to us and passed us. I had stopped whipping. Heading for the finish, he suddenly dipped underneath me, and I could tell he was in pain."

The Belmont was the fifth stakes race in two months for Charismatic, who gained a reputation as an iron horse: fourth in the Santa Anita Derby on April 3, first in a record-setting performance in the Lexington Stakes on April 15, first in the Kentucky Derby on May 1 at odds of 31-1, first in the Preakness on May 15 at 8-1—and then, finally the favorite, at 3-2, in the fateful Belmont yesterday.

Lemon Drop Kid, a son of Kingmambo owned by Jeanne Vance and trained by Scotty Schulhofer, won the Belmont Futurity last September, ran ninth in the Kentucky Derby, finished third in the Peter Pan at Belmont after skipping the Preakness, and came roaring back in the Belmont under his regular jockey, Jose Santos. For one mile, he ran eighth while the filly Silverbulletday was holding a thin lead in a duel with Charismatic. A quarter of a mile from home, the filly grew weary, Charismatic made his move and took the lead, and Lemon Drop Kid nudged up to fourth place.

As they flashed past the finish line, it was a race of the long shots: Lemon Drop Kid, at 29-1, holding off Vision and Verse, at 54-1, by the length of his head. Charismatic was a length and a half farther back in third, but hurting.

"All week long, we talked about how maintenance-free this horse was and how durable he is," said D. Wayne Lukas, who trained Charismatic. "It's racing, these things happen and we have to deal with them. He had a good run, but it's unfortunate. It's not an easy part of the game."

And it was a painful ending to a race so full of anticipation and intrigue.

Silverbulletday, who had won eight straight races and 11 of her 12 starts and went off as the 5-1 third choice, set the pace for more than a mile in her tiring duel with Charismatic before fading and finishing seventh in the field of 12. It was her first race against colts, and her jockey, Jerry Bailey, eased off her in the stretch.

"We were taking a shot," said Bob Baffert, her trainer. "If she could slow them down, she'd have something to kick home. But when they turn for home after a mile in 1:36, they were just tired. We were afraid she'd get bounced around. Our only chance was to go get there and dictate the pace. I thought we could win it. If not, Charismatic would win it."

Bailey acknowledged that the filly had contested things most of the way with Charismatic and said: "I can't believe he ran away with her. It's tough to go head and head that far. It wasn't a killer pace, but you just hate to go eyeball to eyeball early in the race."

Lemon Drop Kid ran the mile and a half in 2:27 ⅗, paid $61.50 for a $2 bet to win and went home with $600,000. Vision and Verse, trained by Bill Mott, paid $44.40 for place.

Schulhofer also won the Belmont in 1993 with Colonial Affair, a victory that was also overshadowed by an injury to the favorite. In that race, Prairie Bayou fractured his left foreleg and did not survive.

"You can ask them to run a mile and a half," Schulhofer said, "but you can't train them to run that far. Either they do or they don't."

EARLY STUMBLE DOOMS
WAR EMBLEM'S TRIPLE CROWN BID

BY JOE DRAPE

ELMONT, N.Y., JUNE 9, 2002 — Maybe the Triple Crown bid of War Emblem was doomed early yesterday morning when word spread that his owner, Prince Ahmed bin Salman of Saudi Arabia, was not making the trip to Belmont Park to see if his horse could make history. At the Kentucky

Derby and the Preakness, the prince was there to meet his speedy black colt in the winner's circle.

But as soon as the gates popped open for the 134th Belmont Stakes yesterday, it was clear that neither owner nor colt would wind up anywhere near the winner's circle. War Emblem nearly scraped his knees after stumbling at the start, and from there the mile-and-a-half trip that was supposed to end in the record books only got worse. There was the dash between horses into the first turn, the skittish sprint up the backstretch to assert the dominance shown in the Derby and the Preakness. Finally there was exhaustion and retreat around the far turn as one, two, three and finally seven horses blew by War Emblem.

What had been a throaty roar from a record crowd of 103,222 gave way to muffled murmurs as Sarava, a 70-1 shot, ran down Medaglia d'Oro in the stretch for a half-length victory. War Emblem lost by more than 19 lengths, and Sarava became the biggest long shot to win the Belmont.

It was as if bad news had been given to a family gathered for a celebration. The record crowd had come to see War Emblem try to become the first horse in 24 years to complete a sweep of the three classic races, ready to toast the colt in his effort to etch his name alongside Secretariat, Seattle Slew and the last great horse to accomplish the Triple Crown, Affirmed, the winner in 1978. Instead, for the fourth time in six years, a very good horse could not make the leap to an immortal one.

Sarava, who had not run in the first two Triple Crown races, paid $142.50 for a $2 bet to win. The previous Belmont record was $132.10 by Sherluck in 1961.

Sunday Break finished third, 10 lengths off the pace.

No one was more devastated by the result than War Emblem's trainer, Bob Baffert, and his flummoxed jockey, Victor Espinoza. Baffert, usually an ebullient and flamboyant sort who had experienced this heartbreak with Silver Charm in 1997 and Real Quiet in 1998, choked up and let tears trail from behind his ever-present shades.

"It was lost at the start," he said. "If I was on the walkie-talkie, I would have told Victor to pull him up. I didn't want him to go a mile and a half like that."

Espinoza concurred. His head curled over War Emblem's ears as the colt nearly planted his snout in the dirt out of the starting gate. Jockey and colt bounced off Magic Weisner on their outside and then angled toward the rail with a hurried dash to regain position.

"I was thinking about where I could save him," Espinoza said.

But it was already too late—Kent Desormeaux aboard Medaglia d'Oro and Jorge Chavez atop Wiseman's Ferry, along with Mike Smith and Proud Citizen, had War Emblem walled off. The fractions were sensible—48.09

for a half-mile, 1:37:01 for the mile—but in War Emblem's three previous losses, he had demonstrated an unwillingness to pass horses when pinned behind them.

War Emblem tried this time, polishing the rail down the backstretch to gain a brief lead at the half-mile pole. But the extra effort was crippling.

"He doesn't like dirt getting kicked in his face," Ken McPeek, Sarava's trainer, said of War Emblem.

"HICKS FROM STICKS" NOW RACING'S ELITE

BY JOE DRAPE

SACKETS HARBOR, N.Y., JUNE 2, 2003 — Eight years ago on Memorial Day, after a weekend spent consuming several cases of beer, six old high school buddies sat on the front porch of this village's former mayor and acknowledged they were approaching midlife crises. Five of them were small businessmen and one a teacher, and their careers had been good to them. They were family men, but their children were growing up and getting on with their lives.

They were certain of one thing: they had enjoyed the heck out of one another's company since the days in the 1960's that they had played football and wore crew cuts at Sackets Harbor Central, the kindergarten-to-grade 12 school that still educates the children of this village of 1,383. In fact, three of them live close enough to a fourth, J. P. Constance, the former mayor, that when he blows a bugle from the porch, they know it is cocktail hour.

The Sackets Six are still arguing about which Phillips brother, Mark or Pete, came up with the idea to buy a horse over that fateful weekend in 1995, but it cost them each $5,000. They began with the simple goal of winning a race at Saratoga, or the Spa, long a nirvana for good-timers and gamblers, who flock there every August to, well, have a good time and gamble.

In the years since, they have been dragged through the inevitable lows of horse ownership—a bowed tendon that shortened the career of one prospect, the retirement to the show-horse ranks of another. But in the past four weeks, the Sackets Six have experienced what for most is the unfathomable high of the game. The star of their small barn, Funny Cide, captured the Kentucky Derby and the Preakness. With a victory in the Belmont Stakes on Saturday, Funny Cide can become the 12th horse to win the Triple Crown.

"Not bad for some hicks from the sticks," Constance said, beaming in his easy chair at his home on Hounsfield Street, a mere eight furlongs from Lake Ontario. The Phillips brothers, Harold Cring and Larry Reinhardt laugh along with him as they have nearly every night the past two weeks while playing host to the dozens of camera crews and reporters who have trekked to this resort town 31 miles south of the Canadian border to ask how it feels to hit the lottery.

"It's a true blessing," said Mark Phillips, 55, a retired high school math teacher. He knows about these things: he has survived two bouts with cancer. "You got some guys who know absolutely nothing about horses; I'm just learning how to bet. And here we go and win the Derby and the Preakness and have a chance to bring home some history. This has been the ride of our lives."

Indeed, the crew possesses little horse sense, with the exception of the managing partner, Jack Knowlton, who like Reinhardt and Mark Phillips is a member of Sackets Harbor Central's Class of '65. He owned and raced standardbreds after landing in Saratoga Springs as a health care consultant in the early 1980's, and took in additional partners, primarily friends and horseplayers from Saratoga, in the hope of playing the ownership game at a high level. Knowlton owns 20 percent of the partnership and his five childhood buddies own 4 percent each. Four other investors own the remaining 60 percent.

The partnership configuration was not confusing to the old high school buddies, but the name they chose for their operation befuddled at least one of them. Pete Phillips, a retired utility worker, believed for years that Sackatoga Stable was an actual place where the partnership's horses stayed when they were not racing.

There have been potential miscues that could have ended in misfortune. In the fall of Funny Cide's 2-year-old campaign, the partnership considered sending him to Houston for a seven-furlong sprint worth $275,000 as part of a series of races called the Great State Challenge.

Barclay Tagg, his trainer, was not keen on the idea because he wanted to rest Funny Cide, who had already won three times, until his 3-year-old season. He sent a message through Knowlton that going to Houston would compromise Funny Cide's chances of reaching the Kentucky Derby.

Much discussion ensued among the partners, who frankly thought that Tagg was out of his mind. Cring, who had been reluctant to put up the initial $5,000 until Constance chided him that he needed better fodder for his obituary, wanted to race in Houston so he could piggyback a visit to a sister who lives there.

"I was, like, the Kentucky Derby, that's pie in the sky," said Pete Phillips, who also was voting for Houston.

The discussion became moot when Funny Cide came down with a throat infection that he battled into January. Last December, there was another miscommunication that could have proved costly for the partnership.

Knowlton had discovered that Funny Cide was listed in the Kentucky Derby Futures Wager at the sports books of some casinos in Las Vegas. In the futures bet, gamblers can get increased odds months before the Derby on potential competitors. The hitch, however, is that if a horse gets hurt or proves not good enough to make the field, bettors still lose their money. Knowlton called Constance and told him that he was flying to Vegas and would make some bets on behalf of the partners. Checks were written and sent and, in all, Knowlton put down $2,000 in increments at odds ranging from 150-1 to 40-1.

"I thought Jack said we were betting on Funny Cide to be 'in' the Kentucky Derby and I thought, well, that is not too much of a stretch," Constance, 54, said. "When I got back the tickets and saw the bet was to win, I almost fainted."

Constance says he offered to buy everyone's tickets back, a claim that is raucously hooted down as false here in his living room. Instead, sometime after the Belmont, the partners will turn in their various tickets, which in total are worth well more than $100,000.

But each and every one of the Sackets Six insists that neither the last eight years nor the past few weeks have been about money. Funny Cide has already earned nearly $2 million, with another $1 million purse available at the Belmont and a $5 million bonus waiting if he sweeps the Triple Crown, but for the partners the smaller moments they have already experienced are what they will treasure most.

For Mark Phillips, it is the tears that ran down his cheeks in the winner's circle at Churchill Downs and the realization that the moment was priceless. For Cring, it is the postrace celebration after the Preakness, where the Pimlico Race Course bugler played "New York, New York" before the hundred-strong voices of friends and family from this tiny village belted out the alma mater of Sackets Harbor Central.

For Reinhardt and Pete Phillips, it is the scores of cards and letters they receive from neighbors and strangers who are enthralled that something good could happen to a bunch of regular guys who go to work every day. For Constance, it is those triumphant rides home from Churchill Downs and Pimlico aboard a yellow school bus, with his oldest friends all still enjoying the heck out of one other's company.

And for Knowlton, it is knowing that a midlife crisis was not only averted in the most spectacular fashion but that the good times will also continue for summers to come.

"You know, no matter what happens in the Belmont, we still got plenty in front of us," he said. "For all we've accomplished, we've yet to achieve what we set out to do: We haven't won a race at Saratoga yet."

EVEN INTO FUNNY CIDE'S STORIED LIFE, RAIN MUST FALL

BY DAVE ANDERSON

ELMONT, N.Y., JUNE 8, 2003 — Over the Belmont Park loudspeakers, Michael Cavanaugh was singing, "I'm in a New York state of mind." And whether they knew it or not, everybody else among the rain-soaked assembly of 101,864 improvers of the breed was singing it as they awaited the 135th Belmont Stakes.

Never had a New York–bred had the opportunity to win thoroughbred racing's Triple Crown. Funny Cide, a 3-year-old chestnut gelding from the Sackatoga Stable, has 10 owners, including six self-described "hicks from the sticks" from near the Canadian border. And no horse had won the Triple Crown since Affirmed in 1978.

But as more than one bettor was heard to say yesterday from under an umbrella at Belmont, "Into each life some rain must fall." Even a horse's life.

As all those cheers that greeted Funny Cide on the stroll from the paddock turned to groans, the New York state of mind disappeared. Funny Cide, the even-money favorite, lost the lead midway on the far turn and finished a tiring third in the mile-and-a-half slop as Empire Maker and Ten Most Wanted swooped past him.

"I don't know what happened; he won't talk to me," the trainer Barclay Tagg, alluding to Funny Cide, said grumpily on the walk back to the saliva-test barn on the backstretch. "Everything was going well. Maybe he didn't like the mud or it wasn't the right race. I just feel bad for all the people behind us. We had some wonderful feedback."

But later, after Funny Cide disappeared into Barn 6 with a white blanket over him, Tagg spoke freely.

"The track at Pimlico was a little wet but nothing like this," he said, alluding to the effect of close to an inch of steady rain by post time. "Either he didn't like the mud or he didn't like the race."

The jockey Jose Santos said the mud affected Funny Cide's ability to hold the lead he had from the start.

Had Tagg planned to try to win wire to wire?

"I didn't send him to the front, Jose did," Tagg said. "I was watching the fractions and the fractions were fine. I had no problem with him being in front."

Funny Cide's fractions were 23.85 seconds for a quarter-mile, 48.70 for a half-mile, 1 minute 13.51 seconds for three-quarters of a mile, 1:38.05 for a mile and 2:02.61 for a mile and a quarter. Empire Maker's winning time was 2:28.26.

In the paddock, the other five horses were walked around, but Funny Cide mostly stayed in his stall.

"I kept him there," Tagg said, "because all the guys were coming around, making a lot of commotion."

Asked where Funny Cide goes now, Tagg smiled and said, "Into his stall." But he added, "We'll give him a few weeks off."

At the souvenir stands at Belmont Park, there were Funny Cide T-shirts ($20), Funny Cide caps ($20), Funny Cide pins ($6) and Funny Cide buttons ($3).

"Any stuff for another horse?" a salesman was asked.

"Secretariat," he said. "But we're sold out of that."

Thirty years ago Secretariat won the Triple Crown with a 31-length victory in the Belmont Stakes, but it's as if he never left. In the paddock, there is a bronze statue of Secretariat in full stride ride atop a bed of white carnations—the same flower that was draped over Empire Maker in the winner's circle.

On the backstretch, Funny Cide was in Barn 6, next to Barn 5, where Secretariat resided. After Secretariat won the Belmont, he was in the state-test barn having saliva swabbed out of his mouth when a middle-age woman shook her head.

"They're treating him," she said, "like just another horse."

Secretariat was anything but. Secretariat was a celebrity, and he knew it. As he was being walked around the test barn that day, bystanders were snapping photos of him. When he noticed a camera, he would stop, cock his head and stare at the camera. After the flashbulb popped, he would turn and continue his walk around the barn.

"The same with the guy in here," said Bill Miller, the Pinkerton guard at Funny Cide's barn. "He knows he's a celebrity."

But when Funny Cide emerged from the test barn, his hooves plopping through the puddles in the gloom, he was no longer a celebrity. He was just a third-place horse.

ADORATION IS IN THE AIR AT A SMARTY JONES WORKOUT

BY BILL FINLEY

BENSALEM, PA., MAY 22, 2004 — As Smarty Jones galloped past the Philadelphia Park grandstand, the crowd was eerily quiet. There were some 8,500 fans at the track to watch nothing more than a Saturday morning gallop, and the reaction was not feverish excitement but hushed reverence. The crowd was in awe; that is what it has come to with Smarty Jones.

"I'm here for this wonderful Cinderella story," said Lois McKeown, who arrived at Philadelphia Park at 7:30 A.M. so she could get a nice location along the rail for Smarty Jones's public gallop. "He is the Seabiscuit of our times."

A crowd estimated at 5,000 turned out to watch Smarty Jones on display here at his home track in suburban Philadelphia after he captured the Kentucky Derby. But there was a bigger gathering on Saturday morning. Management again allowed fans in to watch the winner of the Kentucky Derby and now the Preakness gallop a routine mile-and-a-half in preparation for the Belmont Stakes on June 5. The official estimate of 8,500 seemed on the short side.

Some said they arrived as early as 5 A.M., and traffic was jammed on Street Road getting into the track. Souvenir stands selling Smarty Jones T-shirts and hats were surrounded by hundreds of fans eager to part with their money.

"Smarty Jones doesn't belong to Bensalem or Philadelphia or, no matter what the governor says, Pennsylvania," Bob Green, Philadelphia Park's president, said after Smarty Jones completed his gallop. "Smarty Jones belongs to the American people, and this is the people's racetrack."

The fans were young, old and every age in between. Some described themselves as hard-core racing fans; others were simply curious onlookers.

"We're in town for a wedding, but we thought we'd come to see this famous horse," Joseph Challenger said. "This is the first time I've ever been to a racetrack. I know absolutely nothing about racing. But when I watched the Derby and Preakness, I cheered for him. I was yelling, 'Go, boy, go!' "

Philadelphia Park had the biggest betting handle in its history on Preakness day, and Sal Sinatra, the director of racing, said the record would be broken again for the simulcast of the Belmont, with Smarty Jones having the chance to become the 12th horse to win the Triple Crown. Sinatra said on-track attendance could top 18,000 that day.

Hundreds of fans waited around for more than two hours after the gallop to listen to a scheduled news conference with Smarty Jones's trainer, John Servis, and his jockey, Stewart Elliott. With the fans outnumbering the reporters, the session became more a Smarty Jones pep rally than a news conference.

"I don't know if I'd use the term overwhelming," Servis said of the morning's festivities. "It's more a joy to me to see the people come out and flock around this horse like they do. It's great for the whole industry. I just hope it carries on and continues to roll. It's a great story and it seems to be snowballing."

Servis said he was delighted with the way Smarty Jones handled his morning exercise and he remained pleasantly surprised that the toll of the Kentucky Derby preps, the Kentucky Derby and his record-setting 11½-length romp in the Preakness seemed to have taken so little out of his horse.

"Today, he was awesome," Servis said. "He relaxed so good. I was a little concerned with all the people. Every day, he impresses me more and more. He was so professional, and that's what's making him the horse that he is. He's learned to really relax."

He said his primary worry about the Belmont was that Smarty Jones might be doing too well.

"My horse came out of the Preakness so good, my two biggest concerns are to keep him from hurting himself, and I don't want him too sharp going into the race," he said. "It's a mile-and-a-half race, so the last thing I want is for him to get rank early on."

Servis remained noncommittal about when he would ship Smarty Jones to Belmont but reiterated that he might wait until late that week, possibly the day before the race. That brought a cheer from the hometown crowd, eager to keep him around as long as possible.

"I'm here to see possibly one of the greatest horses who ever lived," Dan Dougherty said. "People here support athletes who come from Philadelphia. It's an extension of our competitive spirit. Philadelphia loves Smarty Jones."

AT SMARTY JONES'S CORONATION, BIRDSTONE MAKES OFF WITH THE CROWN

BY JOE DRAPE

ELMONT, N.Y., JUNE 6, 2004 — As Smarty Jones squared his chestnut shoulders and eyed that final half-mile to the history books, it looked as if thoroughbred racing really had a Big Horse. His jockey, Stewart Elliott, ratcheted the reins the way he had in eight previous victories and coaxed another gear out of him.

Smarty Jones, the winner of the Kentucky Derby and the Preakness Stakes, had a four-length lead. A Triple Crown, which no horse had won since Affirmed, in 1978, awaited at the finish line. Smarty Jones had repelled one challenger, Purge, early and another, Rock Hard Ten, heading into the far turn. Then he beat back a rush from a third, Eddington.

Elliott was peeking under his shoulder, wondering who else could possibly defy his colt from becoming the 12th Triple Crown champion. So was the crowd of 120,139, a Belmont Park record, as raucous and alive now as they were quiet less than two hours earlier during a moment of silence on the day of Ronald Reagan's death.

Becoming bigger and bigger in Elliott's rearview mirror, however, was Birdstone, with Edgar Prado aboard, a 36-1 shot. They were rolling down the middle of the track. Elliott asked for that one last gear, the one he had found at Churchill Downs and at Pimlico Race Course. It was not there.

"He ran and he ran," Elliott said of Smarty Jones, who had made him the most famous jockey that a second-tier track like Philadelphia Park ever produced. "That horse just came and ran us down."

Inside the sixteenth pole it was heartbreakingly clear: for the sixth time in eight years, racing history was not to be made as Birdstone rumbled past Smarty Jones and beat him by a length. Nobody said he felt worse than the winning rider, Prado, and trainer, Nick Zito. It was Prado who was aboard another impossible long shot, the 70-1 Sarava, who shot down War Emblem's Triple Crown bid in 2002.

Another Zito horse, Royal Assault, finished third, eight lengths behind Smarty Jones. "I'm very sorry that happened, but I had to do my job," Prado said. "I'm happy and sad—sad because I was looking forward to a Triple Crown. This sport needs heroes."

Zito, usually the quintessentially brash New Yorker, professed last week that he would be satisfied if Birdstone finished second to Smarty Jones, racing's breakout celebrity. But he was competing in the Belmont for the 12th time, and he desperately wanted more than the five second-place finishes he had notched.

Still, when he got it, he was muted in his jubilation, offering a heartfelt tribute to Smarty Jones. "He'll always be one of the most famous horses in America," he said.

Thoroughbred racing had been down this road before, but this time it was supposed to be different. In eight previous races, Smarty Jones had won at eight distances over five tracks by an average of six lengths. He earned the flattering comparisons to the only horse to complete the Triple Crown undefeated, Seattle Slew in 1977.

Smarty Jones, a Pennsylvania-bred, made more than $7.4 million in earnings for his owners and breeders, Roy and Pat Chapman. His

Philadelphia connections, the trainer John Servis, and Elliott, a 39-year-old recovering alcoholic, had shown that good horsemen come in all temperaments and from the most obscure corners of racing.

But soon after the gates opened, Servis, from his clubhouse box, recognized that Smarty Jones might not be up to joining Sir Barton, Secretariat and the rest in the pantheon of greats. As the field of nine entered the backstretch, Servis's stomach dropped when he saw that his colt was tugging Elliott down the backstretch.

"I was a little concerned," Servis said. "He didn't look like he settled as well as he had in his previous races. I wasn't feeling good down the backstretch. I was really concerned."

Elliott and Smarty Jones were challenged every step of the Belmont, a mile-and-a-half marathon called the Test of the Champion. It was Purge and Rock Hard Ten who prompted and bottled up Smarty, the 1-to-5 favorite, for the first half-mile. Jerry Bailey, aboard Eddington, took up the duel next. The pressure seemed to rattle Smarty Jones.

"I thought maybe if he gets on the lead by himself, and he'll relax, which he might have, but you know I had a horse on the inside," Elliott said. "Then I had a horse on the outside, then a horse on the inside again. So he never got that chance."

Six lengths back, however, Prado had Birdstone loping along as if they were alone on a Sunday ride.

Prado knew Birdstone liked this grand racetrack; the colt had won the Grade I Champagne Stakes here last year as a 2-year-old. He also knew Birdstone, a son of Grindstone, was bred to relish the added ground, even though he is a smallish colt.

"I hadn't really asked my horse," Prado said. "I was going to sit back and bide my time."

When Prado finally asked Birdstone to go, the colt unleashed a smooth paddlewheel stride that Prado aimed like a boat captain to the widest part of the river, the middle of the track. Suddenly, Zito and the colt's owner, Marylou Whitney, and her husband, John Hendrickson, felt this day belonged to them, not to Smarty Jones and thoroughbred history.

"I knew he was going to keep persevering, which he did," Zito said. "I couldn't believe it. I just kept saying, O.K., like they say, I'll take it from here. Honestly, I just had a good feeling."

So did the few bettors who believed in a colt who had won only one race as a 3-year-old, but roared home a winner here in 2:27.50 and rewarded them $74 for a $2 bet to win.

Last week, Whitney confided to friends that she feared that if Birdstone won, she, her husband and the colt they bred would be booed the way last year's spoiler, Empire Maker, was when he upended Funny Cide.

They were not, but a chilly silence descended on the crowd as Birdstone crossed the finish line, and it had nothing to do with the cool temperature. The crowd had come to see a magnetic horse with a catchy name join Sir Barton, Gallant Fox, Omaha, War Admiral, Whirlaway, Count Fleet, Assault, Citation, Secretariat, Seattle Slew and Affirmed as one of horse racing's greatest champions.

Instead, they saw a very good one falter in the third leg of the Triple Crown as 17 others had before him.

ESSAY: THE BEST OF THE "ALMOST" CROWNS SINCE AFFIRMED

BY STEVEN CRIST

Every time that a 3-year-old has been poised but has failed to become racing's first Triple Crown winner since Affirmed in 1978, his defeat has been widely characterized as heartbreaking, unjust, or at least a dreadful disappointment. On the other hand, did every horse who came close actually deserve to join the immortals, or was justice sometimes better served in defeat than it would have been in victory?

Since Affirmed, there have been 17 horses who won two of the three Triple Crown races. Swale (1984) and Thunder Gulch (1995) won the Kentucky Derby and Belmont Stakes but failed in between in the Preakness. Risen Star (1988), Hansel (1991), Tabasco Cat (1994), Point Given (2001), and Afleet Alex (2005) lost the Derby and then won the next two. It is the other 10, who won the first two legs but lost the Belmont, whose bids are remembered as near-misses.

One way to rank those 10 would be simply by how near those misses were. By that standard, War Emblem in 2002 was the least deserving because he finished eighth, beaten 18½ lengths, while Real Quiet in 1988

came closest, running second by a nose. That mechanical exercise, however, would miss the point. What makes some misses forgettable and others regrettable can only be gleaned from the broader context of how the
races unfolded and how ultimately good these horses proved to be. With
that in mind, here is how one handicapper would rank the 10, in descend-
ing order of worthiness:

10. **Funny Cide** (2003), the likeable New York–bred gelding, would have
    been a popular winner but the truth is that he was not even the best
    three-year-old in his crop. Empire Maker, who denied his Crown bid
    with an authoritative Belmont victory, probably would have won the
    Derby had he not been battling a bruised foot, and he toyed with
    Funny Cide in their two other meetings. Nonetheless, Funny Cide,
    like all 15 of the others who have won two of the three classics since
    Affirmed, was voted the nation's champion three-year-old at year's
    end.

9. **War Emblem** (2002) was a pure front-runner and he won the Derby
    and Preakness on the lead facing only mild pressure from the unac-
    complished Proud Citizen. The Belmont would be a test of both his
    endurance and resilience and he failed on both counts. After stum-
    bling at the start, he was unable to contend early and packed it in late.

8. **Charismatic** (1999) had the most poignant failure because he broke
    down while in contention in the stretch of the Belmont, but he had ac-
    complished little before the Triple Crown and did not appear to be en
    route to victory when the injury occurred. None of his handlers or
    jockeys mention him in the same breath as the best horses they have
    been around.

7. **Pleasant Colony** (1981) was a colt who got good at the right time,
    blossoming in the spring just when things began to go wrong with the
    other top colts in his crop. He was a good racehorse and a worthy
    three-year-old champion but has never been given serious considera-
    tion for racing's Hall of Fame in the twenty years since he became eli-
    gible for induction.

6. **Smarty Jones** (2004) ran as gallant a Belmont in defeat as any of these,
    finishing second to Birdstone after fighting off multiple challenges
    while receiving a highly questionable ride. The question remains how
    good he really was, though. He ducked top competition before the
    Triple Crown; benefited from a sloppy track on Derby Day and very

weak opposition in the Preakness; and was routinely lionized well beyond his accomplishments by promoters and broadcasters who tried to
paint him as a blue-collar longshot that he never really was.

5. **Real Quiet** (1998) may well have the lost the Crown when jockey
    Kent Desormeaux made a premature move to open a five-length lead
    that evaporated an inch or two too soon as Derby and Preakness
    runner-up Victory Gallop ran him down in the tightest of photo fin-
    ishes. Still, Real Quiet retired with a career record of just six victories
    in 20 starts, hardly the stuff of greatness.

4. **Silver Charm** (1997) was a better horse than any of those listed
    above, earned more money than any horse on the list, and accom-
    plished more than most of them, but his Belmont defeat was no injus-
    tice. He was run down by Touch Gold, who would have beaten him in
    the Preakness had he not gotten into a world of trouble. Silver Charm
    went on to become a Hall of Fame–caliber horse, but he wasn't quite
    as good as Touch Gold in the spring of 1997.

3. **Alysheba** (1987) was undoubtedly a great horse but he proved it more
    as a four-year-old than he did at three, when he edged Bet Twice in the
    Derby and Preakness but then was a distant fourth behind him in
    the Belmont. He was a bit like Silver Charm, turning into an even
    faster horse at four, but was slightly better on his best day. Alysheba
    also emerged as the king of what is widely considered the deepest
    three-year-old crop in the last 40 years, a group that also included Bet
    Twice, Cryptoclearance, Demons Begone, Gulch, Lost Code, Java
    Gold, and Polish Navy.

2. **Sunday Silence** (1989) virtually shares this spot with his great rival,
    Easy Goer, either one of whom would have been a clear and worthy
    addition to the roster of Triple Crown winners had they not been born
    the same year, similar to Affirmed and Alydar in 1978. There has been
    no rivalry as compelling as theirs in the years since, and both are right-
    fully in the Hall of Fame, along with Alysheba and the final horse on
    this list:

1. **Spectacular Bid** (1979) would have been the third straight Triple
    Crown winner following Seattle Slew in 1977 and Affirmed, but some-
    thing went hideously wrong on Belmont Day. Whether it was prima-
    rily the terrible ride he received or the safety pin his trainer later said
    he stepped on the morning of the Belmont, Spectacular Bid simply did

not run his race, but spent the rest of his career proving he was in the same league as Secretariat, Seattle Slew, and Affirmed. His four-year-old season in 1980, when he was undefeated and set track records that still stand, may have been the greatest single campaign by any American racehorse.

If indeed there are custodial deities who watch over the Triple Crown and award it only sparingly, they may have been too stingy when it came to Silver Charm, Alysheba, and Sunday Silence or Easy Goer. If they got together after Spectacular Bid was retired at the end of 1980, however, and decreed that no Triple Crown would be awarded until a better horse came along, they have simply been true to their word.

Steven Crist, who covered horse racing for The New York Times *from 1981 to 1990, is the publisher and columnist for* Daily Racing Form.

PART X

"You have to have some divine intervention."
—Steve Cauthen, on what it takes to make a Triple Crown winner.

Citation (the first thoroughbred to win a million dollars) enjoys his retirement at Calumet Farm, September 1951. AP IMAGES

The thirty years since Affirmed became the last Triple Crown champion have not lacked for opinions about why there has not been another one, or if there ever will be another one.

Breeding practices have been scrutinized: Has the industry replaced stamina with fragility in search of fast and precocious horses that fetch more money? How a horse is trained en route to the big races has been examined and re-examined. What is a better—a lightly raced, fresher horse or a seasoned one tested by six to nine previous races?

Some have even suggested changes in the format of the series. They propose making the Derby a mile and a sixteenth, the Preakness a mile and an eighth and shortening the mile-and-a-half Belmont Stakes to a mile and a quarter. Others have asked why not run each leg a month apart or even in the fall when these youngsters are more mature? Or limit them to four-year-old Thoroughbreds rather than still-developing three-year-olds.

So just what does it take to win the Triple Crown, a feat in sport, Jim Squires writes, of which "there can be no more demanding test of talent, endurance and luck"?

Shortly before the Belmont Stakes a few years ago, a group of people whose horses won the Derby, the Preakness and the Belmont in the 1970's—a decade that could be called the Triple Crown's golden age—gave their views, and discussed differences between then and now. They decried the current emphasis on speed over endurance. In their day, these veterans said, racehorses competed more often and were thus tougher. Yet they often received more individual attention. And they pointed to a link between their horses and Belmont Park, where the sweeping turns and that long stretch run have spelled heartbreak for so many. "It's no accident Secretariat, Slew and Affirmed all were at home there," said Mickey Taylor, who owned Seattle Slew with his wife, Karen.

This is, of course, all conjecture. We will know for sure what it takes to make a Triple Crown champion the next time we see one, and perhaps the long wait will make us appreciate it all the more.

"In other sporting events, like the World Series, there is not infrequently the sense that the winner is merely the best of a mediocre field in a mediocre season," Laura Hillenbrand writes. "In this respect, Thoroughbred racing stands alone. Deserving horses have lost the Triple Crown, but no undeserving horse has ever won it, and none ever will."

THE TRIPLE CROWN: FIVE VIEWS FROM THE SADDLE

BY JOSEPH DURSO

JUNE 1, 1997 — Following are the memories of the five surviving Triple Crown–winning jockeys, who were asked what made their horses special enough to win all three classics and what they remembered about the Belmont Stakes, the race that clinched their role in history:

WHIRLAWAY—1941
EDDIE ARCARO, 81, LIVING IN MIAMI

"Whirlaway had great natural speed, he was really a speed horse. But he had a great trainer, Ben Jones, who turned him around so that he would save his speed until it counted the most. It wasn't stamina that won him the Triple Crown. It was timing his move, his speed. He did it in all three races. He was that special.

"Before the Kentucky Derby, I remember Ben Jones telling me: You listen to me, it's the only way we'll win the Derby. He's got one shot. He can run three-eighths faster than any horse in the country. When the man throws the gate open, you stop him or he'll never finish. Don't put the bit against his mouth. Don't pick up the reins. Let him be last. He'll hope, but let him. And don't ever get excited and pick up the reins before the half-mile pole. When he gets there, make his move. He can run that far.

"In the Belmont I stopped him leaving the gate. Down the backside, we were dead last. We were so far back, I couldn't even see the leader. I thought I was crazy to be doing it. But I could still hear Ben Jones's warning: let him stop. No horse can run three-eighths as fast as he can. But don't let him run until the stretch.

"And by the time we were turning for home, he was flying. I put him on the outside, and he was rolling. He ran the last quarter-mile in 23 seconds. There were only three other horses in the race, and he put them all away.

"Ben's son, Jimmy Jones, put it this way before the Belmont: Listen, don't be Eddie Arcaro. Don't be Jimmy Jones. Hold him back. But when you let him run, I want you in the middle of the track, out where he'll see nothing but daylight."

CITATION—1948
EDDIE ARCARO

"Citation was the horse with no weakness. You could make four runs with him, not just one, as with Whirlaway. If anybody tried to run with him, he'd kill them off. He could run four miles. Of all the horses I ever rode, he could start and stop and start again four times in one race. He'd give me the bit back.

"He had great strength. You could do 14 things with him, and he'd respond to all of them. When he was 2 years old, he won 8 of 9 races. When he was 3, he won 19 of 20. I can remember, we used to have four weeks between the Preakness and Belmont, and Jimmy Jones decided to run him in a race. He said: 'Why not? He'll need a workout, anyway.' In the prep, the other jockeys took me to the outside fence. I stayed there, and he won.

"In the paddock before the Belmont, Ben Jones asked, 'What are you going to do with him?' I said that I was concerned that he'd make three or four separate runs. I'd only ridden him three times by then. I said, everybody in this race is going to take a shot at me. And Ben said: 'What difference does it make? He's much the best.' There wasn't any pace for him in the Belmont. I got him back to third or fourth, where he could relax and look around. I sat there, then I put him together, and he started to fly. He won by eight lengths."

SECRETARIAT—1973
RON TURCOTTE, 56, LIVING IN NEW BRUNSWICK, CANADA

"He was one of a kind. Very strong, exceptionally fast, remarkably power-ful. He could take the lead and hold it, or he could come from behind and win it. You could place him anywhere.

"He could handle all kinds of tracks, run all distances. One other thing you need is a special trainer, a professional, and Lucien Laurin was pre-cisely that. He could train the horse under pressure. The year before Sec-retariat, he trained Riva Ridge, who won the Kentucky Derby and the Belmont. The next year, Secretariat.

"Secretariat not only won all three races in the Triple Crown, he won them in record time. In the Kentucky Derby, I took it easy with him be-cause I didn't think he'd gotten enough out of the Wood Memorial. In the Preakness, I thought they were all going too slow, and he still set a record. In the Belmont, well, you know how far he ran and how fast.

"In the Belmont too many people have it in their minds that you have to conserve your horse to go a mile and a half. But I never believed in choking a horse. He had trained so superbly, he was just coming up to his own peak. When we got under way, there were only five horses in the race, and I was amazed at how easily he was running, and leading. I never asked him to run. I clucked to him in the last few yards, that was all. He was 31 lengths in front."

SEATTLE SLEW—1977
JEAN CRUGUET, 56, LIVING IN LEXINGTON, KY.

"You could do whatever you wanted to do with Seattle Slew. Anytime, any-thing. Yes, he had great speed. Yes, he had great courage, a very brave horse. He also had great stamina. But he was able to do whatever you wanted, and that's why he was the best from the start.

"I guess that's a sense. He had the sense of doing what the rider wanted. If you asked, he gave. He had to learn what you wanted. But he learned quickly, and he didn't forget.

"You can't do that with all horses. But Seattle Slew was extremely adaptable, besides all that speed and strength and character. You could tell it when he was 2 years old, and everybody came running at him.

"In the Belmont he led from the start by as much as four lengths. I had no doubt that he could go a mile and a half. But when he turned into the stretch, I knew he was home free. Not all horses run when you want them to run. But he never did anything less.

"He ran the first quarter in 24⅕ seconds, the half-mile in 48⅖, the three-quarters in 1:14, the mile in 1:38⅖. At the top of the stretch, Slew had a four-length lead on Run Dusty Run, who had chased him home in the Kentucky Derby and run third in the Preakness. And this day, he was there again, but second again to that magnificent horse."

AFFIRMED—1978
STEVE CAUTHEN, 37, LIVING IN VERONA, KY.

"Affirmed was an all-round athlete with great intelligence, and you could place him wherever you wanted in a race. People doubt that horses have much intelligence, but I think they do. They show it by showing a presence. By liking the people around them. They know they're good, and they like what's going around them. Affirmed used to enjoy it when photographers started taking his picture; he'd pose for them.

"He took it the way an educated person would. If you see another Triple Crown winner, you'll notice his stage presence.

"In the Belmont we were up against Alydar again, just as we were in the Kentucky Derby and the Preakness. So I knew we couldn't afford any mistakes. They hooked up with seven-eighths of a mile to go, and at one point in the homestretch, Alydar got his neck in front. They were this beautifully matched: In the Derby, I never really saw Alydar until I saw the replay. He made up a lot of ground in the last 150 yards, but I knew I had that race won. In the Preakness, I saw him from the head of the lane, and it was a fight to the finish. In the Belmont, I knew he was there with seven furlongs to run, and he stayed there, stride for stride.

"Affirmed may not have been an imposing individual to look at. But he had exceptional courage and intelligence and the desire to win."

COMPLETING THE TRIPLE

The 11 Triple Crown winners raced the same distances for each event except Sir Barton in 1919. That year, the Preakness was a mile and an eighth instead of a mile and three-sixteenths and the Belmont a mile and three-eighths instead of a mile and a half.

1919: Sir Barton
Jockey: John Loftus
Trainer: H. G. Bedwell

RACE - TIME - MARGIN - 2D PLACE
Kentucky Derby - 2:09 ⅘ - 5 lengths - Billy Kelly
Preakness - 1:53 - 4 lengths - Eternal
Belmont - 2:17 ⅔ - 5 lengths - Sweep On

1930: Gallant Fox
Jockey: Earl Sande
Trainer: J. E. Fitzsimmons
RACE - TIME - MARGIN - 2D PLACE
Kentucky Derby - 2:07 ⅗ - 2 lengths - Gallant Knight
Preakness - 2:00 ⅗ - ¾ length - Crack Brigade
Belmont - 2:31 ⅗ - 3 lengths - Whichone

1935: Omaha
Jockey: William Saunders
Trainer: J. E. Fitzsimmons
RACE - TIME - MARGIN - 2D PLACE
Kentucky Derby - 2:05 - 1½ lengths - Roman Solider
Preakness - 1:58 ⅖ - 6 lengths - Firethorn
Belmont - 2:30 ⅗ - 1½ lengths - Firethorn

1937: War Admiral
Jockey: Charles Kurtsinger
Trainer: George Conway
RACE - TIME - MARGIN - 2D PLACE
Kentucky Derby - 2:03 ⅕ - ¾ lengths - Pompoon
Preakness - 1:58 ⅖ - head - Pompoon
Belmont - 2:28 ⅗ - 3 lengths - Sceneshifter

1941: Whirlaway
Jockey: Eddie Arcaro
Trainer: Ben Jones
RACE - TIME - MARGIN - 2D PLACE
Kentucky Derby - 2:01 ⅖ - 8 lengths - Staretor
Preakness - 1:58 ⅘ - 5½ lengths - King Cole
Belmont - 2:31 - 2½ lengths - Robert Morris

1943: Count Fleet
Jockey: Johnny Longden
Trainer: Don Cameron
RACE - TIME - MARGIN - 2D PLACE
Kentucky Derby - 2:04 - 3 lengths - Blue Swords
Preakness - 1:57 ⅖ - 8 lengths - Blue Swords
Belmont - 2:28 ⅕ - 25 lengths - Fairy Manhurst

1946: Assault
Jockey: Warren Mehrtens
Trainer: Max Hirsch
RACE - TIME - MARGIN - 2D PLACE
Kentucky Derby - 2:05 ⅖ - 3 ½ lengths - Coaltown
Preakness - 2:01 ⅖ - neck - Lord Boswell
Belmont - 2:30 ⅘ - 3 lengths - Natchez

1948: Citation
Jockey: Eddie Arcaro
Trainer: Jimmy Jones
RACE - TIME - MARGIN - 2D PLACE
Kentucky Derby - 2:05 ⅖ - 3 ½ lengths - Coaltown
Preakness - 2:02 ⅖ - 5 ½ lengths - Vulcan's Forge
Belmont - 2:28 ⅕ - 8 lengths - Better Self

1973: Secretariat
Jockey: Ron Turcotte
Trainer: Lucien Laurin
RACE - TIME - MARGIN - 2D PLACE
Kentucky Derby - 1:59 ⅖ - 2 ½ lengths - Sham
Preakness - 1:54 ⅖ - 2 ½ lengths - Sham
Belmont - 2:24 - 31 lengths - Twice a Prince

1977: Seattle Slew
Jockey: Jean Cruguet
Trainer: Billy Turner
RACE - TIME - MARGIN - 2D PLACE
Kentucky Derby - 2:02 ⅕ - 1¼ lengths - Run Dusty Run
Preakness - 1:54 ⅖ - 1 ½ lengths - Iron Constitution
Belmont - 2:29 ⅗ - 4 lengths - Run Dusty Run

1978: Affirmed
Jockey: Steve Cauthen
Trainer: Laz Barrera
RACE - TIME - MARGIN - 2D PLACE
Kentucky Derby - 2:01 ⅕ - 1 ½ lengths - Alydar
Preakness - 1:54 ⅖ - neck - Alydar
Belmont - 2:26 ⅘ - head - Alydar

TRIPLE CROWN INSIDERS SHARE
SUCCESS RECIPE

BY JOE DRAPE

JUNE 10, 2006 — The 138th running of the Belmont Stakes will be a bittersweet affair today for a small fraternity of people with direct links to the most recent Triple Crown champions. Penny Chenery, Mickey Taylor and Patrice Wolfson owned Secretariat, Seattle Slew and Affirmed. All of those horses have died. Billy Turner trained Slew, and Steve Cauthen rode Affirmed.

Each knows what an immortal horse looks like and the title that sets him apart: Triple Crown champion. No matter who wins the Belmont today, his connections will not join this rarefied club.

This year's Kentucky Derby winner, Barbaro, is recovering from surgery to his right hind leg, which was shattered by a catastrophic misstep in the opening yards of the Preakness Stakes on May 20. That race's winner, Bernardini, is not running in the Belmont, either, as his owner, Sheik Mohammed bin Rashid al-Maktoum, the crown prince of Dubai, decided to give the colt a rest.

The last Triple Crown triumph came in 1978, and the only direct link to it comes from the small group of owners, jockeys and trainers who were part of the three Triple Crown triumphs of the 1970's. This group does not want to write an obituary for a feat that appears increasingly impossible. Instead, its members prefer to offer a recipe for how horse racing can crown its 12th Triple Crown champion.

The recipe begins with the intentions of breeders, demands the attention of trainers, but ultimately may rely on the most intangible element of all: good fortune.

"You have to have some divine intervention," said Cauthen, who rode Affirmed, the last horse to sweep the series, in 1978. "I'm not sure a Triple Crown champion, or any other great athlete, can be human-made. Someone like Michael Jordan comes around once in a lifetime, and it may be the same for great horses."

The 1970's were a magical time for horse racing. In 1973, Secretariat became the ninth Triple Crown champion, and the first since Citation in 1948, when he won the Belmont by a breathtaking 31 lengths. In 1977, Seattle Slew became the only undefeated horse to sweep the series. The next year, Affirmed outdueled Alydar by a length and a half in the Derby, a neck in the Preakness and a head in the Belmont.

They were different horses with similar traits. Each was the 2-year-old champion, and all were based at Belmont Park and bred to be sound horses with a great deal of stamina. "In those days, we were breeding for the racetrack, not to the market," said Chenery, Secretariat's owner. "Now, breeders are looking for fast, precocious horses that are going to get top dollar at the sales."

The yearling sales have become big business. Last year, owners spent more than $553 million for yearlings across North America compared with about $253 million in 1990, according to the Jockey Club. In the 1970's, breeding was much more of a pastime for well-to-do families.

The sense that horse racing was a game rather than a business extended to the training barns. When Turner campaigned Seattle Slew, the colt was one of 14 horses in his barn. Now, it is not unusual for trainers to have more than 100 horses. Michael Matz, the trainer of Barbaro, runs what is considered a modest operation, but still has 70 horses in training.

"The business has changed in so many ways, and in many respects not for the better," said Turner, who has 20 horses in his barn at Belmont Park. "When you get that big, it means each individual horse is getting less attention, and I think that shows up this time of year."

None of these Triple Crown alumni criticized Matz's unorthodox handling of Barbaro. The colt came to the Derby with only five lifetime starts, which were carefully spaced five to eight weeks apart.

"But in our time, horses were tougher," said Wolfson, who bred and owned Affirmed with her husband, Louis, who is in ill health.

Affirmed was hardly babied by his trainer, Laz Barrera. The colt won seven of nine races at age 2, four of them graded stakes, including the Hopeful at Saratoga and the Futurity at Belmont, both Grade I's. Affirmed started 29 times in his career and won 22 races.

In 1970, each thoroughbred averaged 10.22 starts a year, but in 2005, that number dwindled to 6.45 starts, according to the Jockey Club.

"Laz thought three weeks was a long layoff," Wolfson said.

Taylor, who owned Seattle Slew with his wife, Karen, and their former partner Jim Hill, said a horse's familiarity with Belmont Park should not be underestimated. In six of the past nine years, Triple Crown dreams have died for horses that could not endure the Belmont Stakes mile-and-a-half distance, or navigate the track's sandy surface or wide, sweeping turns.

Slew had won all three of his races as a 2-year-old at Belmont Park in 21 days. In all, the colt won six of seven on his home track.

"There is nothing else like Big Sandy," said Taylor, referring to the track's nickname. "It's no accident Secretariat, Slew and Affirmed all were at home there. It's a unique place and you have to be used to it."

Usually, the members of the Triple Crown club are interviewed on the eve of a horse's bid to capture the Belmont Stakes and enter thoroughbred history. Besides Chenery, the Wolfsons, the Taylors, Hill, Turner and Cauthen, Secretariat's jockey, Ron Turcotte, and Seattle Slew's rider, Jean Cruguet, are alive and waiting for new members. They agree that a Triple Crown has to be earned the old-fashioned way.

"No one should change the scheduling of the races or the distances," Wolfson said. "Winning at three distances, at three different tracks and over five weeks is supposed to be difficult. It's a real achievement and should stay that way."

They also say horse racing will be better off when a 12th Triple Crown champion shows himself.

"We need it to put the style back in racing," Chenery said. "And I mean a real champion that will race beyond his 3-year-old year and compete against the best horses out there. We don't need any more horses that run seven races for the most money and then retire."

WAITING FOR THE NEXT
SECRETARIAT

BY LAURA HILLENBRAND

JUNE 9, 2001 — The running of the 133rd Belmont Stakes today evokes mixed emotions in many. While this year's race promises to be a thriller, pitting Monarchos, the Kentucky Derby winner, against Point Given, the Preakness winner, a Triple Crown is not on the line. Racing fans are frustrated, a sentiment that has become an annual refrain. No horse has claimed the crown in 23 years. Are contemporary horses simply not up to the test?

Historically, horses haven't found it much easier; each of the Triple Crown races is more than 125 years old, yet only 11 horses have managed to capture all three. But after so many failures, some fans wonder if Affirmed, who won the title in 1978, was the final one.

There are myriad reasons why Triple Crown winners emerge so seldom. Trainer error can be disastrous; the rags-to-riches hero, Seabiscuit, whose smashing performances made him a national icon, never made it to any of the 1936 Triple Crown races because his first trainer badly misman-aged him. Jockeys are also critical, making split-second tactical decisions while catapulting through an enormous field of horses at 40 miles an hour. Many deserving horses have lost when their jockeys misjudged the pace and gunned them into suicidal speed duels, moved too early or too late, or steered them into traffic jams. Other horses have been foiled by injury.

But it is the challenge of the event itself that fells most horses.

The Triple Crown is an ingeniously conceived test, probably the most formidable in sport, taking the fullest possible measure of every horse. In three races over three distances at three very different tracks over only five weeks, contenders must reach for their deepest reserves of strength, stamina, versatility, durability and consistency. Courage, too, is at a premium, demonstrated most dramatically in 1937 when War Admiral, unbeknownst to his jockey, sheared off the rear of his hoof while leaving the Belmont starting gate, but won the race and the Triple Crown anyway, setting an American speed record.

The Triple Crown is a test that pits competitors against their own limitations, and a single error or weakness can prove fatal. In other sporting events, like the World Series, there is not infrequently the sense that the winner is merely the best of a mediocre field in a mediocre season. In this respect, thoroughbred racing stands alone. Deserving horses have lost the Triple Crown, but no undeserving horse has ever won it, and none ever will.

In 1973, the racing world was haunted by a mood similar to that felt today. A quarter century had passed since the coming of the last Triple Crown winner, Citation. Fans wondered if they would ever see another horse sweep the series. Then, on June 9, a red colossus named Secretariat roared down the Belmont homestretch on an awesome 31-length lead, winning the Triple Crown in world-record time.

Those who worry that we may never see this again should be patient. True greatness is extremely rare; the next Triple Crown winner will be worth the wait.

Laura Hillenbrand is the author of Seabiscuit: An American Legend.

FAST TRACK TO OBLIVION

BY JOHN JEREMIAH SULLIVAN

MAY 15, 2004 — Think about baseball's so-called perfect game, in which
one pitcher holds the mound for his team through all nine innings without
allowing a single batter on base. It's an all but impossible feat, in large part
because tremendous skill is only the first of the elements that have to be in
place for it to happen. There's toughness. And nerve. Versatility, too: a
pitcher's performance has to be maintained at the highest level even as the
game moves through different phases, as his body changes in response to
the strain, as the opposing team tries different strategies to unseat him.
And once all these are in place, a final requirement remains: huge amounts
of luck.

Now imagine a sport in which an accomplishment roughly analogous
to the perfect game was the central point around which the whole season
revolved, the climax not just of one athlete's ability but of each year's competitive cycle. Imagine, in other words, if the perfect game were to assume
the place of the World Series in terms of importance and public attention.
And should it ever be the case that, in a given year, no pitcher could pull it
off (this would in fact almost always be the case), well . . . get over it. And
please come back next season.

Such a sport exists. It's American thoroughbred racing. And thoroughbred racing's version of pitching the perfect game is to win the Triple Crown.

In 1930, the American turf writer Charles Hatton first used the term
"Triple Crown" to describe three high-stakes races for 3-year-old

horses—the Kentucky Derby, the Preakness, and the Belmont Stakes—
that have been held each spring since the late 19th century. Hatton's decision was somewhat arbitrary: the first horse to win all three races, Sir
Barton, had done so 11 years earlier, and no one had thought of the victories as a unified achievement.

But the notion stuck and, in the way of things, took on its own quiddi-
tas. Very quickly "the Crown" became the grail of thoroughbred racing,
and in 1987 the respective tracks made it a licensed institution by offering
a $5 million bonus to the owner of any horse that could capture all three
races. Today, in the eyes of the casual spectator, thoroughbred racing is the
Triple Crown, and the rest of the year's many lucrative races are dimly understood sideshows.

This is a bit of a problem for the sport, because last year, when Funny
Cide failed to win the Belmont Stakes after having taken the Derby and the
Preakness, we entered a record Triple Crown drought. The last horse to
pull it off was Affirmed, in 1978. That makes 26 years and counting. When
the immortal Secretariat won, in 1973, it had been 25 years since Citation
won in 1948, and fans were wondering then if we'd ever see another one.
Suddenly, there came the "decade of champions," as the 1970's are known
in racing circles—after Secretariat in '73, it was Seattle Slew in '77, then Affirmed in '78. And then, no less suddenly, the stream of champions dried
up. More than a quarter-century later, we're still waiting for rain.

This year's hope is Smarty Jones, the Pennsylvania-bred colt who won
the Derby two weeks ago and goes into the Preakness today as the favorite.
If he wins this afternoon (a bet, of course, but a smart one), only the Belmont Stakes in June will stand between his owners and the Triple Crown.
All the relevant statistics argue that he has a decent shot. He's not an especially fast horse, but he seems to do what it takes to win, over and over.
Amid the unfamiliar competition that he'll face today, or that he might
face two weeks later at the Belmont, no obvious threats pop out.

Why, then, will Smarty Jones almost certainly not win the Triple
Crown?

In the past 26 years, horses have shown a statistically wonky penchant
for winning both the Derby and Preakness only to lose the Belmont. This
has happened 18 times since 1919, and fully half of these have occurred
since 1979. The 80's, 90's, and 00's have been the decades of teasers. Lately
it's been especially cruel—War Emblem and Funny Cide almost got there,
but didn't, in 2002 and 2003, respectively. It's becoming something of a
torment to follow the Triple Crown, and fans have pretty much grown
used to the big story after the Belmont being not about who won the race
but about who lost the Triple Crown.

For years there has been open talk, both within and without the sport, about tinkering with the Triple Crown format. There are as many proposals as there are opinionated observers, but all share a common assumption: it's too hard, in this day and age, to win all three races.

This has never been easy, of course. A horse is still young and inexperienced in the spring of its third year, and the schedule is bruising. The three legs of the Crown are all over the place in terms of length and competition: the Preakness, at a mile and three-sixteenths, is unusually short, and the Belmont is unusually long at a mile and a half. The field at the Derby is always overcrowded; for the Preakness, it's frequently all but empty; then it fills up again in June for the Belmont, which typically sees the introduction of several fresh horses whose trainers have skipped the earlier races. This last phenomenon has become more of an obstacle in the last 25 years; today it's no big thing to deliver an animal based in, say, California, to New York, rested and raring to go, just a day or two before the Belmont.

Suggested reforms, cropping up in sports columns and online forums, range from the radical (make the Triple Crown a contest for 4-year-olds, giving the horses an extra year to toughen up) to the moderate (start the series later in the year, or lengthen the amount of time between each race, allowing the horses to approach each leg at full strength and increasing the chances that individual animals will compete in all three events).

The trainer D. Wayne Lukas has been the most vocal and dogged advocate of the latter adjustment. He thinks, too, that the distances should be altered so that they ramp up from shortest to longest, the idea being that horses could gradually work into the greater lengths and so turn in more consistent performances, winning devoted fans as they went along. Lukas points out that modern breeders are fixated on juvenile speed—if a horse does well as a 2-year-old or 3-year-old sprinter, it can quickly be turned into gold as a stud or broodmare, before injuries or shoddy performances get in the way—and this in turn has left us with generations of horses that simply aren't equipped to win a mile-and-a-half-long race after having just been forced to execute a mad dash like the Preakness. We're not raising all-around runners, yet the sport's exclusive focal point, where network TV and viewers are concerned, remains a contest in which horses are asked to do it all.

One problem with these reforms is that none of them (or none of the plausible ones) really has much to do with the well-being of the animals themselves. No evidence argues that horses who compete in all three legs of the Triple Crown, as it's now designed, are more prone to injury—at the time or later in their careers—than horses who don't.

One could argue that the demands placed on 2-year-old Triple Crown prospects are excessive (and certainly the intense winter prep races in Florida and California are responsible for many of the notorious pre-Derby scratches), but no matter how the series is designed, that won't change. You can't stop a trainer from running a horse if he or she thinks it's ready. Complaints about the physical effects that the Triple Crown has on an animal invariably rest on performance: horses are said to be daunted by the challenge. They don't try as hard after experiencing the shock of the Triple Crown. But, then, maybe they don't want to. The loss is probably not theirs.

A more common line of reasoning is that the Triple Crown should be changed not for the horses, but for the good of the sport. But here it gets even more problematic, because what's good for the sport? What are its greatest assets as a popular amusement: its famous champions and the thrill they generate, or its mystique, which, to an extent not exceeded by any American sport, lies in history and tradition, the sense that each year's Triple Crown represents the enactment of a spring rite?

Would-be reformers point out that there's nothing sacred about the way the series is organized now. The Derby started out a furlong longer than it is today and was held mid-month—not on the hallowed "first Saturday in May"—until 1932; the distance of the Belmont didn't settle at a mile and a half until 1926. The Preakness was run in New York (at Morris Park and the Gravesend Course) for nearly 20 years. So why not structure the Triple Crown along the most fair and rational lines, ones that will make another winner, in the near future, more likely, and save us from a sport that has come to be largely about losing? After all, a Triple Crown champion will still need to beat all comers, no matter how the schedule is arranged.

It's disingenuous, though, to point out that things were not always thus with the Triple Crown; they were thus for War Admiral and Whirlaway and Citation and Secretariat; they were thus during all the years when the Triple Crown was becoming the be-all and end-all of thoroughbred racing. Mess with it, and you risk destabilizing the one spectacle in the sport's calendar that impinges on American mass consciousness. It would take less than some people realize for horse racing to go the way of dog racing. Already—and even taking into consideration the post-*Seabiscuit* boom—the sport fights for what crowds it does attract.

Take away the public's overriding sense of the Triple Crown, won or lost, as an awesome thing, a momentous thing, and you may very well take away its sense that racing is a sport worth getting excited over. For although it may be true that everyone loves a winner, changes to the Triple Crown would leave everyone wondering what had been won. And that diminishment of the magic could be deadly.

Racing will never make sense: these are horses. It's not as if a tournament-style process of elimination could decide the field for the Triple Crown. Victory is about which horse and jockey are best on a given day, or, in cer-

tain magnificent cases, three days. The occasional randomness of this—
that, for instance, the horse that can move at the highest speed can still not
be rewarded in the end, or that in the Belmont a Triple Crown hopeful has
to beat horses that haven't fought like him to be there, or that the distances
change because of mere historical contingency—puts the achievement in
undeniable relief; the randomness is one more thing that the next champion, when we finally see another one, will have defeated, just as his prede-
cessors did.

Calls to rationalize racing are like those calls to get rid of the draw in
soccer; they're anti-subtlety. I say, embrace failure and loss. Learn to savor
their complicated bouquet. Surely it's a great sport that can go 26 years
without a champion and still look forward to spring. If the people who call
the shots are smart, they'll take pains to protect racing's quirkiness and, by
extension, its aura.

John Jeremiah Sullivan is the author of Blood Horses: Notes of a Sportswriter's Son.

ESSAY: A BIT OF SCIENCE, A DASH OF TECHNOLOGY AND A WHOLE LOT OF LUCK

BY JIM SQUIRES

AFTER MONARCHOS RAN THE second fastest Kentucky Derby in history in 2001, an e-mail arrived from a famous horse trainer congratulating
me as "a breeding genius." With pride, it was forwarded to an old newspaper colleague who had belittled as "temporary insanity" my decision to try
to raise racehorses for a living.

The e-mail returned with raised eyebrows: "Breeding genius, hell! The sun will shine on a dog's butt if he stands out in it long enough."

Lucky dog or not, the first Grade 1 stakes winner from my tiny, under-financed breeding program had become the only horse other than the great Secretariat to run the world's toughest mile and quarter race in less than 2 minutes. And the dazzling turn of foot he displayed coming from 13th and passing the favorite and eventual Horse of the Year Point Given like he was a statue raised hopes that Monarchos was capable of the most difficult achievement in sport—winning the Triple Crown.

He didn't. Like all but eleven of the 126 Derby winners before him and each since, Monarchos could not withstand the rigors of the Triple Crown trail, a minefield of training that culminates in a grueling stretch of three races in five weeks at different distances on three dissimilar racetracks. And like the 2006 Derby winner, the ill-fated Barbaro, his place in history as a truly great horse alongside Citation, Seattle Slew and the other Triple Crown champions had been snatched away by the most frequent derailment to racing glory—injury—specifically a hairline crack in the knee of his right foreleg from a year-long pounding on hard racetracks in preparation for the Derby.

Horses get only one chance at the Triple Crown, due to its restriction to three-year-olds. Breeders, on the other hand, can keep trying. Because the Kentucky Derby is first in the series and therefore key to the Crown, it is the most sought-after prize in racing and their most difficult challenge. When Citation won it in 1948, the Thoroughbred crop worldwide was only about 5,000 or so. A handful of rich sportsmen owned all of the good breeding stock, so breeding more than one Kentucky Derby winner was difficult but not impossible. The famous Calumet Farm bred nine between 1941 and 1991. Two of those went on to win the Triple Crown, a feat matched only by one other breeder, Belair Stud, in the 1930's when crops were even smaller. But today with 36,000 foals a year, coming up with a Derby winner is akin to catching lightning in a bottle, and winning the Triple Crown even more improbable.

A handful of rich sportsmen still own most of the good Thoroughbred breeding stock. Some own hundreds of the best-blooded broodmares and literally have spent billions of dollars buying, raising and racing horses for decades without coming close to winning the Derby, much less the Crown. So the disparaging assessment of my own meager effort—based on match-ing eight cheap mares with inexpensive, unproven stallions—as "insane" was entirely accurate.

But I had been recklessly emboldened by a lifetime of learning about horses and surprising success in raising equine athletes of other breeds, in-cluding dozens of top-level competitors for specific equine athletic achievements like jumping, sprinting short distances, sliding, stopping, and wheeling on a dime—all precision feats demanding horses with particular capabilities. Besides, thirty years in the newspaper business had skewed my definition of insanity and raised my tolerance for failure. Billy Turner, the man who trained the great Seattle Slew, maintains you can't breed a Kentucky Derby winner, or buy one, "they just show up." He is right about that to a point. But mating horses in pursuit of an offspring with a specific athletic prowess is a combination of art and science, requiring the creativity of the first and knowledge of the latter. It is akin to engineering a running machine with exactly the right blend of fast muscle for speed, slow muscle for endurance, and a structure with no imbalance of fore and hind quarters and no weakness of back or limb or joint or brain to hinder efficient movement or waste energy. For example, horses with long sloping shoulders cover more ground in fewer strides than those with short, straight shoulder angles. Since the intake of oxygen occurs in mid-stride, the longer the better, explaining why the giant strides of Man o' War and Secretariat were not coincidental.

Modern-day science and technology now allows breeders to measure the pumping capacity of a horse's heart, the ground-covering efficiency of a gait, the proficiency of respiratory system and hardness of bone. Monarchos was analyzed as possessing one of the most efficient combinations of gait and respiration ever tested. But a barely noticeable structural flaw—a slightly flat and imperfect right knee—ultimately proved his undoing.

Genetic research is rapidly discovering how and when such traits—visible and invisible—are passed on, and what bloodlines contain them. Blending it all is the breeder's challenge. It demands a grounding in bloodlines, an understanding of equine physiology as related to form and function and a willingness to ignore the market demands for big, precocious males that can run blistering 10-second furlong sprints in the popular juvenile training sales. Muscle-bound sale-topping yearlings and two-year-old speedsters are seldom around when well-engineered little running machines like Afleet Alex and Birdstone win the mile-and-a-half Belmont Stakes that completes the Triple Crown.

For one reason or another some of the best racehorses in history—Man o' War and John Henry, for example—did not compete in the Derby. Other horses physically capable of winning didn't because of accidents, illness, bad human management or the extraordinary challenge of surviving that adrenaline-fueled, collision-marred cavalry charge beneath the Twin Spires every first Saturday in May.

But all the extraordinarily fast Triple Crown horses have one thing in common. They are genetically designed to carry speed for a distance. Derby winners Count Fleet, who won the Triple Crown, and Swaps, who did not, were among the fastest horses that ever lived. Two male siblings of Monarchos, though never stakes winners, competed at the highest levels and were just as swift and structurally efficient. All came from the same female family, as did Barbaro's sire Dynaformer.

All four graded stakes winners from my breeding program resulted from inexpensive matings with stud fees of $10,000 or less. All have the same physical characteristics and are products of a single, simple pattern of bloodline blending based on the repetition of great females known for producing classic horses. Any skilled horseman can figure out my good fortune by looking at my horses and their six-generation pedigrees.

Similarly, any artful breeder can assemble in mind's eye all the pieces of the classic running machine. All shrewd buyers can recognize the aerodynamics, the power, the strength, the perfect angles and well-formed joints. Some maybe can even spot a glint of the delicately balanced temperament of a potential Triple Crown champion.

But what cannot be determined by slow-motion photography, digital imaging of structure or measurement of oxygen efficiency are the most elusive and vital qualities of a Triple Crown winner. Even DNA testing cannot now—and hopefully never will—measure the grit and determination of a racehorse to overtake an equally well-bred and talented opponent in the stretch and out-gut him to wire. And even if that becomes possible, no electronic means or human judge of horseflesh among us can ever be sure they see in a horse's eye the measure of luck necessary to win the Kentucky Derby or the Triple Crown.

Jim Squires, who breeds horses in Kentucky, is the author of Horse of a Different Color.

PART XI

---◆◆◆---

"Grief is the pain we all pay for love."
—GRETCHEN JACKSON, OWNER OF BARBARO

Pimlico Race Course: Jockey Edgar Prado after Barbaro suffered a leg injury at the start of the Preakness Stakes in 2006. ELIOT J. SCHECHTER/EPA/CORBIS

Barbaro burst on the scene with an emphatic six-and-a-half-length victory in the 132nd running of the Kentucky Derby. He was the first undefeated horse to win the first leg of the Triple Crown since Seattle Slew, and that performance promised to keep horsemen and horseplayers on the edge of their seats for the next five weeks as Barbaro took aim at the Triple Crown. The colt's trainer, Michael Matz, had signaled his intention for Barbaro to sweep the series when he adopted an unorthodox training regimen. Barbaro was given an unusual amount of rest between races—anywhere from five to eight weeks—and came into the Derby with only five lifetime starts.

"We were training for the Triple Crown," Matz said. "It has been so long since anyone has won it, why not try something different?"

But two weeks later, on May 20, the colt took a misstep in the opening yards of the Preakness and was pulled up, his right hind leg horribly shattered.

For those in the press box, the race stopped right there. No one watched as the other horses headed into the clubhouse turn. We all understood that the worst thing that can possibly occur in a race, just had. There were some moist eyes, and shared sense of dread. While a stunned crowd watched in silence, Barbaro was carefully loaded into an ambulance and sped 80 miles north to the George D. Widener Hospital for Large

Animals at the University of Pennsylvania's New Bolton Center in Kennett Square, Pa. That night, Dr. Dean Richardson operated on Barbaro, placing 27 steel pins in his broken leg. Suddenly, instead of sports fans being briefly captivated by a horse story, the nation, even the world, was riveted for eight months by Barbaro's determined fight for his life.

Flowers, fruit baskets and get-well cards flooded into the hospital. Beyond its grounds, many debated whether Barbaro should have been euthanized immediately on the racetrack. His saga, along with efforts of those who tried to save him, became one of the most compelling stories of 2007.

THINKING TRIPLE CROWN BEFORE
FIRST RACE WAS RUN

BY JOE DRAPE

ELKTON, MD., MAY 10, 2006 — A year ago, after the big dark bay horse arrived at the European-styled training center here, the trainer Michael Matz and his assistant, Peter Brette, shared a transcendental thought about a colt by the ho-hum name of Barbaro. But they dared not say it aloud.

Barbaro was a superhorse, Brette believed, after he first took him onto the racetrack for a morning workout. Barbaro could sweep the Triple Crown, Matz said he kept thinking. It was the beginning of what would become a most unorthodox plan to chase after one of sport's most elusive prizes.

"We were training for the Triple Crown," Matz said, daring to tempt racing's fates. "It has been so long since anyone has won it, why not try something different?"

In the Kentucky Derby on May 6, Barbaro validated Brette's opinion with a stunningly effortless victory. On May 20 in Baltimore, Matz says, his undefeated colt will take the second step toward fulfilling his prophecy by jetting away from the field in the 131st running of the Preakness Stakes.

Matz says he thinks his horse can succeed where six others in the last nine years, from Silver Charm to Smarty Jones, failed after coming so close to horse racing immortality. He has thrown out a regimen that has been regarded by trainers as commandments etched in stone, opting instead for a new schedule forged by his own personal setback and inspired by a brilliant colt.

While most trainers organize training to maximize fitness and build race readiness, Matz has given Barbaro an unusual amount of rest between races in his budding career. Trainers usually prefer to have their horses experienced in having dirt kicked in their face, maneuvering through crowded fields and reacting to adversity before they run in the Triple Crown races.

Barbaro, though, ran only five times before winning the Derby, and started his career only when Matz decided he was ready, in October, relatively late for a horse with Triple Crown ambitions.

Matz, 55, came upon his fresh-horse theory at the lowest point of what turned out to be an illustrious career in show jumping.

In 1976, he was on the cusp of making the United States Olympic team and was forced to push his horse in the trials. Matz became an Olympian, but at the Montreal Games, he and his tired horse staggered through the competition, suffering 28 faults and knocking down 7 poles.

"When I watched the replay, I felt agony," he said. "No one, none of my teammates, wanted to get close to me. I decided then, I was never going to put a tired horse in a competition or race."

Matz says that a horse needs every advantage to win the Triple Crown, the most exacting and enduring challenge in the sport. It was back in 1978 that Affirmed became the last horse to sweep the Derby, the Preakness and the Belmont Stakes. In recent years, Matz has watched as six horses, weary from their Triple Crown campaigns, have fallen short.

As a group, those six horses competed in an average of 8.5 races before the Derby, and an average of 3.8 of those races were as 3-year-olds, usually in the 12 weeks before the first Saturday in May. Bob Baffert trained three of those horses, and two—Silver Charm and Real Quiet—fell three-quarters of a length and a nose short from completing the sweep in the grueling mile-and-a-half Belmont Stakes. Eking out those last few gallops from a tired horse in the Triple Crown's third leg has vexed trainers in recent years.

"It's a tricky balance to keep, and a lot of it depends on your horse and how he is progressing," said Baffert, who raced Silver Charm six times before the Derby and ran Real Quiet 12 times. "You want him to be ready for anything in the Derby. I think most of us focus on winning the Derby.

"Then you try to hold them together for the Preakness and Belmont. It looks like Michael had a horse that he could think Triple Crown with, and he believed enough in his colt's talent to try a different route."

Barbaro pulled into Churchill Downs having raced only once in the 13 weeks before the Derby. Between his starts, he was rested for five to eight weeks. His racing career looks odder still because his first three victories were on the grass—not on dirt, the surface of the Triple Crown—at distances of a mile, a mile and a sixteenth, and a mile and an eighth.

Usually, Triple Crown hopefuls begin their careers on the dirt in races shorter than a mile involving one turn of the track before stretching to two-turn races in their third year.

Matz said he knew that Barbaro, as the son of Dynaformer—an accomplished sire known for producing turf horses with stamina—would relish those grass races. Actually, the trainer was listening to his horse.

"We took our time with him because he needed to grow up mentally," Matz said. "I would have run him on dirt, but the grass race at Delaware Park was the only one that came up that fit our schedule."

Following the trainer's regimen of allowing plenty of time to recover between races, Barbaro did not compete on the dirt until Feb. 4, in the Holy Bull Stakes at Gulfstream Park. When rain pelted South Florida and the racing surface became sloppy, Matz thought about pulling him from the race. But Brette, unworried about how Barbaro would handle a wet track, talked him out of it.

"We had to try the dirt, as well as stay on schedule," Brette said. Barbaro was impressive winning the Holy Bull, but traditionalists were puzzled by Matz's decision to wait until the Florida Derby eight weeks later. By that time, Matz and Brette were well aware that they had a maturing colt with more gears than a bicycle in the Tour de France.

To keep his horses happy, Mr. Matz has based his stable at the Fair Hill Training Center here in Elkton, which is a sort of equine spa with Fifth Avenue amenities. Its 350 acres are next to the 5,600-acre Fair Hill Preserve, once the fox-hunting estate of William du Pont Jr., and is veined by riding trails, dotted with pastures and home to a dirt, turf and more forgiving wood-chip training track. It is an oasis where horses can be treated as horses.

On Wednesday morning, Barbaro grazed quietly after an effortless mile jog that once more had Brette feeling as if he had been atop a winged horse. "If he is feeling this good four days after running a mile and a quarter, I can't imagine what he will be like in 10 days," he said, referring to the Preakness at Pimlico Race Course.

Matz and Brette say they know they are tempting fate by talking of the Triple Crown when two legs remain. But they also have been unable to suppress thoughts of sweeping the series, then taking Barbaro to Europe in the fall to run on grass again, perhaps in the Prix de l'Arc de Triomphe, the most famous race in Europe.

It is with this confidence that Matz has entered Barbaro to run against

a compact field of perhaps six horses at Pimlico on May 20. When he gives
Edgar Prado a leg up on Barbaro before the Preakness, Mr. Matz said he
would offer him the same succinct instructions that he did at the Derby:
"Just ride him like he's the best horse."

STARTLING INJURY AT PREAKNESS
ENDS BARBARO'S QUEST

BY JOE DRAPE

BALTIMORE, MAY 20, 2006 — The Preakness Stakes was supposed to be
a walkover for Barbaro, the undefeated colt who looked every bit the
superhorse when winning the Kentucky Derby two weeks ago. Since that
first Saturday in May, he was being talked about as a potential Triple
Crown champion.

Those hopes ended horrifically in the first sixteenth of a mile at Pimlico Race Course on Saturday, when Barbaro sustained potentially life-
threatening fractures above and below his right hind ankle. His jockey,
Edgar Prado, felt the colt's pain immediately; he slowed Barbaro gradually
to a standstill in front of a clubhouse brimming with stunned onlookers.

As the eight remaining horses disappeared into the first turn of a race
that Bernardini eventually won, the real drama was unfolding in the opening straightaway. Barbaro was holding his awkwardly bent leg aloft as an
equine ambulance raced to his aid.

His trainer, Michael Matz, ran from the clubhouse to the racetrack;
Barbaro's owners, Roy and Gretchen Jackson, trailed behind him. But it
was Matz's assistant, Peter Brette, who was watching near the paddock and
reached Barbaro and Prado first. The two horsemen dissolved into a hug as
veterinarians tried to comfort Barbaro.

"There are some major hurdles here," said Dr. Larry Bramlage, a renowned equine surgeon who was the on-call veterinarian for the American Association of Equine Practitioners. "This is a significant injury. His career is over. This is it for him as a racehorse. We're trying to save him as a stallion."

Bramlage, who examined the X-rays, said that Barbaro broke the bone above the ankle first. The break below the ankle occurred sometime in the next several yards, he said, because Barbaro was coursing with energy and adrenaline and wanted to keep running.

He likened the injury to a runner who twists his ankle but continues, then sustains more damage with every step. Bramlage praised Prado for acting swiftly; he said that could be critical to Barbaro's survival.

He said horses had two small arteries in their legs, and the concern was that blood flow to the lower limb might be impeded.

"That's what you worry about as life-threatening," Bramlage said. "Secondly, if this kind of injury happened to us, we'd be put up in bed for six weeks. But you can't do that for a horse."

A horse's physiology and temperament are not designed for long stretches of inactivity. A horse with a severely injured leg will try to put weight on it; if a horse is forced to recline, its internal organs may not react properly.

Prado was visibly shaken. On the racetrack, in a loud, quivering voice, he tried to tell Matz and the Jacksons of the strange, uncharacteristic sensation he felt on Barbaro, the horse he had said was the best he had ever ridden. On the rail nearby, many in the crowd of 118,402, a record for the Preakness, were in tears.

Only moments earlier, a seemingly rambunctious Barbaro had prematurely broken through the gate, delaying the start of the race.

"When he went to the gate, he was feeling super and I felt like he was in the best condition for this race," Prado said. "He actually tried to buck me off a couple of times. He was feeling that good. He just touched the front of the gate and went right through it."

Barbaro got 10 or so yards before being escorted by outriders to his No. 6 post position. He was checked by a track veterinarian and found to be uninjured. When the gates opened, Barbaro bounded out effortlessly.

"He took a bad step, and I can't tell you what happened," Prado said. "I heard a noise about 100 yards into the race and pulled him right up." Bramlage said the injury occurred during the race and not in the gate incident.

Barbaro was only the sixth horse to come to the Preakness undefeated. Matz had carefully planned a racing schedule to minimize wear and tear on Barbaro, in hopes of his becoming just the 12th Triple Crown champion and the first since Affirmed in 1978.

Matz had raced Barbaro only five times before the Derby, and gave him five to eight weeks of rest between outings. On Saturday, when the 131st running of the Preakness was complete, an eerily calm Barbaro was on the racetrack, standing gingerly on three legs as the track veterinarian, Dr. Dan Dreyfuss, fitted him for a splint.

Matz was unavailable for comment after the race. His wife, Dorothy, met briefly with reporters outside the stakes barn after Barbaro was taken from the track at 7:22 P.M. by ambulance and with a police escort to the George D. Widener Hospital for Large Animals in Kennett Square, Pa.

"Barbaro is behaving like the true champion he is, and hopefully, he'll get the best treatment possible and will be all right," she said.

As soon as Barbaro can be stabilized, Bramlage said, equine surgeons will begin the hours-long process of trying to repair his leg. This is not the first time horse enthusiasts have seen heartbreak on what were supposed to be triumphant days: in the 1990 Breeders' Cup at Belmont Park, Go for Wand broke down in the Distaff race and had to be euthanized; and on July 7, 1975, Ruffian was fatally injured in a match race with Foolish Pleasure.

Barbaro's injury put a chill on the human connections of his eight rivals, all of whom knew that the second jewel of horse racing's Triple Crown had been scuffed, perhaps irreparably.

"The whole story is this: Let's just hope Barbaro lives," said Nick Zito, trainer of the third-place finisher, Hemingway's Key.

Even the winning jockey, Javier Castellano, who rode Benardini, found little joy in capturing his first victory in a Triple Crown race. He seemed puzzled when he turned Bernardini for home, peeked under his arm and did not see Barbaro or Prado behind him.

Moments later, however, shortly before crossing the finish line five and a quarter lengths in front of the field, Castellano finally laid eyes on them. His heart sank.

"I saw the jockey in the middle of the track," Castellano said, seeing Prado, Barbaro and the equine ambulance still near the first turn. "It was really sad."

BARBARO OUT OF SURGERY, BUT NOT YET IN THE CLEAR

BY JOE DRAPE

KENNETT SQUARE, PA., MAY 21, 2006—Barbaro's racing career is over, but a valiant and costly effort was made Sunday to repair the right hind leg of the horse that sustained a catastrophic ankle break before an audience of millions early in the Preakness Stakes on Saturday.

On Sunday night at the University of Pennsylvania's George D. Widener Hospital for Large Animals, Barbaro emerged from an operation that lasted more than four hours and a post-operation recovery that took another three.

While the surgeon who performed the operation, Dr. Dean Richardson, was pleased enough with how things went to remark that Barbaro "practically jogged" to his stall, his prognosis was more grave. "To be brutally honest, there's still enough chance for things going bad that it's still a coin toss even though everything went well," Richardson said.

It was remarkable that the surgery was attempted at all. Most horses with injuries as severe as Barbaro's, Dr. Richardson acknowledged, would have been euthanized on the racetrack. Dr. Richardson said that the injury was far worse than originally thought.

But this colt was the Kentucky Derby winner with an estimated value of $30 million, and his owners, Roy and Gretchen Jackson, were well heeled enough to foot the bill for the costly, and risky, surgery and rehabilitation.

In the operating room, Richardson worked with a team of eight: two residents, an intern, two anesthesiologists and three nurses.

"I could see no evidence of pre-existing injury," Dr. Richardson said. "It was just a bad step."

Richardson praised Barbaro's jockey, Edgar Prado, for skillfully bringing the horse to a stop and preventing further injury Saturday.

Barbaro, relatively unknown before his dazzling performance in the Kentucky Derby, had been considered one of the best horses to come along in the past 25 years, one with a legitimate chance to sweep the Triple Crown for the first time since 1978. On Sunday, bouquets of roses, bundles of carrots and green apples awaited Barbaro in the lobby of this prestigious veterinary hospital. Hand-painted signs stating simply "We Love You, Barbaro" hung outside its gates.

For Barbaro's trainer, Michael Matz, the end of the surgery came as a relief after he endured his worst day as a thoroughbred trainer. "From what I saw last night, I feel much more confident that now he has a chance," Matz said.

In the delicate assemblage of bones that make up a horse's ankle, Barbaro had practically shattered it. To fuse the ankle, the surgeons used a locking compression plate with 27 screws and put his leg in a cast.

"It's about as bad as it could be," Richardson said of the injury before the surgery. After the operation, Barbaro was lifted from the operating table by a sling and placed in a recovery pool. He was suspended in the water as well as fitted with a raft until the anesthesia wore off. It prevented him from thrashing and possibly reinjuring the leg.

He was lifted by a sling and placed on a monorail, which carried him to his stall. When Barbaro was lowered on four legs, standing, he reared up, startling Mr. Matz and giving hope to Richardson.

"He's a genuine athlete," Richardson said.

Whether Barbaro can recover to lead the lucrative life of a stallion depends on his convalescence. Horses, by nature, are animals of flight and are not designed for long periods of recumbence. Richardson said it would take many months for Barbaro's leg to fuse properly. The cost, already in the "tens of thousands," would increase.

"Some way has to be devised to support the limb long enough for the fractures to mend," said Dr. Paul Thorpe, an equine surgeon with the Hagyard, Davidson and McGee Veterinary Clinic in Lexington, Ky. "We're talking about four months in some sort of stabilizing cast or splinting device."

It is likely that Barbaro was insured for a great deal of money—a $300,000 premium buys an average of $10 million of insurance on a top-flight racehorse, according to several owners and breeders. The Jacksons

have bred and owned thoroughbreds for 30 years. They have acknowledged turning down several offers for Barbaro stretching into millions of
dollars as the colt won one race after another.

They were not here on Sunday, and were unavailable for comment.

Barbaro is a son of Dynaformer, a noted distance and turf sire who
stands for $100,000 a session. Barbaro offered potentially added value as a
stallion because he had demonstrated versatility, winning three races on
the grass, three on the dirt and at distances up to a mile and a quarter.

In 2005, Smarty Jones was syndicated for $40 million after winning the
Derby and the Preakness, and losing his only race, the Belmont Stakes,
narrowly to Birdstone.

"Had Barbaro won the Preakness, his value would have easily climbed
to the $30 million range," said Dr. Rolf Embertson, a surgeon with Rood
and Riddle Equine Hospital in Lexington.

How the colt sustained the injury will most likely remain a puzzle to
casual fans, and a gruesome reminder of the cruel vagaries of a sport that
dates back centuries.

Veterinarians have ruled out that the injury occurred when Barbaro
broke through the starting gate before the race. "Edgar said he just hit the
gate with his nose and it opened," Matz said.

A track veterinarian checked him before he was reloaded, and replays
of the race show that Barbaro broke cleanly and was running smoothly for
about a hundred yards.

"Why does a football player turn their ankle, break their tibia, why does
a basketball player blow out their knee?" Dr. Larry Bramlage, a prominent
equine veterinarian, said. "It has to be some sort of bad step that loaded the
weight unevenly."

Bramlage explained that 1,200-pound horses had more than six times
the body weight of the average-size person but strikes the ground on about
the same surface area as the human foot.

"Those really elegantly built lower legs are very vulnerable to twisting
it at just exactly the wrong angle and create the fracture," he said.

Barbaro had come to the Preakness as only the sixth undefeated horse
to compete in the second leg of the Triple Crown, and off a breathtaking
sixth-and-a-half-length romp in the Derby, the largest margin of victory
in 50 years.

Judi Hunt of Aberdeen, Wash., who said she had listened to or watched
each Triple Crown race since 1948, was among those watching. "I cried
yesterday when the horse came up lame," she said by phone. "I just want to
know how the horse is going to do."

Bill Mooney contributed reporting from Lexington, Ky., for this article.

AN UNKNOWN FILLY DIES, AND THE CROWD JUST SHRUGS

BY WILLIAM C. RHODEN

ELMONT, N.Y., MAY 25, 2006 — There was no array of photographers at Belmont Park yesterday, no sobbing in the crowd as a badly injured superstar horse tried to stay erect on three legs. There was no national spotlight.

Instead, there was death. In the seventh race at Belmont, a 4-year-old filly named Lauren's Charm headed into the homestretch. As she began to fade in the mile-and-an-eighth race on the grass, her jockey, Fernando Jara, felt her struggling, pulled up and jumped off.

As the race concluded, Lauren's Charm collapsed. No one, except those associated with the horse and two track veterinarians, seemed to notice.

The scene was in stark contrast to what unfolded at Pimlico last Saturday when the Kentucky Derby winner, Barbaro, severely fractured his ankle in the opening burst of the Preakness. A national audience gasped; an armada of rescuers rushed to the scene. In the days that followed, as the struggle to keep Barbaro alive took full shape, there was an outpouring of emotion across the country and heartfelt essays about why we care so much about these animals.

But I'm not so sure we do, and I'm not so sure the general public fully understands this sport. When people attempt to rationalize the uneasy elements of racing, they often say: "That's part of the business. That's the game."

But there was nothing beautiful or gracious or redeeming about the seventh race at Belmont. This was the underside of the business. The nuts-and-bolts part, where animals are expendable parts of a billion-dollar industry.

The two vets raced to the stricken horse, followed by the assistant trainer Anthony Rodriguez; his mother, Doreen, who served as the hot-walker; and the groom. By the time they reached her, Lauren's Charm was dead.

Dr. Jennifer Durenberger, the second vet to reach the horse, said the filly had apparently died of a heart attack. "This was very uncommon," she said afterward in a telephone interview from her office. "It happens to 1 in 20,000 horses."

I'm not sure how many fans in the meager crowd of 3,741 paid attention to the white equine ambulance that pulled onto the track, or saw the filly being loaded in it.

The filly's owner, Joseph Dirico, was watching a simulcast of the race at a track in Massachusetts with his father and uncle. "She started dropping back," he said last night of the horse he had named after his wife. "That's what I saw. I didn't expect to get a phone call saying she'd had a heart attack. I'm glad I wasn't there. I would have run down to the track, I would have had tears in my eyes. She was a nice horse, a really correct filly."

Last Saturday evening, Barbaro's devastated owners said that these things happened in racing, that it is part of the sport. Yesterday, Dirico said, "I guess that's part of the game."

What is the nature of this game?

Horses go down much more frequently than the general public realizes, and many in the business have noted that had Barbaro not been the winner of the Kentucky Derby, he might have been destroyed after being injured.

Jara, an 18-year-old Panamanian, seemed to take Lauren's Charm's death in stride. He had finished fourth aboard Jazil in the Kentucky Derby, his first Triple Crown race. He said that in his four years of racing, this was the first time he was in the saddle when a horse died.

Asked if he was going to think about the horse during the rest of the day, he said no. "There is another race to come," he said. "You have to think about the next race."

"Everything is equal," he added as he compared Barbaro to Lauren's Charm, who won one race in her career and earned all of $77,363. "But Barbaro could have won the Triple Crown."

The dead animal was loaded in the ambulance and carted to the track's stable area, where it was put on its side, legs bent as if it were still running. The horseshoes had not been removed. The carcass was then half carried and half pushed into an area designated for autopsies. An earthmover helped push the horse against a concrete wall.

I asked one of the track supervisors what would happen now. He said if the horse was insured, there would be an autopsy. If not, then he would wait to hear from the owner to determine if there would be an autopsy at the owner's expense.

Dirico said he indeed might order an autopsy. "I had no insurance on her," he said. "If reasonable, I'd like to have it done for my own peace of mind."

I wondered why he didn't have the horse insured. "Insurance is so expensive," he said. "I never thought it would come to this. I've had good luck with horses."

The gate to the fenced-in area was closed. I glanced back at Lauren's Charm, lying on the ground. Just days ago, the cameras were trained on Pimlico, and a nation cried for Barbaro. I wonder what the nation would have thought about this.

One animal breaks an ankle on national television in a Triple Crown race and sets off a national outpouring of emotion. A 4-year-old collapses and dies in full view on a sunny afternoon and not many seem to notice. Or care.

As they say, it's the business.

But what kind of business is this?

EQUINE EVOLUTION; OUR CREATION, OUR CONCERN

BY LINDA GREENHOUSE

MAY 28, 2006 — Few scenes in sports could ever be more poignant than the image of the racehorse Barbaro holding his hind leg awkwardly in the air as the people on whom his life now depended clustered around him. A human athlete with an equivalently catastrophic injury would have been writhing in pain or cursing fate. But Barbaro stood stock still, his face registering nothing that could be interpreted as emotion. He felt pain, clearly, but only the people around him sensed doom.

The huge audience that had tuned in the Preakness Stakes expecting to toast a once-in-a-generation champion remained gripped all week by the story of Barbaro's injury, surgery and outlook for recovery. In sports, human disasters seldom hold our attention for so long or so strongly.

Athletes ski into trees, are swept away by rogue waves or suffer career-ending injuries on the playing field, and we shake our heads in sympathy and move on to the next contest. The undiminished fascination with the fate of a 3-year-old colt, even among people who have never been near a racetrack, does at least raise the question of whether the public cares more for horses than for humans.

The answer is that we care about horses in a different way. Human athletes choose to put themselves in danger. Even in sports where risk-taking is not a central element, people choose their own path. When a weekend warrior suffers a heart attack on the tennis court, it is not uncommon to hear the cliché: "At least he died doing what he loved to do."

We have no idea whether Thoroughbred horses love to race. We like to think they do, and maybe, on a glorious spring day in Triple Crown season, a 40-mile-an-hour run around a dirt oval under a jockey's whip in front of a cheering crowd really does feel wonderful to an animal that has, after all, been bred and trained for just such an activity. But we don't know, and it is hard to sustain an illusion of joy for anyone who has sat in a nearly deserted grandstand on a dreary afternoon, watching horses cross the finish line covered with mud from a sloppy track. And do even champions really love being loaded into vans or onto airplanes for a trip to a distant racetrack when the reward, for them, is little more than a blanket of roses?

I have been a racing fan for years, and my point is not that horse racing is cruel or morally ambiguous. I will let others make that argument, as many have in the past week. Yes, we feel a special obligation to these fragile, beautiful creatures whom we place in harm's way for our own sporting pleasure. And yes, when their perfection is marred, we shudder as we would at the destruction of a work of art. But I think the sense of obligation runs at a deeper, even subliminal level. We are responsible for racehorses because we in a very real sense created them.

Today's Thoroughbreds are a result of more than 300 years of selective breeding that has carried them very far from their roots on the steppes and deserts of the Middle East. Every Thoroughbred is descended from one of three stallions, the Darley Arabian, Godolphin, and the Byerly Turk, brought to England toward the close of the 17th century and bred to mares initially under the patronage of King Charles II. A great-great-grandson of the Darley Arabian, bred by a son of King George II, was born during a solar eclipse in 1764 and named Eclipse. An undefeated champion on the track, he sired 344 winners, and his powerful bloodline literally eclipsed all others. In fact, 95 percent of the Thoroughbreds alive today are his descendants.

During the ensuing centuries, theories about the best strategies for fulfilling the injunction to "breed the best to the best" have come and gone, but almost nothing has been left to chance. Barbaro's sire, Dynaformer, stands for a stud fee of $100,000. Human intervention has been so pervasive that on some level these are scarcely horses any longer but centaurs, part equine and part human, their lives so intermingled with ours that there is no separating the two.

Or to evoke another mythical creature: facing months of confinement and recuperation in a padded 12-by-12-foot stall, Barbaro is the "unicorn in captivity" of the medieval tapestry, fenced-in, bleeding from his wounds, the chase at an end.

Even casual horseplayers know the experience of urging a struggling horse down the stretch, as if this object of a $2 bet or a selection in the daily double carried their own fate on its back. But the image is backward. It is the horse's fate that is at stake, now as ever in our hands.

WITH LOVING AND COSTLY CARE, BARBARO'S LONG ODDS IMPROVE

BY JOE DRAPE

KENNETT SQUARE, PA., AUGUST 21, 2006— Barbaro was reclined on his side in a stall. His left hind foot curled out beneath him, revealing a fitting that his surgeon called a foam-lined rubber sneaker. His right hind leg, the one that has been in a cast for 90 days, was hidden beneath a carpet of knee-deep straw.

Barbaro wears a bandage around his neck to protect a catheter, and his left hip has a few white splotches, healing blisters from a combination of his sweat and the antiseptics used in his initial operation. When he awakened from a serene slumber, however, his eyes burned as bright as a Kentucky Derby champion's. After all, he is a Derby champion.

Barbaro's owners, Roy and Gretchen Jackson, notice that look in his eyes, as does his trainer, Michael Matz, and the medical staff at the George D. Widener Hospital for Large Animals. It is why they have never left this horse for dead.

They refused to do so when Barbaro took a catastrophic misstep and shattered his right hind leg in the opening yards of the Preakness Stakes on May 20. They forged on in early July when the colt developed severe laminitis, a painful and often-fatal condition that afflicts horses that bear excessive weight on a limb.

Instead, they have combined aggressive medical treatment with tender loving care in one of the most extraordinary efforts ever mounted to save a top-flight racehorse. Gretchen Jackson comes here twice a day with fresh grass clippings to feed Barbaro. Matz also arrives daily to change the leg bandages on the best horse that he has ever trained. Barbaro is also fed the carrots and apples that continue to arrive here from the public. He has been doused with holy water sent by well-wishers.

This holistic and community approach seems to be working, not to mention the untold tens of thousands of dollars in medical care.

The sling Barbaro once needed to keep weight off his legs now hangs in storage in another stall, and the epidurals he required for pain have not been necessary for weeks. Best of all, for almost two weeks, Barbaro has been walked outside for 20 or 30 minutes a day in a field, where he grazes on grass and looks every bit like a normal horse.

"He's been very, very good on his legs," said Dr. Dean Richardson, his surgeon and the man who leads him outside each day. "It's exciting. He's improving."

Richardson warned that Barbaro was hardly out of the woods and that a full recovery would not be evident for months. Still, he said he was encouraged by the progress.

On July 13, Richardson had to compose himself when he announced that laminitis had ravaged Barbaro's left hind hoof wall and that the chances of survival were poor. Now, his hoof wall is growing back, and his fractured right hind leg appears to be mending, Richardson said. But he cautioned that until the cast was removed, he could not be certain the leg would be strong enough to bear Barbaro's weight.

"I think he's got a 50-50 shot," said Richardson, echoing the prognosis he gave May 21, after performing an operation on the colt's leg for more than five hours. "He's back to that level. Now, if you would have asked me the same question six weeks ago, I would have told you they were a lot—a lot—less than that."

Luck, too, will continue to play a part in Barbaro's convalescence. Gretchen Jackson said good fortune was with them even on May 20, when the colt hobbled to a stop at Pimlico Race Course in Baltimore.

"When the accident happened right there on the track, Michael Matz and the track veterinarians told us that Barbaro had to go to the New Bolton Center and Dean Richardson," she said. "They knew Dean was a magician putting horses back together, and fortunately, we were just an hour or so away."

The New Bolton Center is part of the University of Pennsylvania, and the Jacksons have long been among its benefactors; Gretchen Jackson is on the board of the veterinary school.

The Jacksons have been involved in thoroughbred racing for nearly 30 years and have a reputation for going to great lengths for their injured horses. Roy Jackson, whose grandfather William Rockefeller was once the president of Standard Oil, and his wife, Gretchen, have spared no expense when it comes to Barbaro's recovery.

The Jacksons had long known of Richardson's reputation, but in the days since the Preakness, they have come to admire the skill and dedication of his team. Beyond the complicated operation he performed to put back together a leg shattered in more than 20 pieces, Richardson oversaw a pain-management and after-care program that kept Barbaro comfortable and progressing smoothly for seven weeks.

"I've never in my life used more pain medication on a horse," Richardson said. "It meant that he needed around-the-clock nursing care to keep everything hooked up and clean and to make sure he was all right. He was rarely alone."

When the laminitis appeared, however, the Jacksons faced a wrenching decision: whether to end Barbaro's life. Richardson met here at the hospital with the couple and Matz and explained that the colt had severe laminitis, which he described as "exquisitely painful."

"Most owners would have called it a day," Richardson said.

But nobody—not the Jacksons, not Richardson, not Matz—saw any signs of suffering from Barbaro. They agreed to remove 80 percent of the ruined hoof wall and to give the colt some more time.

"We agreed that the moment the colt was in pain, the veterinarians would put him down," Gretchen Jackson said.

Not only has Barbaro not shown signs of distress, he appears to be growing stronger each day. The foam sneaker is changed daily as the veterinarians continue to watch for the regrowth of his hoof wall.

"I go over there with the grass because I love him and want to break up his day," Gretchen Jackson said. "Now that he is getting outside, he is an even happier horse."

Barbaro, who faces long odds of ever becoming a lucrative stallion, appears to be a healthier horse, too. He receives only antibiotics and a mild analgesic, the equivalent of aspirin for a horse. He is eating well and maintaining his muscle tone. The more uneventful days that pass, the better off he will be.

No one close to Barbaro is predicting a full recovery, but they remain optimistic and seem grateful for each good day. By the cards and gifts that continue to arrive, they know that Barbaro has touched people far beyond them.

"Everyone who cares about this horse is doing their best," Michael Matz said, "and, hopefully, we can pull Barbaro through."

AFTER EIGHT MONTHS FILLED BY HOPE, SETBACK ENDS BARBARO'S BATTLE

BY JOE DRAPE

KENNETT SQUARE, PA., JANUARY 29, 2007 — In eight months of waiting for Barbaro's shattered bones to heal, the horse's owners and his veterinarian said they had not seen the Kentucky Derby–winning colt become so uncomfortable that he would refuse to lie down and rest. Until Sunday night.

So on Monday morning, the owners, Roy and Gretchen Jackson, and the veterinarian, Dr. Dean Richardson, decided enough was enough. At 10:30 A.M., Barbaro was euthanized, ending an extraordinary effort to save the life of a remarkable racehorse whose saga had gripped people around the world.

In recent weeks, Barbaro's ailments had become overwhelming: complications with his left hind leg lingered, an abscess in his right hind heel was discovered last week and, finally, a new case of the painful and often fatal condition called laminitis developed in both of his front feet.

"That left him with not a good leg to stand on," Dr. Richardson said Monday at an emotional news conference here at the George D. Widener Hospital for Large Animals. "He was just a different horse. You could see he was upset. That was the difference. It was more than we wanted to put him through."

The Jacksons were red-eyed as they explained that it had become clear their horse could not live without pain after a setback over the weekend that required a risky surgical procedure on his right hind leg. The couple had spent tens of thousands of dollars trying to save Barbaro's life, and Gretchen Jackson thanked the people who had expressed support for Barbaro through cards, letters, messages and even holy water.

"Grief is the pain we all pay for love," she said.

Fifty feet away, in the hospital's lobby, flowers and notes of condolences continued to arrive. The eight-month effort to nurse Barbaro back to health had riveted people around the world and had reminded casual fans about the beauty, mystery and heartbreak that is part of Thoroughbred racing.

The day after his breakdown at the Preakness in May, Barbaro endured more than five hours of surgery as Richardson and his team used 27 screws to piece the right hind leg back together. In July, after laminitis had developed in Barbaro's left rear hoof, Richardson proclaimed the chances for survival as poor. The condition is frequently caused by uneven weight distribution among a horse's legs.

Despite having 80 percent of his hoof removed, Barbaro bounced back, and by mid-August, he was grazing outside the hospital here each day as Richardson fed him by hand.

The Jacksons visited the colt here each day and fed him grass from their farm in nearby West Grove, Pa. Before Christmas, they were encouraged enough by Barbaro's recovery that they were making plans to move him to a farm in Kentucky, where he could roam the bluegrass and avoid the Northeast winter.

Earlier this month, however, veterinarians discovered that Barbaro's left hind hoof was not growing back properly, and they had to remove some damaged tissue. Last week, the horse developed a deep bruise in his right heel, which Richardson tried to protect by performing a risky surgery Saturday. He tried to build a framework of metal pins, bars and a plate around the right hind leg to take all the weight off the fragile bone structure, which was already being held together with a matrix of screws.

By Sunday night, laminitis had begun to ravage Barbaro's front legs, and the Jacksons decided there was little else left to do. Barbaro was in too much distress. When they and Richardson saw the colt struggling Sunday night in a sling designed to take pressure off his legs, they determined Barbaro had lost his will to live.

"We just reached a point where it was going to be difficult for him to go on without pain," Jackson said. "It was the right decision. It was the right thing to do. We said all along if there was a situation where it would become more difficult for him, then it would be time."

As news of Barbaro's death became known early Monday, horsemen felt the loss deeply. Like Seattle Slew, Barbaro left Churchill Downs undefeated in six races. His victories were remarkable for their versatility: on grass, on dirt and at distances of a mile to a mile and a quarter.

The trainer Michael Matz, a former equestrian who won a silver medal in the 1996 Atlanta Olympics, decided as soon as Barbaro arrived as a 2-year-old at his training center in Maryland that this was a preternaturally talented colt.

Beyond Barbaro's burgeoning talent, all of his human connections were beguiled by his personality, which blended intelligence with an old soul's temperament, as one of Matz's assistants, Peter Brette, said.

Gretchen Jackson, who with her husband had been breeding and racing thoroughbreds for more than 30 years, broke the golden rule of horse ownership: She fell in love with Barbaro.

So did much of the world. The gates of the hospital here have been adorned with signs proclaiming love for Barbaro and beseeching him to heal—"Grow Hoof Grow"—since his arrival. The fruit baskets filled with green apples and carrots, elaborate flower arrangements and get-well cards arrived by the truckload. Since early June, a Barbaro Fund has attracted more than $1.2 million in donations for the hospital, which is part of the New Bolton Center at the University of Pennsylvania.

Online message boards were swamped with Barbaro news and for months became a virtual waiting room. On Monday, one of them, operated by Alex Brown, an exercise rider at the nearby Fair Hill Training Center, had its daily traffic nearly double to 15,000 visitors in a single hour.

"I love you Barbaro," read one message posted by Cheryl—NY. "Everyone in my family is praying for you & lighting candles. Stay strong & don't give up! XXOO."

The Jacksons said they would remember most the good things that had come from Barbaro's brief but brilliant life—from his Kentucky Derby victory to how he had raised the public's awareness about everything from veterinary medicine to anti-slaughterhouse legislation.

"Our hope is that some of these issues don't die," Jackson said.

While the couple acknowledged that the decision to put Barbaro down was difficult, neither they nor Richardson expressed regrets. Even after months on end of being confined in a stall here in the intensive care unit, Barbaro had never been anything but calm and relaxed, Richardson said.

"The vast majority of the time he was a happy horse," he said.

When that was no longer true Sunday night, all agreed on what had to be done.

Barbaro ate some grass for breakfast Monday morning. He was tranquilized and then a slight overdose of anesthetic was fed to him through a catheter that had already been fitted to him. "It could not have been more peaceful," Richardson said. He fought back tears throughout the news conference.

When he was asked to make sense of the deep feelings Barbaro had summoned from complete strangers and from those who knew him best, Richardson perhaps wrote Barbaro's epitaph:

"People love greatness," he said. "People love the story of his bravery."

EDITORIAL: ONE HORSE DIES

JANUARY 30, 2007 — Why should we feel so much grief at the loss of one horse? After all, this is a world in which horses are sacrificed again and again for the sport of humans. Barbaro was euthanized yesterday, eight months after he shattered his right hind leg at the start of the Preakness Stakes. After an injury like that, most racehorses would have been put down minutes later. But every race is a complex equation—a balance of economics, athleticism, equine grace and conscience. Conscience often comes in last, but not in this case. Barbaro's owners gave that horse exactly what he had given them, which is everything. It was the very least they could do, and yet it seemed truly exceptional in a sport that is barbarous as often as it is beautiful.

Barbaro was exceptional because he won the Kentucky Derby and looked as if he might have a chance at the Triple Crown. But nearly everyone who met him also talked of the life he displayed, a vivid presence that was so much more visible to us because it happened to belong to a winner.

Humans are not especially good at noticing horses, but Barbaro was easy to notice. And if his life caused us to pay attention to the possibilities of all horses, his death should cause us to pay attention to the tragedy inherent in the end of so many horses. Barbaro's death was tragic not because it was measured against the races he might have won or even against the effort to save his life. It was tragic because of what every horse is.

You would have to look a long, long time to find a dishonest or cruel horse. And the odds are that if you did find one, it was made cruel or dishonest by the company it kept with humans. It is no exaggeration to say that nearly every horse—Barbaro included—is pure of heart. Some are faster, some slower. Some wind up in the winner's circle. But they should all evoke in us the generosity of conscience—a human quality, after all— that was expended in the effort to save this one horse.

ESSAY: IS IT WORTH IT?

BY JANE SMILEY

In 1997, I had a thoroughbred mare that came down with colic in the night, and was too far gone to save by the time she was found at 6 A.M. After she was euthanized, I remember staring at her body, which was stretched out in the grass, running my hands over her. Her coat was shining. Her haunch was rounded and firm. Her feet and legs were perfect. Only that one thing had been wrong, that twist in her gut, but it was enough, and it killed her. So it is with all horses—they are engineered so close to the margins of what is physically possible that when one thing fails, it can cause the failure of the whole animal.

I watched the Preakness in 2006 with some lifelong racing people. When Barbaro was injured, we turned the TV off. All of us had seen it before; everyone who loves racing has seen it all too many times. There are horrible things you can see on TV, and I'm not going to rank them, but for me, one of the most disturbing is that dangling leg or foot—the appendage that is normally stiff and strong suddenly shattered in two. The horse himself is pumping so much adrenaline that he barely knows it yet, and all around it, distracting things are happening, but it is there, terribly wrong and terribly ominous. That's why we turned off the TV—the one thing wrong, the unbearable sight.

My mare had a foal, then a month old, by a stallion named Golden Act. He ran in the Triple Crown against Spectacular Bid. Spectacular Bid ran first, first, and third. Golden Act ran third, second, and second. My mare's pedigree was mostly French, but three of her ancestors ran in the Triple Crown. She did not. But she did something I thought of when they were trying to save Barbaro, when he seemed so game and ready to be saved— she struggled to her feet because her foal wanted to nurse, and she kept standing until she fell down. Five minutes later she was dead.

It is the paradox of racing. Barbaro's dynamic beauty and his exceptional heart were gifts Barbaro inherited from his racing forebears, who had the luck and toughness to run and win and prove themselves worthy of reproducing. Great thoroughbreds press on and prevail where other horses throw in the towel. When we saw Barbaro in last May's Kentucky Derby fly away from the field so gracefully and effortlessly, he was doing something thoroughbreds have been bred to do for 300 years—to sense the encroaching fatigue of three-quarters of a mile at top speed and want only to run faster, to push ahead and take the lead.

Barbaro's vets warned us all along that the odds were against him, but we didn't really believe them. They had hope, too. How could a horse who appeared so full of life break his leg and be so suddenly close to death? His head was fine. His back was fine. His lungs and heart and chest were fine. In fact, after a while, his broken leg was fairly fine. It was laminitis in the other hind leg that was so worrisome, since the weight of his body constantly bearing down on the delicate structures inside his foot eventually damaged and destroyed them.

A horse's hoof is wondrous structure—the outside horn is lined with delicate membranes and blood vessels that feed and support the bones of the foot. The bones of the foot are analogous to a person's fingertips, since a horse's knee is analogous to a person's wrist. The racehorse carries a thousand pounds at 35 to 40 miles per hour using a few slender bones supported by an apparatus of ligaments and tendons that have no analogues in human anatomy. Every part of the system depends on every other part. What happened to Barbaro was that the engineering couldn't take it. When it was right, as in the Kentucky Derby, it was perfectly right, and when it became wrong, it became irredeemably wrong.

During his medical saga, he showed that he was intelligent as well as beautiful, strong, and fast. According to a friend of mine who talked to trainer Michael Matz in the summer, Barbaro knew when he needed some pain relief—he would stand by the sling and shake it until they put him in it, and when he was tired of it, he would shake himself so that it rattled, signaling he was ready to be taken out. And then he would go to his stall and lie down. Just after Christmas, Dr. Dean W. Richardson, Barbaro's surgeon, wrote about the case in the *Thoroughbred Times*. He remarked, "When the four of us—the Jacksons, trainer Michael Matz, and me—were discussing the gravity of the situation, there were no dry eyes. But the nice thing is that there was one other individual there taking part in the decision who didn't have tears in his eyes. That was Barbaro! Because he was just standing there—looking like a great horse—telling us that he wanted to go on."

Did he want to survive? It seemed as though he did. Was he special or unique? Dr. Richardson was not quite willing to go that far. It was rather, according to Dr. Richardson, that they lived with Barbaro longer and got to know him better. The implication here, I think, is no disrespect to Barbaro, but rather an invitation to greater respect for other horses.

In a great racehorse, the heart and mind do the running, and the body tries to hold up. In Golden Act's pedigree, there is a horse named Your Host, who ran ninth in the Kentucky Derby of 1950, then returned to California and shorter distance races. In 1951, Your Host had an accident as devastating as Barbaro's. He clipped heels with another horse in the race and fell. According to Wikipedia, "The ulna bone of his right foreleg was fractured in four places, his right shoulder and upper leg were also fractured." His insurers, Lloyd's of London, paid the owners and took possession of him. Dr. John Walker saved him, and in 1957, he sired Kelso, who raced for eight seasons.

Everyone who loves thoroughbred horses has to contend with the fact that racing is a tough game, compounded of supreme effort and erratic luck, but if there were no racing, there would be no thoroughbreds as we know them. No one knows why Barbaro broke his leg leaving the gate in the 2006 Preakness. In the Kentucky Derby two weeks earlier, he looked happy and invincible. His training up to the Preakness was uneventful. Every breeder is always looking for that miracle combination of speed and stamina, heart, intelligence, and sheer good fortune that leads to the Triple Crown, or the Kentucky Derby, or to any graded stakes race. Few find it. But every thoroughbred lover must also recognize that the serendipitous consequence of racing's difficulty and tragedy is the very athleticism, toughness, and fire that we see in our humbler horses—the ones who never got to the track, or the ones that tried and came home to jump or do dressage or ride the trails. The ones who became broodmares.

When I think of Barbaro, I like to think also of Secretariat, and Whirlaway, and a horse I bred a mare to once named Loyal Pal. Among the three of them, they ran hundreds of times. They managed to avoid the bad steps and the bad luck, to go to the races as if a race were a trot in the park, coming back afterward to a bucket of grain and a long nap. Sometimes, thousands of fans thrilled to their exploits. Sometimes, the only ones watching were the owner, the trainer and a few punters. Like Barbaro, they did it because they were born and bred to do it, because thoroughbreds love to run, and because they didn't know what it meant not to keep on trying.

Jane Smiley's most recent novel is Ten Days in the Hills.

PART XII

◆◆◆

"If this isn't a Triple Crown horse, I don't know what one looks like."
—TRAINER BARCLAY TAGG ON NO BIZ LIKE SHOWBIZ

Belmont Park, June 2007: Rags to Riches, John Velazquez up, edges out Curlin, ridden by Robby Albarado, to win the Belmont—the first filly winner since 1905. AP IMAGES/JULIE JACOBSON

In a perfect world, this twelfth and final chapter would have been about the twelfth and newest Triple Crown champion. The trainer Barclay Tagg, who won the Derby and Preakness in 2003 with Funny Cide, thought he had that horse last year in Nobiz Like Shobiz. He didn't—nor did the owners of 34,642 thoroughbreds foaled in the United States in 2004, and who had the first Saturday in May 2007 circled in their fantasies. The odds of even getting a horse to the Kentucky Derby are staggering. By 2006, only 10,390 from that crop made it to the racetrack. On May 5, 2007, twenty of them made it to the starting gate at Churchill Downs.

The pursuit of a Derby champion has humbled people like George Steinbrenner, the principal owner of the New York Yankees; the [late] television impresario Merv Griffin; Sheik Mohammed bin Rashid al-Maktoum, the ruler of Dubai, and a who's who of business titans. In 2006, horse owners spent more than $1.26 billion at North American thoroughbred auctions in search of them.

But if 2007 didn't produce a new Triple Crown champion, it did have three very good horses each winning a leg in great style—Street Sense, Curlin and Rags to Riches, who outran the boys to become the first filly since 1902 to win the Belmont Stakes. The year's series also provided a well-rounded portrait of where the sport is today, which perhaps does not differ much from Red Smith's perception of horse racing during its Golden Era.

It still offers rich and authentic stories, such as Calvin Borel, an uneducated journeyman jockey from Cajun Country who not only captured the biggest race of his life when he triumphed in the Kentucky Derby aboard Street Sense but also lived a fantasy a couple days later when Queen Elizabeth II of England made him her guest of honor at a state dinner in the White House. There remains a hint of old-fashioned chicanery: two of the owners of Curlin, both lawyers, were found to have defrauded 400 plaintiffs out of $64.4 million—money intended to pay for injuries caused by the diet drug fen-phen—and were indicted in the week after the colt finished second in the Belmont. In the Belmont, horse racing's magic was on display when Rags to Riches overcame a stumble at the gate to duel Curlin in the stretch, instantly turning 46,870 spectators into fans of the courageous filly.

It was one of the most competitive and compelling Triple Crowns in years, and was more than enough to satisfy racing fans until the next season.

BLOODLINES WORTH THEIR WEIGHT IN GOLD

BY JOE DRAPE

MAY 1, 2007—The dream of Sheik Mohammed bin Rashid al-Maktoum to win the Kentucky Derby died this year in the same place it took flight: his desert kingdom, Dubai. His last 3-year-old prospect, a colt named Day Pass, struggled to finish ninth in the U.A.E. Derby.

The sheik did not appear disappointed that his run for the roses ended at Nad Al Sheba racetrack on March 31 rather than at Churchill Downs on Saturday. He shuttled between the multilevel royal boxes, which he shared with dozens of the male members of his family, to the paddock where some of the best thoroughbreds in the world were saddled over seven races in the hope of taking home $21.25 million of the sheik's purse money.

Sheik Mohammed switched from a gold dishdasha to a black one, gave out one trophy after another, and indicated that the Dubai World Cup, the world's richest race, was going to get richer because he intended to plump its $6 million purse to $10 million.

Like no other horseman in the world, the sheik has learned that it is easier to build the world's tallest building or create artificial islands—endeavors are under way in Dubai—than it is to win a Kentucky Derby.

In 1999, he sent Worldly Manner to the Derby, proclaiming that if the colt did not win the race, one of his horses would do so within four years.

From 1999 to 2002, however, his stable went 0 for 5 in the Derby, with a top finish of sixth, by China Visit in 2000.

He has not been back since.

"We'll go to the Derby when we've got the horses," said Simon Crisford, the manager of the Maktoum family's Godolphin Stable, which is based in Dubai and has sent horses to victories in many of the most prestigious races around the globe.

There is little doubt that the sheik is spending a great deal of money to return to Churchill Downs. He has been the leading buyer at Keeneland's September yearling sales over the past eight years, spending $245.6 million. The sheik has also built a commercial breeding and racing business on more than 4,000 acres in the bluegrass of Kentucky.

James Tafel can match the sheik's passion for finding a Kentucky Derby winner, but not his bankroll. Nearly 25 years ago, Tafel retired as the chairman and chief executive of a publishing company near Chicago and began racing, and then breeding, horses.

"You know the appeal of the Kentucky Derby is pretty spectacular and straightforward," said Tafel, who is 83 and lives in Boynton Beach, Fla. "It's the aspiration of all horsemen to have a horse in the race. It's our gold standard. I make the case it's the greatest race in the world, because if you're on a plane or waiting in line, and you tell someone you're in the horse business, the only question they have is, 'Have you won the Kentucky Derby?'"

Now, the two men are linked. On Saturday, Tafel will be in the paddock at Churchill Downs for the Derby with Street Sense, a colt who was the 2-year-old champion last year and will be among the favorites. His sire, Street Cry, is owned by Sheik Mohammed, as is the colt's mother, Bedazzle, who was purchased last year by the sheik's breeding operation, Darley America.

The sheik may not have a horse running in the Derby, but his impact on American thoroughbred racing is being felt. Another one of the sheik's Kentucky-based sires, Cherokee Run, is the father of the Derby starter Zanjero. If Street Sense or Zanjero wins, Darley America will be able to command bigger breeding paydays for years to come.

The value of Street Cry, for example, has increased largely because of the accomplishments of Street Sense, who won last year's Breeders' Cup Juvenile. When Tafel matched Bedazzle with the recently retired Street Cry, he was gambling a $30,000 stud fee on a new sire. Now, Street Cry stands for $50,000, a figure that will most likely double if Street Sense wins the Derby.

Last fall, the sheik acknowledged that he had made a mistake by buying too many horses with pedigrees better suited to the turf racing in Europe than the dirt in America. Tafel says he understands how Sheik Mohammed has repositioned his operation for a more effective Kentucky Derby run. He has done so, too, but on a much smaller scale. Tafel culled his brood-mares to 6 from 12; the sheik has more than 160 in Kentucky.

"You get into the racing side of the game, and you end up with some nice fillies or mares, and their value is greater as breeding stock," said Tafel, who has had one other Derby horse, Vicar, who finished 18th in 1999. "So you back into the breeding game, and it sustains the racing operation in lean times."

The making of Street Sense is perhaps further evidence that beating the long odds of getting a horse to the Derby has more to do with luck than with money or strategy.

In 2002, Tafel watched as his horse Unshaded, who had won the 2000 Travers Stakes, was trounced by an impressive-looking horse in the Stephen Foster Handicap at Churchill Downs. It was Street Cry.

"I remembered what a great back end he had and how much balance," Tafel said. "It just stuck with me."

When he showed Street Sense to Carl Nafzger, his trainer of 23 years, both men were impressed. Here was a perfectly proportioned weanling he had produced in the fields of Kentucky. When the offers to buy the yearling began coming in, they knew they had a reason to be impressed.

"Well, he was about as perfect a specimen as you've seen, as a weanling, as a yearling to now," Nafzger said. "You couldn't buy one that looked this good all the way through."

Tafel has refused to hear any offers for the horse, especially from the sheik, who last year offered $17 million to Elizabeth Valando, the owner of Nobiz Like Shobiz, after the colt won a maiden race. Valando turned it down, and Nobiz will be among the Derby favorites on Saturday.

In 2005, Tafel sold Bedazzle to a group led by Nafzger for $180,000 at the Keeneland November breeding stock sale. Last fall, after Street Sense ran off to a record 10-length victory in the Breeders' Cup Juvenile, Nafzger sold the mare to Darley America for an undisclosed price.

Tafel says he has no regrets. In Street Sense, win or lose, he has a valuable stallion prospect. A victory Saturday, however, would increase the colt's value to as much as $30 million. But that is not what Tafel or, he suspects, Sheik Mohammed views as the point of racing and breeding.

"It's the Kentucky Derby," Tafel said. "And just thinking about walking a horse over there as good as this one is more excitement than a guy my age should be able to have."

STREET SENSE WINS DERBY AFTER GIVING FIELD A HEAD START

BY JOE DRAPE

LOUISVILLE, MAY 5, 2007 — Calvin Borel had Street Sense in 19th place and about a half a block behind the leaders as the field hit the backstretch in the 133rd running of the Kentucky Derby. Was he worried? Hardly. He had the agile colt next to his beloved rail, and they don't call the jockey "Bo-Rail" here at Churchill Downs for nothing.

"I had a bomb," Borel said.

He and Street Sense picked up one horse after another, hugging the rail on the far turn as if it were magnetized. Finally, the explosion: Street Sense vaulted from the rail with a quarter-mile to go, took aim at the leader, Hard Spun, and then he was gone.

In the charts, it will say Street Sense circled the mile and a quarter in 2:02.17 for a two-and-a-half-length victory. In the racing history books, it will say that Street Sense became the first winner of the Breeders' Cup Juvenile to win the Kentucky Derby, and the first 2-year-old champion to wear the roses since Spectacular Bid in 1979.

Street Sense's performance, however, was far more than that. Not only was he dominating, but he also did it so effortlessly that Borel said that he had yet to see the best of the colt.

"I really don't know how good he is," said Borel, a 40-year-old journeyman who captured his first Derby in his fifth try. "He is a push-button horse. He'll put you in a spot where you want to be at any time and then relax."

Street Sense, a son of Street Cry out of the mare Bedazzle, was plenty good yesterday. While Hard Spun, Cowtown Cat and Teuflesberg took the field through a brisk half-mile of 46.26 seconds, Borel actually asked Street Sense to slow down.

"I knew they were going quick and so I backed him up," Borel said.

In a box at the finish line, the colt's trainer and owner, Carl Nafzger and Jim Tafel, liked what they saw.

"Calvin has a clock in his head that is unreal," said Nafzger, who won his second Kentucky Derby 17 years after he captured his first with Unbridled in 1990.

Tafel, 83, began believing that the prophecy Nafzger recited to him last October was about to be fulfilled. "We're going to win the Kentucky Derby," Nafzger had told the owner he had served for 23 years after Street Sense had finished third in a race at Keeneland in Lexington, Ky.

Even though Street Sense did not win that race, the Breeders' Cup Futurity, he demonstrated an ability to relax behind horses and rocket past them when Borel asked.

"He had learned his lessons," Nafzger said.

The crowd of 156,635, which was the third largest in Derby history and included Queen Elizabeth II, was about to see how well Street Sense had comprehended the racing business. They had sent him off as the 9-2 betting favorite.

As Street Sense hit the far turn, Cowtown Cat and Teuflesberg started backing up. Borel and his colt were picking up steam.

"Street Sense came blowing through there and it was like a big old wave," said Garrett Gomez, the jockey aboard the eighth-place finisher Any Given Saturday.

Hard Spun, however, was still running. First, he beat back the challenge of Sedgefield.

"I said, 'Let's go,' and he got to running," Hard Spun's rider, Mario Pino, said.

Borel was not worried. The rail was open and Street Sense was polishing it.

"The ones in front of me were getting tired and drifting apart," he said. "It was wide open."

It was time. Street Sense came off the turn like a slingshot and zoomed outside of Sedgefield. Hard Spun was next. From the middle of the track, Borel took aim at the leader. He said he knew the race was over.

"It was just a matter of how far he wins by," Borel said.

In an instant, Street Sense streaked into the lead. Hard Spun's trainer, Larry Jones, held faint hope that his colt was about to win the Derby. "I felt pretty good around the turn," he said. "I could only see one horse moving. But he came with authority."

Borel crossed the reins one, two, three, four, five times. He looked back again.

In the clubhouse box, Nafzger nudged Tafel.

"Mr. Tafel, we're clear, we're clear," he said. "It's up to him now."

Borel showed Street Sense the whip once, then twice and then he could not help himself. He lifted his whip high in celebration.

He was yards from the wire. It did not matter.

Street Sense was on his way to his fourth victory in eight starts and, with the $1.45 million first-place check, his earnings were about to grow to nearly $3 million.

Nafzger had been in the winner's circle of America's greatest race before. Tafel had not. He had bred the colt himself, to some criticism from his friends. Street Cry was a new—and thus unproven—stallion at the time. Bedazzle was an unproven dam.

"This is the epitome of anybody in the horse business," he said. "It's the most difficult race in the world to win."

For Borel, the victory was even more monumental. He had grown up in Louisiana and learned to ride on the region's fabled Cajun bush tracks. Borel knew horses. He dropped out of school in eighth grade and devoted his life to them.

He still comes to the track here at dawn each morning to help his brother, Cecil, a trainer. He mucks stalls, exercises and rubs down horses. But Borel always wondered if he would get the opportunity to ride a great one, a horse good enough to win the most famous race in the world.

"I always knew I had the ability," he said. "I just had to find the horse to get me there."

Borel has found him. His name is Street Sense. And today, he is the only colt in the world with the opportunity to become the next, and only the 12th, Triple Crown champion.

A HARD RACE FROM THE BACKSTRETCH TO THE WHITE HOUSE

BY JOE DRAPE

LOUISVILLE, MAY 10, 2007—There was the hug from President Bush, and small talk with Chief Justice John G. Roberts Jr., and the introduction to Queen Elizabeth II. Calvin Borel blushed as he recounted the fairy tale evening at the White House, a grin cracking across a face as well worn as an old saddle.

There he was, all 5 feet 4 inches and 114 pounds of him, amid the heavyweights of politics and culture. Borel, 40, was in that company because he had ridden a colt named Street Sense to victory in the Kentucky Derby two days earlier. Had he not been intimidated by their star power and tongue-tied by his grade school education, Borel could have told them a remarkable tale about how a son of a sugar cane farmer came to win the United States' biggest horse race.

How he learned to ride as an 8-year-old tied to the saddle in match races against horses carrying roosters at bush tracks like Cajun Downs in southern Louisiana. How the whip he carried to school each day was more important to him than his textbooks. How by eighth grade, his father finally let him quit school to chase the horses.

Borel's brother Cecil, older by 13 years and a trainer, became a loving taskmaster for an advanced education in horsemanship. It is a family tradition in Acadiana, a region known for fighting roosters and sawdust-floored honky-tonks as well as some of the finest jockeys, including the Hall of Famers Eddie Delahoussaye and Kent Desormeaux.

"He told me to go out and work hard and be the best jockey I could be," Borel said in a melodic Cajun singsong, referring to his father. "He just wanted me to do things the right way and be happy."

Borel's brave, rail-skimming ride of Street Sense in the Derby attests to his skills, but the fact that he is back here at Churchill Downs to work out some far less expensive horses speaks volumes about how well he has heeded his father's advice.

"You don't forget the people who brung you here," Borel said. "Just 'cause I've gotten on a million-dollar horse doesn't mean I can't still get on a $5,000 one."

Until Borel heads to Baltimore to ride Street Sense on May 19 in the Preakness Stakes, he will spend his days the same way he always has: on top of, taking care of or thinking about horses.

It has been the rhythm of his life since he began his apprenticeship in Vinton, La., where Cecil had a stable of 60 horses at Delta Downs. Borel remains Boo, short for Boo-Boo, which his parents, Clovis and Ella, thought they had made when their fifth son was born. On the racetrack, he is called Bo-Rail for his insistence on taking the shortest route.

Borel learned the business from the ground up, mucking out stalls, changing horses' bandages, rubbing their legs, working them out in the mornings and racing them in the afternoons. Fourteen-hour days were the norm, and Cecil was a demanding teacher.

"We didn't have much book education," Cecil Borel said. "But we've worked very hard. I'm proud that Calvin has earned everything he's gotten."

When Borel broke ribs, punctured a lung and had his spleen removed after a spill at Evangeline Downs in Lafayette, La., Cecil was among the first to comfort him. When Borel returned to the track, however, Cecil put him on the same horse, a filly named Miss Touchdown, for his first race.

They won.

"You know with Cecil it's always been about hard work, and having no fear," Borel said. "Those are pretty simple rules, and I owe him everything for passing that on to me."

Simplicity remains a hallmark of Borel's life. Each morning at 5:30, he drives his seven-year-old pickup with more than 130,000 miles to the track, where his agent, Jerry Hissam, will have up to eight horses for him to work. Each race afternoon, Borel maneuvers an inexpensive horse with the same fierce focus as he does a Triple Crown contender like Street Sense.

Some horses come from established barns like that of Carl Nafzger, Street Sense's trainer. Some are from barns like Sam Dorsey's. A week before the Derby, Dorsey watched as Borel won with his filly Deputy Sammie in a low-level race at 34-to-1 odds.

"He loves winning, period," said Hissam, who has been Borel's agent since 1991. "I think he likes winning for the guys who have a couple of horses and are trying to make a living a little bit more than the big outfits. They are his people."

Borel's Derby victory has been a popular one on the backside of Churchill Downs, which is a far more humble precinct than the White House. Security guards, grooms, riders and owners have congratulated him or swallowed him in hugs here this week. Although Borel has won more than 4,300 races, as well as riding titles from here to Louisiana Downs and Oaklawn Park in Arkansas, he has yet to break into the top tier of the nation's jockeys.

Nafzger, for one, does not understand why. Borel has been the pilot for all eight of Street Sense's races and virtually all of his important workouts. In 1990, when Nafzger won the Derby with Unbridled, another rider with deep Louisiana roots, Craig Perret, was in the irons. It was no accident.

"Before there was glamour, girls and money, these guys were learning how to communicate with horses," Nafzger said. "I rely on Calvin to tell me how Street Sense is feeling, what he needs, what he's lacking. He's a horseman as good as they come."

Borel hardly feels slighted. He wears his emotions close to his skin.

When Cecil found him in the winner's circle and told him the Derby was for their father, who died three years ago, Borel cried. Their mother, partly paralyzed by a stroke, is in a nursing home. Borel cries for her, too.

He mists up when he tells how much Cecil has given him and how lucky he is to have a woman who loves him. Lisa Funk met Borel seven years ago at Ellis Park in Kentucky. She was a 21-year-old college student; he was 33. There was an age difference and a cultural divide, but their friendship turned into romance and they are engaged to be married.

"I had never met a man who was so happy about his life, about what he was doing," said Funk, who graduated from the University of Louisville and is pursuing a teaching certificate. "He loves his family. He loves his horses. He wants to go to work every day."

She was his date Monday at the White House, and perhaps they were the most unlikely couple at the ball. As much as Borel will cherish the memory of putting on a white tie and tails, he made it clear that the experience had not gone to his head.

On Thursday at Churchill Downs, Neil Howard was atop a stable pony when he encountered Borel. Howard trains horses for William S. Farish, a prominent breeder and former United States ambassador to Britain, who was host to the queen at the Derby.

Howard teased Borel about the heady company he had been keeping.

"I hear you won't ride claiming horses anymore," Howard said. "I hear that you're a big-time rider now."

Borel smiled wide. He eased up to Howard's horse and began stroking its nose.

"You know that ain't true, Mr. Neil," he said. "I know who my people are. I'd ride this here pony if you asked me to. You know I would."

IN FINAL STRIDES, CURLIN ENDS BID FOR THE CROWN

BY JOE DRAPE

BALTIMORE, MAY 19, 2007—As Street Sense angled out of the final turn past Hard Spun, much as he did two weeks ago in the Kentucky Derby, Carl Nafzger, the colt's trainer, nudged Jim Tafel, his owner, and tight, satisfied smiles spread across their faces. Street Sense was en route to the Belmont Stakes with a chance to sweep the Triple Crown.

Even Calvin Borel, aboard Street Sense, believed he was home free: "I thought it was all over," he said.

Robby Albarado, however, was atop a colt named Curlin and knew the real running in the Preakness Stakes was just beginning. He had his colt out in the middle of the track poised to pounce. Like Borel, Albarado had learned his craft on the bush tracks of Louisiana. Like Borel, he had toiled just below the nation's elite jockeys.

Two races earlier, Albarado took a hard fall on the turf course trying to avoid a fallen horse and rider. His day got worse when Curlin stumbled out of the gate, nearly scraping his knees. But an eighth of a mile to the wire, Curlin was only a length and a half from Street Sense.

First, Borel heard the big chestnut rolling behind him. Then he peeked beneath his shoulder and saw Albarado looming larger.

Each jockey pulled the head of his horse toward his rival, asking each to dig deeper and be better than the other. For 40 yards, the two powerful colts moved as if they were a crew rowing on a river: Borel fanned his whip with his left hand, Albarado with his right.

When they hit the wire, the record crowd of 121,263 at Pimlico Race Course needed a photo finish to sort out the duel.

Albarado and Borel did not.

"You got me," Albarado said Borel told him immediately.

Nafzger and Tafel did not need a photo either. They knew their Triple Crown dreams were over.

"They nipped us," Nafzger said, the smile turning into a grimace.

The margin of Curlin's victory was actually a head, and the two colts covered the mile and three-sixteenths in 1 minute 53.46 seconds, equaling the Preakness Stakes record set by Tank's Prospect in 1985 and tied by Louis Quatorze in 1996.

"Heartbreaking, that's what it was," said Nafzger, whose colt looked invincible galloping off with the Kentucky Derby by two and a quarter lengths. "We only needed a nose. Curlin ran a hell of a race, but we had Curlin. We should have never let him come back and get us."

The drama of a wonderfully run race could not capture the ebullience displayed by Albarado and the colt's trainer, Steve Asmussen, who had just captured their first victory in a Triple Crown race.

They had done the seemingly impossible: Curlin did not race as a 2-year-old, but now has gone from maiden winner to Classic champion in four races over three months. To do so, the colt, a son of Smart Strike out of the mare Sheriff's Deputy, had to recover from a momentum-wrecking stumble at the gate, which was all too reminiscent of the Derby.

At Churchill Downs, Curlin failed to break cleanly from the gate and was blocked three times as Albarado guided him around the track. He still finished third. It was a gallant effort for a horse that showed so much promise in his first race that a consortium of owners purchased 80 percent of him for $3.5 million.

"We threw the Derby out of mind," said Jess Jackson, one of Curlin's owners and the founder of Kendall Jackson Vineyards. "We never lost faith in him."

But when Curlin faltered in the opening strides Saturday, Asmussen's heart sank.

"Robby was nudging on him early," he said. "I was worried about the replay of the Derby at that point."

So was Albarado. He was not having a good day. Aboard Einstein in the Dixie Stakes, a mile-and-an-eighth turf race, he was unseated trying to avoid a horse named Mending Fences and his jockey, Eddie Castro. Both riders came out uninjured, but Mending Fences had to be euthanized after sustaining a fracture.

"I was on the grass course, so I kind of slid for 10, 15 feet," he said. "I was very, very lucky I didn't get hurt."

In the main event, Albarado had to overcome his unlucky start, which meant adopting, in his words, "Plan B." It essentially entailed riding Curlin every stride.

"I had to step on him a bit and get him in the race," Albarado said.

Curlin is a mammoth chestnut colt with a high cruising speed. Albarado found it in the backstretch while Hard Spun, Xchanger and Flying First Class set wickedly fast fractions of 45.75 for a half-mile, and 1:09.80 for three-quarters of a mile.

As the three speedsters collapsed in front of them, Borel and Albarado started to make their moves. Borel went inside, Albarado outside. It looked as if Borel had the faster horse as he surged into the stretch and seemed to leave Curlin behind him. Albarado knew better.

"I think I got enough time to get to him," Albarado said. "Curlin just has this way about him, the last part of the race he wants to win."

Curlin has won four of five lifetime starts, and he increased his career winnings to $1.6 million.

Street Sense also has a way about him that has concerned Borel and Nafzger in previous races: He loses focus after he passes horses and lets them catch up to him.

"He hung a bit, started looking around about 40 yards from home," Borel said. "He just got outrun."

Nafzger was gracious in defeat. He conceded Street Sense was defeated "fair and square," and hailed the effort not only of Curlin but of Hard Spun, who followed his runner-up finish at the Derby by hanging on for third here.

When Street Sense won the Derby, Borel was invited to a White House dinner to meet Queen Elizabeth II. All week here, Nafzger was confident in his colt and confessed to enjoying his status as "king of the mountain."

Now, Curlin has a claim on that crown. Unfortunately, it will not be that of a Triple Crown champion, a fact modern horsemen have grown accustomed to since Affirmed was the last to sweep the Triple Crown races in 1978.

"We have two good horses here—we might have an Alydar-Affirmed thing," said Nafzger, referring to the colt that pushed Affirmed in each of the classic races. "Curlin is a racehorse. If he wasn't a racehorse, he wouldn't have overcome the lead that we had on him. How good is he? Hell, that's why we run them."

A GREAT HORSE, BUT WHO TAKES THE WINNINGS?

BY JOE DRAPE

JUNE 4, 2007—When Curlin chased down the Kentucky Derby winner Street Sense to capture the Preakness Stakes, his owners bounded to the winners' circle at Pimlico Race Course. They were an eclectic bunch that included a winemaker, a computer magnate, an investment banker and two lawyers.

W. L. Carter was just as ecstatic while his wife narrated the race over his cellphone as he drove through the horse country of Ocala, Fla. "They could hear me all the way up to Gainesville," he said.

But his delight depends on the answer to one of racing's thorniest questions: who will Curlin be running for in the Belmont Stakes on Saturday?

Carter believes he has a piece of Curlin, a mammoth chestnut colt whose value increases with every stride of his brief but brilliant career and who is already worth as much as $30 million as a stallion prospect.

Carter is among more than 400 plaintiffs in a civil suit who were found to have been defrauded by their lawyers out of $64.4 million—money intended to pay for injuries caused by the diet drug fen-phen.

Two of those lawyers, William J. Gallion and Shirley A. Cunningham Jr., together own a fifth of Curlin and were in the Pimlico winners' circle.

"We own part of that horse—there's about 400 of us," Carter said. "We may not have our names on the papers, but it's our horse. He was bought with our blood money."

It may soon be up to the courts to determine just who owns Curlin.

Gallion and Cunningham have had their law licenses suspended. A federal grand jury has begun to investigate potential criminal wrongdoing arising from the fen-phen settlement.

Angela M. Ford, who represents Carter and most of the other plaintiffs, argues that her clients own all of Curlin. She contends that Gallion and Cunningham originally purchased the colt with ill-gotten gains—they paid $57,000 for the colt at the 2005 Keeneland September Yearling Sale — and had no legal right to sell 80 percent of the horse for $3.5 million, as they did in February.

Gallion's and Mr. Cunningham's new partners are no strangers to the vagaries of the horse business.

One partner, Jess Jackson, the founder of Kendall-Jackson wines, has sued several of his former advisers, charging they defrauded him out of $3 million by overcharging him for horses he purchased and taking kickbacks from sellers.

Another partner, Satish Sanan, who made his fortune addressing the computer concerns brought on by Y2K, said he, too, had been victimized by slick horse traders. It prompted him to push for a code of ethics for sellers and buyers. Mr. Sanan is now in the forefront of the industry's reform movement.

Sanan said that he and his partners were not aware of the legal problems faced by Gallion and Mr. Cunningham when they purchased their portion of Curlin. He says that the lawyers that worked on the contract on their behalf have, however, assured them that their interest in the colt is protected.

Still, Sanan concedes that having a colt competing in Triple Crown races under a legal cloud is not the face he or the sport of thoroughbred racing wants to put forward.

"I don't think it says a whole lot good about the industry, to be honest with you," said Sanan, who said he had spent $150 million breeding and racing horses.

"It takes the limelight away from the horse," he said. "At the end of the day, racing is all about the horses. Unfortunately, now the focus is on the ownership and the team."

The pursuit of a Kentucky Derby champion can make for strange bedfellows. When Curlin demolished eight other horses, romping by 12¾ lengths in his very first race, on Feb. 3 at Gulfstream Park in Florida, Gallion and Cunningham were bombarded with dozens of offers to sell the colt.

Most of them were for far more than the $3.5 million offered by Jackson, Sanan and George Bolton, an investment banker in San Francisco. But the higher bids were for the whole horse. Jackson, Sanan and Bolton were willing to let Midnight Cry Stable, the banner under which Gallion and Cunningham race, retain a piece of Curlin and chase a Kentucky Derby victory.

In the days before the Derby, in which Curlin finished third, photographs of Cunningham and Gallion in connection with the colt appeared in a couple of Kentucky newspapers. It did not go unnoticed among the fen-phen plaintiffs in a horse-crazy state.

The $200 million fen-phen settlement, paid by American Home Products Corporation in 2001, was earmarked to compensate the plaintiffs for claims of heart damage caused by the drug combination, which had been withdrawn from the market at the request of the Food and Drug Administration.

When the plaintiffs sued the drug maker, they agreed to pay the lawyers 30 percent to 33 percent of any money that was recovered, in addition to expenses. In this case, that would have left the 440 clients to divide perhaps $135 million. The clients, however, received only $74 million and, on average, received less than 40 percent of what the settlement agreement specified, instead of the roughly 70 percent to which they were entitled.

Sanan said he and the other partners are focused solely on Curlin and have found Cunningham and Gallion pleasant team members. On the night before the Preakness, the group met for dinner at a farm near Pimlico owned by Bolton's father. They will unite in New York on Saturday to see if Curlin can win for the fifth time in six races when he goes in the Belmont Stakes, the final leg of thoroughbred racing's Triple Crown.

W. L. Carter cannot be as benevolent. But Carter, a builder of industrial models from Lawrenceburg, Ky., will be watching the Belmont intently, rooting for a horse and its growing worth, a value he someday hopes to share in.

"I'm cheering for the colt," Carter said. "He was bought with stolen money, but I want Curlin to do well. He is one magnificent racehorse, and I'm invested in him."

[Note: In October, 2007 a state judge in Kentucky ruled that the former clients of William Gallion and Shirley Cunningham were entitled to a 20 percent stake in Curlin. Gallion and Cunningham were in jail awaiting trial on a charge of conspiracy to commit wire fraud.]

IN A STIRRING BELMONT, THE FILLY
BEATS THE FELLAS

BY JOE DRAPE

JUNE 10, 2007 — No, it did not start well for Rags to Riches, or for that matter the filly's jockey, John Velazquez, or her trainer, Todd Pletcher. She stumbled out of the gate for the 139th running of the Belmont Stakes, and for a heart-in-your-throat moment, Velazquez and Pletcher had a simultaneous and bitter thought: Why did we do this? Why did we run this girl against the boys when history told us it was foolish?

Two minutes later, however, Velazquez had Rags to Riches eyeball-to-eyeball with the Preakness champion, Curlin, and Pletcher was on his feet in a clubhouse box, his heart thumping in his chest, his voice uncharacteristically growing louder.

"Come on, baby! Come on, baby! Come on, baby!" Pletcher cried.

He is a placid man by nature, and a humbled one when it comes to Triple Crown races. He has been the nation's leading trainer three years running, but before yesterday he had saddled 28 horses in the Kentucky Derby, the Preakness Stakes and the Belmont, and had not visited the winner's circle.

Both Rags to Riches and Curlin had 4-for-5 records, but Curlin was a mammoth colt and Rags to Riches was just the 22nd filly to enter the Belmont. Only two had won the race, the last a filly named Tanya in 1905.

Now, they were alone in the final quarter-mile of the Belmont's grueling and once-in-a-lifetime distance of a mile and a half, rolling like a pair of freight trains, with Curlin taking the inside rail and Rags to Riches, a head in front of him, simply refusing to give up. Suddenly, the 46,870 spectators at this grand old racetrack on Long Island were on their feet and echoing Pletcher's cry of "Come on, baby!"

This was a Belmont for the ages. No matter which horse anyone here had bet on, it was clear in the final strides that the only payoff anyone wanted was to witness something they would not forget. When Rags to Riches crossed the finish line an elegant head in front of Curlin, Pletcher was pumping his arm in full exultation, as was Velazquez aboard the filly, and the crowd erupted in a deafening ovation.

"It hadn't been done in 102 years," said Pletcher, his face flushed from Rags to Riches' feat.

Velazquez, too, was stunned. In 2004, he was awarded the Eclipse Award as the nation's outstanding jockey, but he entered yesterday's race 0 for 20 in Triple Crown races.

"My heart stopped," Velazquez said of the initial stumble. "Good thing this was a mile and half and she had time to get herself together."

The Belmont's marathon distance, indeed, played to Rags to Riches' strengths. Her father, A. P. Indy, won the Belmont in 1992, and her mother, Better Than Honour, produced last year's winner, Jazil. While C P West and Slew's Tizzy led the field of seven around the track for the first mile in a tepid 1:40.23, Velazquez angled Rags to Riches to the outside and let her settle into fifth place, still within four lengths of the leaders.

"Todd and I had talked and all we wanted was to give her a good chance around the turn," Velazquez said. "We didn't want her jumping up and wasting a lot of energy. We didn't want too much dirt kicked in her face."

Robby Albarado aboard Curlin knew exactly where Rags to Riches was located. First, he bulled Hard Spun and jockey Garrett Gomez out of the way.

"The filly jumped right on top of me," Albarado said.

She inched ahead of Curlin in the stretch. Still, there was a long half-mile to go, and Albarado believed that Curlin was going to run down Rags to Riches just as he did the Kentucky Derby winner Street Sense in the Preakness.

But it was not happening this time. "They came home fast and he never stopped," Albarado said of Curlin.

Rags to Riches and Curlin were actually going super fast—they covered the last quarter-mile in 23 ⅘ seconds, trading head bobs like painted horses on a carousel.

"I thought at one point he could come back and get her, but she is tough," Albarado said.

How tough? Beyond the dismal record of fillies in the Belmont, consider the fact that only 38 of them have started in the Kentucky Derby since it began in 1875, and only 3 have won: Regret in 1915, Genuine Risk in 1980 and Winning Colors in 1988. In the Preakness, which was first run in 1873, a total of 52 have tried to beat the boys and 4 came out winners, the last being Nellie Morse in 1924.

The owners of Rags to Riches, Michael Tabor and Derrick Smith, knew what they were up against when they decided to try her here. They hoped their move would be received as a sporting gesture because, beyond the $600,000 first-place check, it hardly increased the horse's value.

"It was all about prestige," Tabor said.

When Velazquez guided Rags to Riches back to the winner's circle with the blanket of white carnations draped over her neck, Smith, Tabor, Pletcher and Velazquez knew it was about much more than prestige. What had started with a stumble out of the starting gate was ending with a coronation for an unlikely queen in the sport of kings.

Rags to Riches was greeted with raucous cheers by a crowd that understood it had witnessed something special. Why had Tabor, Smith and Pletcher entered Rags to Riches in a grueling race when history told them they were likely to end up looking like fools?

"We thought it was something the public would like to see," Tabor said. "It was a fantastic feat."

He was correct on both counts.

ESSAY: THE VIEW FROM AFAR

BY GINA RARICK

When I was growing up on a dairy farm in Wisconsin, I wanted a horse more than anything. I can't explain the equine fascination that so often grips children, but like many little girls, I was taken in, first by the Misty books, then the Black Stallion stories. But maybe more than any of those fictitious friends, what captured my imagination every spring were the Triple Crown races.

I looked forward to that first Saturday in May when *Wide World of Sports* devoted an entire hour of coverage to the Kentucky Derby. I was glued to the TV, devouring the profiles of each horse, the pomp and ceremony of the post parade, the celebration in the winner's circle. Most of all, I loved the moment when Jim McKay took the winning jockey aside and reviewed the race film with him, discussing every stride toward victory.

I never was allowed to have a horse ("smelly, dangerous and useless," was what my grandmother, the matriarch of our farm, thought of the beasts), and when I grew up and went to college, the urge faded. But it did not die; it just hibernated until a premature midlife crisis found me in the saddle at 30, taking riding lessons for the first time. At 44, I'm training my own racehorses in France, a world away from Churchill Downs, Pimlico or Belmont Park.

Now, Longchamp, Chantilly, Newmarket and Ascot are the epicenter of my racing world. I pay more attention to the French and English derbies than the one in Kentucky. I have learned a lot about horses since those early days in front of television, but I know now that my early instincts were right on the money: the horses running in those prestigious races deserved every bit of admiration I had for them. The odds against training a horse capable of running at the top level are staggering. Everything has to go right. The horse needs the right breeding, conformation, talent, heart and a good dose of luck to be in peak condition on the big day.

While European and American racing are very different, trainers on both sides of the Atlantic share the same frustrations. You can leave the stable after tucking your star in for the night and come back the next morning to find him mysteriously standing on three legs—or worse.

But the challenge of preparing an equine athlete, of finding out what makes each individual horse tick, the thrill when it all comes together at the right time, keeps us all going.

It's unlikely that a horse based in Europe will ever tackle the American Triple Crown. The races fall too early in the three-year-old season; it would be a huge risk for a European trainer to ship an essentially unproven young horse to the United States in May. The Breeders' Cup races are a more practical target, because they are run in the autumn, when the cream of the three-year-old crop has already risen to the top and the older horses have solidified their credentials.

There's also a big difference between Churchill Downs and Longchamp—and not just in racing surfaces. The main track at Churchill, which looked so imposing on TV all those years ago, is only a mile in circumference, tiny by European standards. The Grande Piste at Longchamp is a sweeping 2,750 meters, or about a mile and three quarters.

American horses also are allowed to use several medications on race day, all of which are banned in Europe. But a European horse running in America is almost obligated to run on medication in order to compete.

I am a convert to European racing; it has proven the axiom that, no, you really can't go home again. Still, my American roots come through now and again. I have a quick little three-year-old that I like to race on the synthetic sand track at Deauville, a style of racing not far from what I used to watch growing up.

And when a Seattle Slew colt came through the sales ring here a few years ago, I had to bid, and ended up taking him home. He was called So Long Slew, and he didn't cost very much so I knew there had to be something wrong with him. There was: he had a wind problem. I trained him for a few months anyway, mostly just because it was fun riding a son of Seattle Slew around for awhile.

I sold him to a stud in Belgium; his pedigree was so impressive that he could be a stallion without ever having run. He has a few foals on the ground, and some of them show signs of being useful racehorses.

I remember watching his father sweep the Triple Crown in 1977; So Long looked quite a lot like his dad. It's unlikely I'll ever have a closer brush with greatness in horses. It takes a lot of money—or a lot of luck—to possess a true champion.

I'm also unlikely ever to run a horse in my native country. But on the first Saturday in May, my thoughts still drift toward Kentucky, and I still stay up until midnight with a mint julip to watch the race.

While I love European racing, I miss the American spirit. Racing people are more reserved on this side of the pond. When Ouija Board kicked off her glorious Group 1 career with a victory in the English Oaks, Lord Derby turned to his trainer, Ed Dunlop, with a reserved "well done." By comparison, who could forget moments like the one in 1990 when Carl Nafzger, the trainer of Unbridled, yelled into the ear of the horse's aging owner, Frances Genter, "Mrs. Genter, you've won the Kentucky Derby!"?

When I am lucky enough to see one of my horses charging up the home stretch with a chance, my European friends will make no mistake about my origins. I still scream like an American.

Gina Rarick is an editor and reporter at The International Herald Tribune *who has trained thoroughbred racehorses in Maison-Lafittes, France.*

APPENDIX: THE TRIPLE CROWN

(continued)

YEAR	HORSE	KENTUCKY DERBY	PREAKNESS STAKES	BELMONT STAKES
1967	Damascus	3rd	1st	1st
1966	Kauai King	1st	1st	4th
1964	Northern Dancer	1st	1st	3rd
1963	Chateaugay	1st	2nd	1st
1961	Carry Back	1st	1st	7th
1958	Tim Tam	1st	1st	2nd
1956	Needles	1st	2nd	1st
1955	Nashua	2nd	1st	1st
1953	Native Dancer	2nd	1st	1st
1950	Middleground	1st	2nd	1st
1949	Capot	2nd	1st	1st
1944	Pensive	1st	1st	2nd
1942	Shut Out	1st	5th	1st
1940	Bimelech	2nd	1st	1st
1939	Johnstown	1st	5th	1st
1936	Bold Venture	1st	1st	dns
1932	Burgoo King	1st	1st	dns
1931	Twenty Grand	1st	2nd	1st
1923	Zev	1st	12th	1st
1922	Pillory	dns	1st	1st
1920	Man o' War	dns	1st	1st
1895	Belmar	dns	1st	1st
1881	Saunterer	dns	1st	1st
1880	Grenada	dns	1st	1st
1878	Duke of Magenta	dns	1st	1st
1877	Cloverbrook	dns	1st	1st

* - won on a disqualification

		KENTUCKY DERBY			
YEAR	WINNER	JOCKEY	TRAINER	SECOND	THIRD
2007	Street Sense	Calvin Borel	Carl Nafzger	Hard Spun	Curlin
2006	Barbaro	Edgar Prado	Michael Matz	Bluegrass Cat	Steppenwolfer
2005	Giacomo	Mike Smith	John Shirreffs	Closing Argument	Afleet Alex
2004	Smarty Jones	Stewart Elliott	John Servis	Lion Heart	Imperialism
2003	Funny Cide	Jose Santos	Barclay Tagg	Empire Maker	Peace Rules
2002	War Emblem	Victor Espinoza	Bob Baffert	Proud Citizen	Perfect Drift
2001	Monarchos	Jorge Chavez	John Ward Jr.	Invisible Ink	Congaree
2000	Fusaichi Pegasus	Kent Desormeaux	Neil Drysdale	Aptitude	Impeachment
1999	Charismatic	Chris Antley	D. Wayne Lukas	Menifee	Cat Thief
1998	Real Quiet	Kent Desormeaux	Bob Baffert	Victory Gallop	Indian Charlie
1997	Silver Charm	Gary Stevens	Bob Baffert	Captain Bodgit	Free House
1996	Grindstone	Jerry Bailey	D. Wayne Lukas	Cavonnier	Prince of Thieves
1995	Thunder Gulch	Gary Stevens	D. Wayne Lukas	Tejano Run	Timber Country
1994	Go for Gin	Chris McCarron	Nick Zito	Strodes Creek	Blumin Affair
1993	Sea Hero	Jerry Bailey	Mack Miller	Prairie Bayou	Wild Gale
1992	Lil E. Tee	Pat Day	Lynn Whiting	Casual Lies	Dance Floor
1991	Strike the Gold	Chris Antley	Nick Zito	Best Pal	Mane Minister
1990	Unbridled	Chris Perret	Carl Nafzger	Summer Squall	Pleasant Tap
1989	Sunday Silence	Pat Valenzuela	Chas. Whittingham	Easy Goer	Awe Inspiring
1988	Winning Colors (F)	Gary Stevens	D. Wayne Lukas	Forty Niner	Risen Star
1987	Alysheba	Chris McCarron	Jack Van Berg	Bet Twice	Avies Copy
1986	Ferdinand	Bill Shoemaker	Chas. Whittingham	Bold Arrangement	Broad Brush
1985	Spend a Buck	Angel Cordero Jr.	Cam Gambolati	Stephan's Odyssey	Chief's Crown
1984	Swale	Laffit Pincay Jr.	Woody Stephens	Coax Me Chad	At The Threshold
1983	Sunny's Halo	E. Delahoussaye	David Cross Jr.	Desert Wine	Caveat
1982	Gato Del Sol	E. Delahoussaye	Eddie Gregson	Laser Light	Reinvested
1981	Pleasant Colony	Jorge Velasquez	John Campo	Woodchopper	Partez
1980	Genuine Risk (F)	Jacinto Vasquez	LeRoy Jolley	Rumbo	Jaklin Klugman
1979	Spectacular Bid	Rron Franklin	Bud Delp	General Assembly	Golden Act
1978	**Affirmed**	Steve Cauthen	Laz Barrera	Alydar	Believe It
1977	**Seattle Slew**	Jean Cruguet	Billy Turner	Run Dusty Run	Sanhedrin
1976	Bold Forbes	Angel Cordero Jr.	Laz Barrera	Honest Pleasure	Elocutionist
1975	Foolish Pleasure	Jacinto Vasquez	LeRoy Jolley	Avatar	Diabolo
1974	Cannonade	Angel Cordero Jr.	Woody Stephens	Hudson County	Agitate
1973	**Secretariat**	Ron Turcotte	Lucien Laurin	Sham	Our Native
1972	Riva Ridge	Ron Turcotte	Lucien Laurin	No Le Hace	Hold Your Peace
1971	Canonero II	Gustavo Avila	Juan Arias	Jim French	Bold Reason
1970	Dust Commander	Mike Manganello	Don Combs	My Dad George	High Echelon
1969	Majestic Prince	Bill Hartack	Johnny Longden	Arts and Letters	Dike
1968	x-Forward Pass	Ismael Valenzuela	Henry Forrest	Francie's Hat	T. V. Commercial
1967	Proud Clarion	Bobby Ussery	Loyd Gentry	Barbs Delight	Damascus
1966	Kauai King	Don Brumfield	Henry Forrest	Advocator	Blue Skyer
1965	Lucky Debonair	Bill Shoemaker	Frank Catrone	Dapper Dan	Tom Rolfe
1964	Northern Dancer	Bill Hartack	Horatio Luro	Hill Rise	The Scoundrel
1963	Chateaugay	Braulio Baeza	James Conway	Never Bend	Candy Spots
1962	Decidedly	Bill Hartack	Horatio Luro	Roman Line	Ridan
1961	Carry Back	John Sellers	Jack Price	Crozier	Bass Clef
1960	Venetian Way	Bill Hartack	Victor Sovinski	Bally Ache	Victoria Park
1959	Tomy Lee	Bill Shoemaker	Frank Childs	Sword Dancer	First Landing

(continued)

YEAR	WINNER	JOCKEY	TRAINER	SECOND	THIRD
1958	Tim Tam	Ismael Valenzuela	Jimmy Jones	Lincoln Road	Noureddin
1957	Iron Liege	Bill Hartack	Jimmy Jones	Gallant Man	Round Table
1956	Needles	David Erb	Hugh Fontaine	Fabius	Come On Red
1955	Swaps	Bill Shoemaker	Mesh Tenney	Nashua	Summer Tan
1954	Determine	Raymond York	Willie Molter	Hasty Road	Hasseyampa
1953	Dark Star	Hank Moreno	Eddie Hayward	Native Dancer	Invigorator
1952	Hill Gail	Eddie Arcaro	Ben Jones	Sub Fleet	Blue Man
1951	Count Turf	Conn McCreary	Sol Rutchick	Royal Mustang	Ruhe
1950	Middleground	William Boland	Max Hirsch	Hill Prince	Mr. Trouble
1949	Ponder	Steve Brooks	Ben Jones	Capot	Palestinian
1948	**Citation**	Eddie Arcaro	Ben Jones	Coaltown	My Request
1947	Jet Pilot	Eric Guerin	Tom Smith	Phalanx	Faultless
1946	**Assault**	Warren Mehrtens	Max Hirsch	Spy Song	Hampden
1945	Hoop Jr.	Eddie Arcaro	Ivan Parke	Pot o' Luck	Darby Dieppe
1944	Pensive	Conn McCreary	Ben Jones	Broadcloth	Stir Up
1943	**Count Fleet**	Johnny Longden	Don Cameron	Blue Swords	Slide Rule
1942	Shut Out	Wayne Wright	John Gaver	Alsab	Valdina Orphan
1941	**Whirlaway**	Eddie Arcaro	Ben Jones	Staretor	Market Wise
1940	Gallahadion	Carroll Bierman	Roy Waldron	Bimelech	Dit
1939	Johnstown	James Stout	Jim Fitzsimmons	Challedon	Heather Broom
1938	Lawrin	Eddie Arcaro	Ben Jones	Dauber	Can't Wait
1937	**War Admiral**	Charley Kurtsinger	George Conway	Pompoon	Reaping Reward
1936	Bold Venture	Ira Hanford	Max Hirsch	Brevity	Indian Broom
1935	**Omaha**	Willie Saunders	Jim Fitzsimmons	Roman Soldier	Whiskolo
1934	Cavalcade	Mack Garner	Bob Smith	Discovery	Agrarian
1933	Brokers Tip	Don Meade	Dick Thompson	Head Play	Charley O.
1932	Burgoo King	Eugene James	Dick Thompson	Economic	Stepenfetchit
1931	Twenty Grand	Charley Kurtsinger	James Rowe Jr.	Sweep All	Mate
1930	**Gallant Fox**	Earl Sande	Jim Fitzsimmons	Gallant Knight	Ned O.
1929	Clyde Van Dusen	Linus McAtee	Clyde Van Dusen	Naishapur	Panchio
1928	Reigh Count	Chick Lang	Bert Micchell	Misstep	Toro
1927	Whiskery	Linus McAtee	Fred Hopkins	Osmand	Jock
1926	Bubbling Over	Albert Johnson	Dick Thompson	Bagenbaggage	Rock Man
1925	Flying Ebony	Earl Sande	William Duke	Captain Hal	Son of John
1924	Black Gold	John Mooney	Hanley Webb	Chilhowee	Beau Butler
1923	Zev	Earl Sande	David Leary	Martingale	Vigil
1922	Morvich	Albert Johnson	Fred Burlew	Bet Mosie	John Finn
1921	Behave Yourself	Charles Thompson	Dick Thompson	Black Servant	Prudery (F)
1920	Paul Jones	Ted Rice	Billy Garth	Upset	On Watch
1919	**Sir Barton**	Johnny Loftus	H. Guy Bedwell	Billy Kelly	Under Fire
1918	Exterminator	William Knapp	Henry McDaniel	Escoba	Viva America (F)
1917	Omar Khayyam	Charles Borel	C.T. Patterson	Ticket	Midway
1916	George Smith	Johnny Loftus	Hollie Hughes	Star Hawk	Franklin
1915	Regret (F)	Joe Notter	James Rowe Sr.	Pebbles	Sharpshooter
1914	Old Rosebud	John McCabe	F.D. Weir	Hodge	Bronzewing (F)
1913	Donerail	Roscoe Goose	Thomas Hayes	Ten Point	Gowell (F)
1912	Worth	C.H. Shilling	Frank Taylor	Duval	Flamma (F)
1911	Meridian	George Archibald	Albert Ewing	Governor Gray	Colston
1910	Donau	Fred Herbert	George Ham	Joe Morris	Fighting Bob
1909	Wintergreen	Vincent Powers	Charles Mack	Miami	Dr. Barkley
1908	Stone Street	Arthur Pickens	J.W. Hall	Sir Cleges	Dunvegan
1907	Pink Star	Andy Minder	W.H. Fizer	Zal	Ovelando

(continued)

YEAR	WINNER	JOCKEY	TRAINER	SECOND	THIRD
1906	Sir Huon	Roscoe Troxler	Pete Coyne	Lady Navarre (F)	James Reddick
1905	Agile	Jack Martin	Robert Tucker	Ram's Horn	Layson
1904	Elwood	Shorty Prior	C.E. Durnell	Ed Tierney	Brancas
1903	Judge Himes	Hal Booker	J.P. Mayberry	Early	Bourbon
1902	Alan-a-Dale	Jimmy Winkfield	T.C. McDowell	Inventor	The Rival
1901	His Eminence	Jimmy Winkfield	F.P. Van Meter	Sannazarro	Driscoll
1900	Lieut. Gibson	Jimmy Boland	Charles Hughes	Florizar	Thrive
1899	Manuel	Fred Taral	Robert Walden	Corsini	Mazo
1898	Plaudit	Willie Simms	John E. Madden	Lieber Karl	Isabey
1897	Typhoon II	Buttons Garner	J.C. Cahn	Ornament	Dr. Catlett
1896	Ben Brush	Willie Simms	Hardy Campbell	Ben Eder	Semper Ego
1895	Halma	Soup Perkins	Byron McClelland	Basso	Laureate
1894	Chant	Frank Goodale	Eugene Leigh	Pearl Song	Sigurd
1893	Lookout	Eddie Kunze	William McDaniel	Plutus	Boundless
1892	Azra	Lonnie Clayton	John Morris	Huron	Phil Dwyer
1891	Kingman	Issac Murphy	Dud Allen	Balgowan	High Tariff
1890	Riley	Issac Murphy	Edward Corrigan	Bill Letcher	Robespierre
1889	Spokane	Thomas Kiley	John Rodegap	Proctor Knott	Once Again
1888	Macbeth II	George Covington	John Campbell	Gallifet	White
1887	Montrose	Isaac Lewis	John McGinty	Jim Gore	Jacobin
1886	Ben Ali	Paul Duffy	Jim Murphy	Blue Wing	Free Knight
1885	Joe Cotton	Babe Henderson	Alex Perry	Bersan	Ten Booker
1884	Buchanan	Issac Murphy	William Bird	Loftin	Audrain
1883	Leonatus	Billy Donohue	John McGinty	Drake Carter	Lord Raglan
1882	Apollo	Babe Hurd	Green Morris	Runnymede	Bengal
1881	Hindoo	Jim McLaughlin	James Rowe Sr.	Lelex	Alfambra
1880	Fonso	George Lewis	Tice Hutsell	Kimball	Bancroft
1879	Lord Murphy	Charlie Shauer	George Rice	Falsetto	Strathmore
1878	Day Star	Jimmy Carter	Lee Paul	Himyar	Leveler
1877	Baden-Baden	Billy Walker	Ed Brown	Leonard	King William
1876	Vagrant	Bobby Swim	James Williams	Creedmore	Harry Hill
1875	Aristides	Oliver Lewis	Ansel Anserson	Volcano	Verdigris

Notes

BOLD denotes Triple Crown winners
(F) denotes Fillie
x-Dancer's Image finished first, but was disqualified after traces of prohibited medication were found in his system

Race Changes

1.5 miles from 1887–1995, 1.25 miles in 1896

	PREAKNESS				
YEAR	WINNER	JOCKEY	TRAINER	SECOND	THIRD
2007	Curlin	Robby Albarado	Steve Asmussen	Street Sense	Hard Spun
2006	Bernardini	Javier Castellano	Tom Albertrani	Sweetnorthernsaint	Hemingway's Key
2005	Afleet Alex	Jeremy Rose	Timothy Ritchie	Scrappy T	Giacomo
2004	Smarty Jones	Stewart Elliott	John Servis	Rock Hard Ten	Eddington
2003	Funny Cide	Jose Santos	Barclay Tagg	Midway Road	Scrimshaw
2002	War Emblem	Victor Espinoza	Bob Baffert	Magic Weisner	Proud Citizen
2001	Point Given	Gary Stevens	Bob Baffert	A P Valentine	Congaree
2000	Red Bullet	Jerry Bailey	Joe Orseno	Fusaichi Pegasus	Impeachment
1999	Charismatic	Chris Antley	D. Wayne Lukas	Menifee	Badge
1998	Real Quiet	Kent Desormeaux	Bob Baffert	Victory Gallup	Classic Cat
1997	Silver Charm	Gary Stevens	Bob Baffert	Free House	Captain's Bodgit
1996	Louis Quatorze	Pat Day	Nick Zito	Skip Away	Editor's Note
1995	Timber Country	Pat Day	D. Wayne Lukas	Oliver's Twist	Thunder Gulch
1994	Tabasco Cat	Pat Day	D. Wayne Lukas	Go For Gin	Concern
1993	Prairie Bayou	Mike Smith	Tom Bohannan	Cherokee Run	El Bakan
1992	Pine Bluff	Chris McCarron	Tom Bohannan	Alydeed	Casual Lies
1991	Hansel	Jerry Bailey	Frank Brothers	Corporate Repot	Mane Minister
1990	Summer Squall	Pat Day	Neil Howard	Unbridled	Mister Frisky
1989	Sunday Silence	Pat Valenzuela	Chas. Whittingham	Easy Goer	Rock Point
1988	Risen Star	E. Delahoussaye	Louie Roussel III	Brian's Time	Winning Colors (F)
1987	Alysheba	Chris McCarron	Jack Van Berg	Bet Twice	Cryptoclearance
1986	Snow's Chief	Alex Solis	Melvin Stute	Ferdinand	Broad Brush
1985	Tank's Prospect	Pat Day	D. Wayne Lukas	Chief's Crown	Eternal Prince
1984	Gate Dancer	Angel Cordero Jr.	Jack Van Berg	Play On	Fight Over
1983	Deputed Testimony	Donald Miller Jr.	Bill Boniface	Desert Wine	High Honors
1982	Aloma's Ruler	Jack Kaenel	John Lenzini Jr.	Linkage	Cut Away
1981	Pleasant Colony	Jorge Velasquez	John Campo	Bold Ego	Paristo
1980	Codex	Angel Cordero Jr.	D. Wayne Lukas	Genuine Risk (F)	Colonel Moran
1979	Spectacular Bid	Ron Franklin	Bud Delp	Golden Act	Screen King
1978	**Affirmed**	Steve Cauthen	Laz Barrera	Alydar	Believe It
1977	**Seattle Slew**	Jean Cruguet	Billy Turner	Iron Constitution	Run Dusty Run
1976	Elocutionist	John Lively	Paul Adams	Play The Red	Bold Forbes
1975	Master Derby	Darrel McHargue	Smiley Adams	Foolish Pleasure	Diablo
1974	Little Current	Miguel Rivera	Lou Rondinello	Neopolitan Way	Cannonade
1973	**Secretariat**	Ron Turcotte	Lucien Laurin	Sham	Our Native
1972	Bee Bee Bee	Eldon Nelson	Red Carroll	No Le Hace	Key To The Mint
1971	Canonero II	Gustavo Avila	Juan Arias	Eastern Fleet	Jim French
1970	Personality	Eddie Belmonte	John Jacobs	My Dad George	Silent Screen
1969	Majestic Prince	Bill Hartack	Johnny Longden	Arts and Letters	Jay Ray
1968	Forward Pass	Ismael Valenzuela	Henry Forrest	Out Of the Way	Nodouble
1967	Damasacus	Bill Shoemaker	Frank Whiteley	In Reality	Proud Clarion
1966	Kauai King	Don Brumfield	Henry Forrest	Stupendous	Amberoid
1965	Tom Rolfe	Ron Turcotte	Frank Whiteley	Dapper Dan	Hail To All
1964	Northern Dancer	Bill Hartack	Horatio Luro	The Scoundrel	Hill Rise
1963	Candy Spots	Bill Shoemaker	Mesh Tenney	Chateaugay	Never Bend
1962	Greek Money	John Rotz	V.W. Raines	Ridon	Roman Line
1961	Carry Back	John Sellers	Jack Price	Globemaster	Crozier
1960	Bally Ache	Bobby Ussery	Jimmy Pitt	Victoria Park	Celtic Ash
1959	Royal Orbit	William Harmatz	R. Cornell	Sword Dancer	Dunce
1958	Tim Tam	Ismael Valenzuela	Jimmy Jones	Lincoln Road	Gone Fishin'

(continued)

YEAR	WINNER	JOCKEY	TRAINER	SECOND	THIRD
1957	Bold Ruler	Eddie Arcaro	Jim Fitzsimmons	Iron Leige	Inside Tract
1956	Fabius	Bill Hartock	Jimmy Jones	Needles	No Regrets
1955	Nashua	Eddie Arcaro	Jim Fitzsimmons	Saratoga	Traffic Judge
1954	Hasty Road	Johnny Adams	Harry Trotsek	Correlation	Hasseyampa
1953	Native Dancer	Eric Guerin	Bill Winfrey	Jamie K.	Royal Bay Gem
1952	Blue Man	Conn McCreary	Woody Stephens	Jampol	One Count
1951	Bold	Eddie Arcaro	Preston Burch	Counterpoint	Alerted
1950	Hill Prince	Eddie Arcaro	Casey Hayes	Middleground	Dooly
1949	Capot	Ted Atkinson	J.M. Gaver	Palestinian	Noble Impulse
1948	**Citation**	Eddie Arcaro	Jimmy Jones	Vulcan's Forge	Bovard
1947	Faultless	Doug Dodson	Jimmy Jones	On Trust	Phalanx
1946	**Assault**	Warren Mehrtens	Max Hirsch	Lord Boswell	Hampden
1945	Polynesian	W.D. Wright	Morris Dixon	Hoop Jr.	Darby Dieppe
1944	Pensive	Conn McCreary	Ben Jones	Platter	Stir Up
1943	**Count Fleet**	Johnny Longden	Don Cameron	Blue Swords	Vincentive
1942	Alsab	Basil James	Sarge Swenke	Requested and Sun Again (dead heat)	
1941	**Whirlaway**	Eddie Arcaro	Ben Jones	King Cole	Our Boots
1940	Bimelech	F.A. Smith	Bill Hurley	Mioland	Gallahadion
1939	Challedon	George Seabo	Louis Schaefer	Gilded Knight	Volitant
1938	Dauber	Maurice Peters	Dick Handlen	Cravat	Menow
1937	**War Admiral**	Charley Kurtsinger	George Conway	Pompoon	Flying Scot
1936	Bold Venture	George Woolf	Max Hirsch	Granville	Jean Bart
1935	**Omaha**	Willie Saunders	Jim Fitzsimmons	Firehorn	Psychic Bid
1934	High Quest	Robert Jones	Bob Smith	Cavalcade	Discovery
1933	Head Play	Charley Kurtsinger	Thomas Hayes	Ladysman	Utopian
1932	Burgoo King	Eugene James	Dick Thompson	Tick On	Boatswain
1931	Mate	George Ellis	J.W. Healy	Twenty Grand	Ladder
1930	**Gallant Fox**	Earl Sande	Jim Fitzsimmons	Crack Brigade	Snowflake (F)
1929	Dr. Freeland	Louis Schaefer	Thomas Healey	Minotaur	African
1928	Victorian	Sonny Workman	James Rose Sr.	Toro	Solace
1927	Bostonian	Whitey Abel	Fred Hopkins	Sir Harry	Whiskery
1926	Display	John Maiben	Thomas Healey	Blondin	Mars
1925	Coventry	Clarence Kummer	William Duke	Backbone	Almadel
1924	Nellie Morse (F)	John Marinee	A.B. Gordon	Transmute	Mad Play
1923	Vigil	B. Marinelli	Thomas Healey	General Thatcher	Rialto
1922	Pillory	L. Morris	Thomas Healey	Hea	June Grass
1921	Broomspun	F. Coltiletti	James Rowe Sr.	Polly Ann (F)	Jeg
1920	Man o' War	Clarence Kummer	L. Feustel	Upset	Wildair
1919	**Sir Barton**	Johnny Loftus	H. Guy Bedwell	Eternal	Sweep On
1918	Jack Hare Jr.	Charles Peak	F.D. Weir	The Porter	Kate Bright (F)
1918	War Cloud	Johnny Loftus	W.B. Jennings	Sunny Slope	Lanius
1917	Kalitan	E. Haynes	Bill Hurley	Al M. Dick	Kentucky Boy
1916	Damrosch	Linus McAtee	A.G. Weston	Greenwood	Achievemant
1915	Rhine Maiden (F)	Douglas Hoffman	F. Devers	Half Rock	Runes
1914	Holiday	A. Schuttinger	J.S. Healy	Brave Cunarder	Defendum
1913	Buskin	James Butwell	J. Whalen	Kleburne	Barnegat
1912	Colonel Holloway	C. Turner	D. Woodford	Bwana Tumbo	Tipsand
1911	Watervale	Eddie Dugan	J. Whalen	Zeus	n/a
1910	Layminister	R. Estep	J.S. Healy	Dalhousie	Sager
1909	Effendi	Willie Doyle	F.C. Frisbie	Fashion Plate	Hill Top (F)
1908	Royal Tourist	Eddie Dugan	A.J. Joyner	Live Wire	Robert Cooper
1907	Don Enrique	G. Mountain	J. Whalen	Ethon	Zambesi

(continued)

YEAR	WINNER	JOCKEY	TRAINER	SECOND	THIRD
1906	Whimsical (F)	Walter Miller	T.J. Gaynor	Content (F)	Larabie
1905	Cairngorm	W. Davis	A.J. Joyner	Kiamesha (F)	Coy Maid (F)
1904	Bryn Mawr	E. Hildebrand	W.F. Presgrave	Wotan	Dolly Spanker
1903	Flocarline (F)	W. Gannon	H.C. Riddle	Mackey Dwyer	Rightful
1902	Old England	L. Jackson	G.B. Morris	Major Daingerfield	Namtor
1901	The Parader	F. Landry	T.J. Healey	Sadie S. (F)	Dr. Barlow
1900	Hindus	H. Spencer	J.H. Morris	Sarmation	Ten Candles
1899	Half Time	R. Clawson	F. McCabe	Filigrane	Lackland
1898	Sly Fox	W. Simms	H. Campbell	The Huguenot	Nuto
1897	Paul Kauvar	T. Thorpe	T.P. Hayes	Elkins	On Deck
1896	Margrave	H. Griffin	Byron McClelland	Hamilton II	Intermission (F)
1895	Belmar	F. Taral	E. Feakes	April Fool	Sue Kittie (F)
1894	Assignee	F. Taral	W. Lakeland	Polentate	Ed Kearney
1893	Not Held				
1892	Not Held				
1891	Not Held				
1890	Montague	W. Martin	E. Feakes	Philosophy	Barrister
1889	Buddhist	W. Anderson	J. Rogers	Japhet	(2 horse race)
1888	Refund	F. Littlefield	R.W. Walden	x-Bertha B.	Glendale
1887	Dunboyne	W. Donohue	W. Jennings	Mahoney	Raymond
1886	The Bard	S. Fisher	J. Huggins	Eurus	Elkwood
1885	Tecumseh	Jim McLaughlin	C. Littlefield	Wickham	John C.
1884	Knight of Ellerslie	S. Fisher	T.B. Doswell	Welcher	(2 horse race)
1883	Jacobus	G. Barbee	R. Dwyer	Parnell	(2 horse race)
1882	Vanguard	T. Costello	R.W. Walden	Heck	Colonel Watson
1881	Saunterer	T. Costello	R.W. Walden	Compensation	Baltic
1880	Grenada	L. Hughes	R.W. Walden	Oden	Emily F. (F)
1879	Harold	L. Hughes	R.W. Walden	Jericho	Rochester
1878	Duke of Magenta	C. Holloway	R.W. Walden	Bayard	Albert
1877	Cloverbrook	C. Holloway	J. Walden	Bombast	Lucifer
1876	Shirley	G. Barbee	W. Brown	Rappahannock	Compliment
1875	Tom Ochiltree	L. Hughes	R.W. Walden	Viator	Bay Final
1874	Culpepper	W. Donohue	H. Gaffney	King Amadeus	Scratch
1873	Survivor	G. Barbee	A.D. Pryor	John Boulger	Artist

Notes

BOLD denotes Triple Crown winners
(F) denotes Fillie
x-Later named Judge Muray

Race Changes

1.5 miles from 1873–88, 1.25 miles in 1889, 1.5 miles from 1890–93, 1.0625 miles from 1894–1900, 1 mile and 70 yards from 1901–07, 1.0625 in 1908, 1 mile from 1909–10, 1.125 miles from 1911–24, 1.1875 miles from 1925 to present

BELMONT STAKES

YEAR	WINNER	JOCKEY	TRAINER	SECOND	THIRD
2007	Rags to Riches	John Velazquez	Todd Pletcher	Curlin	Tiago
2006	Jazil	Fernando Jara	Kiaran McLaughlan	Bluegrass Cat	Sunriver
2005	Afleet Alex	Jeremy Rose	Tim Richey	Andromeda's Hero	Nolan's Cat
2004	Birdstone	Edgar Prado	Nick Zito	Smarty Jones	Royal Assault
2003	Empire Maker	Jerry Bailey	Bobby Frankel	Ten Most Wanted	Funny Cide
2002	Sarava	Edgar Prado	Ken McPeek	Medaglia d'Oro	Sunday Break
2001	Point Given	Gary Stevens	Bob Baffert	A P Valentine	Monarchos
2000	Commendable	Pat Day	D. Wayne Lukas	Aptitude	Unshaded
1999	Lemon Drop Kid	Jose Santos	Scotty Schulhofer	Vision and Verse	Charismatic
1998	Victory Gallup	Gary Stevens	Elliott Walden	Real Quiet	Thomas Jo
1997	Touch Gold	Chris McCarron	David Hofmans	Silver Charm	Free House
1996	Editor's Note	Rene Douglas	D. Wayne Lukas	Skip Away	My Flag
1995	Thunder Gulch	Gary Stevens	D. Wayne Lukas	Star Standard	Citadeed
1994	Tabasco Cat	Pat Day	D. Wayne Lukas	Go For Gin	Strodes Creek
1993	Colonial Affair	Julie Krone	Scotty Schulhofer	Kissin Kris	Wild Gale
1992	A.P. Indy	E. Delahoussaye	Neil Drysdale	My Memoirs	Pine Bluff
1991	Hansel	Jerry Bailey	Frank Brothers	Strike the Gold	Mane Minister
1990	Go And Go	Michael Kinane	Dermot Weld	Thirty Six Red	Baron de Vaux
1989	Easy Goer	Pat Day	Shug McGaughey	Sunday Silence	Le Voyageur
1988	Risen Star	E. Delahoussaye	Louie Roussel III	Kingpost	Brian's Time
1987	Bet Twice	Craig Parret	Jimmy Croll	Cryptoclearance	Gulch
1986	Danzig Connection	Chris McCarron	Woody Stephens	John's Treasure	Ferdinand
1985	Creme Fraiche	Eddie Maple	Woody Stephens	Stephan's Odyssey	Chief's Crown
1984	Swale	Laffit Pincay Jr.	Woody Stephens	Pine Circle	Morning Bob
1983	Caveat	Laffit Pincay Jr.	Woody Stephens	Slew o' Gold	Barberstown
1982	Conquistador Cielo	Laffit Pincay Jr.	Woody Stephens	Gato Del Sol	Illuminate
1981	Summing	George Martens	Laz Barerra	Highland Blade	Pleasant Colony
1980	Temperence Hill	Eddie Maple	Joseph Cantey	Genuine Risk	Rockhill Native
1979	Coastal	Ruben Hernandez	David Whiteley	Golden Act	Spectacular Bid
1978	**Affirmed**	Steve Cauthen	Laz Barrera	Alydar	Derby Creek Road
1977	**Seattle Slew**	Jean Cruguet	Billy Turner	Run Dusty Run	Sanhedrin
1976	Bold Forbes	Angel Cordero Jr.	Laz Barrera	McKenzie Bridge	Great Contractor
1975	Avator	Bill Shoemaker	Tommy Doyle	Foolish Pleasure	Master Derby
1974	Little Current	Miguel Rivera	Lou Rondinello	Jolly Johu	Cannonade
1973	**Secretariat**	Ron Turcotte	Lucien Laurin	Twice A Prince	My Gallant
1972	Riva Ridge	Ron Turcotte	Lucien Laurin	Ruritania	Cloudy Down
1971	Pass Catcher	Walter Blum	Eddie Yowell	Jim French	Bold Reason
1970	High Echelson	John Rotz	John Jacobs	Needles N Pens	Naskra
1969	Arts and Letters	Braulio Boeza	Elliott Burch	Majestic Prince	Dike
1968	Stage Door Johnny	Gus Gustines	John Gaver	Forward Pass	Call Me Prince
1967	Damasacus	Bill Shoemaker	Frank Whiteley	Cool Reception	Gentleman James
1966	Amberoid	Williams Boland	Lucien Laurin	Buffle	Advocator
1965	Hail to All	John Sellers	Eddie Yowell	Tom Rolfe	First Family
1964	Quadrangle	Manuel Ycaza	Eddie Burch	Roman Brother	Northern Dancer
1963	Chateaugay	Braulio Boeza	James Conway	Candy Spots	Shoker
1962	Jaipur	Bill Shoemaker	B. Mulholland	Admiral's Voyage	Crimson Satan
1961	Sherluck	Braulio Boeza	Harold Young	Globemaster	Guadalcanal
1960	Celtic Ash	Bill Hartack	Tom Barry	Venetian Way	Disperse

(continued)

YEAR	WINNER	JOCKEY	TRAINER	SECOND	THIRD
1959	Sword Dancer	Bill Shoemaker	Elliott Burch	Bagdad	Royal Orbit
1958	Cavan	Pete Anderson	Tom Barry	Tim Tam	Flamingo
1957	Gallant Man	Bill Shoemaker	John Nerud	Inside Tract	Bold Ruler
1956	Needles	David Erb	Hugh Fontaine	Career Boy	Fabius
1955	Nashua	Eddie Arcaro	Jim Fitzsimmons	Blazing Count	Portersville
1954	High Gun	Eric Guerin	Max Hirsch	Fisherman	Limelight
1953	Native Dancer	Eric Guerin	Bill Winfrey	Jamie K.	Royal Bay Gem
1952	One Count	Eddie Arcaro	Oscar White	Blue Man	Armageddon
1951	Counterpoint	David Gorman	Syl Veitch	Battlefield	Battle Morn
1950	Middleground	William Boland	Max Hirsch	Lights Up	Mr. Trouble
1949	Capot	Ted Atkinson	John Gaver	Ponder	Palestinian
1948	**Citation**	Eddie Arcaro	Jimmy Jones	Better Self	Escadru
1947	Phalanx	R. Donoso	Syl Veitch	Tide Rips	Tailspin
1946	**Assault**	Warren Mehrtens	Max Hirsch	Natchez	Cable
1945	Pavot	Eddie Arcaro	Oscar White	Wildlife	Jeep
1944	Bounding Home	G.L. Smith	Matt Brady	Pensive	Bull Dandy
1943	**Count Fleet**	Johnny Longden	Don Cameron	Fairly Manhurst	Deseronto
1942	Shut Out	Eddie Arcaro	John Gaver	Alsab	Lochinvar
1941	**Whirlaway**	Eddie Arcaro	Ben Jones	Robert Morris	Yankee Chance
1940	Bimelech	Fred Smith	Bill Hurley	Your Chance	Andy K.
1939	Johnstown	James Stout	Jim Fitzsimmons	Belay	Gilded Knight
1938	Pasteurized	James Stout	George Odom	Dauber	Cravat
1937	**War Admiral**	Charley Kurtsinger	George Conway	Sceneshifter	Vamoose
1936	Granville	James Stout	Jim Fitzsimmons	Mr. Bones	Hollyrood
1935	**Omaha**	Willie Saunders	Jim Fitzsimmons	Firethorn	Rosemont
1934	Peace Chance	W.D. Wright	Pete Coyne	High Quest	Good Goods
1933	Hurryoff	Mack Garner	H. McDaniel	Nimbus	Union
1932	Faireno	Tom Malley	Jim Fitzsimmons	Osculator	Flag Pole
1931	Twenty Grand	Charley Kurtsinger	James Rowe Jr.	Sun Meadow	Jamestown
1930	**Gallant Fox**	Earl Sande	Jim Fitzsimmons	Whichone	Questionnaire
1929	Blue Larkspur	Mack Garner	C. Hastings	African	Jack High
1928	Vito	Clarence Kummer	Max Hirsch	Gene	Diavolo
1927	Chance Shot	Earl Sande	Pete Coyne	Bois de Rose	Flambino
1926	Crusader	Albert Johnson	George Conway	Espino	Haste
1925	American Flag	Albert Johnson	G.R. Tompkins	Dangerous	Swope
1924	Mad Play	Earl Sande	Sam Hildreth	Mr. Mutt	Modest
1923	Zev	Earl Sande	Sam Hildreth	Chickvale	Rialto
1922	Pillory	C.H. Miller	T.J. Healey	Snob II	Hea
1921	Grey Lag	Earl Sande	Sam Hildreth	Sporting Blood	Leonardo II
1920	Man o' War	Clarence Kummer	L. Feustel	Donnacona	(2-horse race)
1919	**Sir Barton**	Johnny Loftus	H. Guy Bedwell	Sweep On	Natural Bridge
1918	Johren	Frank Robinson	A. Simons	War Cloud	Cum Sah
1917	Hourless	James Butwell	Sam Hildreth	Skeptic	Wonderful
1916	Friar Rock	E. Haynes	Sam Hildreth	Spur	Churchill
1915	The Finn	George Byrne	E.W. Heffner	Half Rock	Pebbles
1914	Luke McLuke	Merritt Buxton	J.F. Schorr	Gainer	Charlestonian
1913	Prince Eugene	Roscoe Troxler	James Rowe Sr.	Rock View	Flying Fairy
1912	Not Held				
1911	Not Held				
1910	Sweep	James Butwell	James Rowe Sr.	Duke of Ormonde	(2-horse race)
1909	Joe Madden	E. Dougan	Sam Hildreth	Wise Mason	Donald MacDonald
1908	Colin	Joe Notter	James Rowe Sr.	Fair Play	King James

(continued)

YEAR	WINNER	JOCKEY	TRAINER	SECOND	THIRD
1907	Peter Pan	G. Mountain	James Rowe Sr.	Superman	Frank Gill
1906	Burgomaster	Lucien Lyne	J.W. Rogers	The Quail	Accountant
1905	Tanya	E. Hildebrand	J.W. Rogers	Blandy	Hot Shot
1904	Delhi	George Odom	James Rowe Sr.	Graziallo	Rapid Water
1903	Africander	John Bullman	R. Miller	Whorler	Red Knight
1902	Masterman	John Bullman	J.J. Hyland	Renald	King Hanover
1901	Commando	H. Spencer	James Rowe Sr.	The Parader	All Green
1900	Ildrim	Nash Turner	H.E. Leigh	Petruchio	Missionary
1899	Jean Beraud	R. Clawson	Sam Hildreth	Half Time	Glengar
1898	Bowling Brook	F. Littlefield	R.W. Walden	Previous	Hamburg
1897	Scottish Chieftain	J. Scherrer	M. Byrnes	On Deck	Octagon
1896	Hastings	H. Griffin	J.J. Hyland	Handspring	Hamilton II
1895	Belmar	Fred Taral	E. Feakes	Counter Tenor	Nanki Poo
1894	Henry of Navarre	Willie Simms	B. McClelland	Prig	Assignee
1893	Commanche	Willie Simms	G. Hannon	Dr. Rice	Rainbow
1892	Patron	W. Hayward	L. Stuart	Shellbark	(2 horse race)
1891	Foxford	Ed Garrison	M. Donovan	Montana	Laurestan
1890	Burlington	Pike Barnes	A. Cooper	Devotee	Padishah
1889	Eric	W. Hayward	J. Huggins	Diablo	Zephyrus
1888	Sir Dixon	Jim McLaughlin	F. McCabe	Prince Royal	(2 horse race)
1887	Hanover	Jim McLaughlin	F. McCabe	Oneko	(2 horse race)
1886	Inspector B	Jim McLaughlin	F. McCabe	The Bard	Linden
1885	Tyrant	Paul Duffy	W. Claypool	St. Augustine	Tecumseh
1884	Panique	Jim McLaughlin	James Rowe Sr.	Knight of Ellerslie	Himalaya
1883	George Kinney	Jim McLaughlin	James Rowe Sr.	Trombone	Renegade
1882	Forester	Jim McLaughlin	L. Stuart	Babcock	Wyoming
1881	Saunterer	T. Costello	R.W. Walden	Eole	Baltic
1880	Grenada	L. Hughes	R.W. Walden	Ferncliffe	Turenne
1879	Spendthrift	George Evans	T. Puryear	Monitor	Jericho
1878	Duke of Magenta	L. Hughes	R.W. Walden	Bramble	Sparta
1877	Cloverbrook	C. Holloway	J. Walden	Loiterer	Baden-Baden
1876	Algerine	Billy Donohue	Major Doswell	Fiddlesticks	Barricade
1875	Calvin	Bobby Swim	W. Williams	Aristides	Milner
1874	Saxson	G. Barbee	W. Prior	Grinstead	Aaron Pennington
1873	Springbok	James Roe	D. McDaniel	Count d'Orsay	Strachino
1872	Joe Daniels	James Roe	D. McDaniel	Meteor	Shylock
1871	Harry Bassett	W. Miller	D. McDaniel	Stockwood	By the Sea
1870	Kingfisher	W. Dick	R. Colston	Foster	Midday
1869	Fenian	C. Miller	J. Pincus	Glenelg	Invercauld
1868	General Duke	Bobby Swim	A. Thompson	Northumberland	Fanny Ludlow
1867	Ruthless	J. Gilpatrick	A.J. Minor	DeCourcey	Rivoli

Notes

- Horses in bold indicate winners of the triple crown.
- 1 mile and 5 furlongs from 1867–89, 1.25 miles from 1890–1905, 1.375 miles from 1906–25, 1.5 miles from 1926–present.
- Held at Jerome Park from 1867–89, Morris Park from 1890–1904, Belmont Park 1905–present.

INDEX

(Page numbers in boldface indicate photographs)